TOUCH MONKEYS
Nonsense Strategies for Reading
Twentieth-Century Poetry

THEORY / CULTURE

Editors:
Linda Hutcheon, Gary Leonard,
Janet Paterson, and Paul Perron

Touch Monkeys

Nonsense Strategies for Reading Twentieth-Century Poetry

———◆———

Marnie Parsons

UNIVERSITY OF TORONTO PRESS
Toronto Buffalo London

© University of Toronto Press Incorporated 1994
Toronto Buffalo London
Printed in Canada

ISBN 0-8020-2983-3

Printed on acid-free paper

Canadian Cataloguing in Publication Data

Parsons, Marnie
  Touch monkeys : nonsense strategies for reading
  twentieth-century poetry

  (Theory/culture)
  Includes bibliographical references and index.
  ISBN 0-8020-2983-3

  1. Poetry, Modern – 20th century – History and
  criticism – Theory, etc. 2. Poetics. I. Title.
  II. Series.

  PN1042.P37 1994   801'.951   C93-094817-3

This book has been published with the help of a grant from the Canadian
Federation for the Humanities, using funds provided by the Social Sciences
and Humanities Research Council of Canada.

For Stan, Rachel, Marty, and Patrick,
and especially
– for Don

Contents

———◆———

Acknowledgments

—◆◆—

Before any other thanks are given, I want to acknowledge the many friends and family members who helped care for my daughter, Rachel, while I worked on this book. Some were able to offer a few hours, others whole days and weeks; but all provided Rachel with excellent care, and me with much needed pockets of time for thought. Two people, however, stand out from among the rest: Alanna Reabel, who was, for four years, Rachel's other mother, and gave her a second home and family; and my husband, who thought he'd given up single parenthood.

Most thought is developed over a long period of time, and is indebted to a large community of peers; this book is no exception. Many readers and friends have, knowingly or not, left their mark on this study. An earlier version of 'What then is a window' appeared in *Brick* 38; Linda Spalding's editorial suggestions helped make the review and the resulting interchapter better pieces of work. Mike Groden's graduate course on *Finnegans Wake* initiated this whole process. And Jan Zwicky patiently tried to teach me about Wittgenstein, and gave generously of her time to read and comment upon several sections of this work; whatever wrinkles remain in my treatment of philosophy are despite, not because of, her careful and lucid explanations. As well, I would like to thank Laura Macleod and the others at the University of Toronto Press for their help and encouragement, and those friends and colleagues who read this work, or discussed these ideas with me, at various stages; especially worthy of thanks are Danny O'Quinn, who set me reading on a path that grew 'curiouser & curiouser,' and Linda Hutcheon, who saw a book where I saw much less. Brenda Carr, Elisabeth Köster, Sue Leclaire, T.J. Lovegrove, Dorothy Nielsen, Sue Schenk, and Jill Siddall are important not only for their intellectual engagement, but also for their continuing emotional (and musical) support. Thanks, too, to Kinny with the keen eyes.

Martin Kreiswirth and Patrick Deane deserve special thanks. Their astute judgment and wonderful advice, all given in the spirit of this study, and their confidence in it, were much needed and continue to be valued as greatly as their friendship. Don McKay has for years been a model for me of intellectual, pedagogical and poetic excellence, and humanity. His participation in this project has been a continual pleasure. Always comprehensive, thoughtful, and witty, his responses have added to this book as no one else's could.

Finally my families, in Leamington and London, deserve *many* thanks for various encouragements. Their continuing interest urged me on. To my husband and daughter, of course, go greatest thanks; to Stan – for patience and suggestions and patience and support and patience again; to Rachel – for letting me fall in love with language all over again, as I watched her do so for the first time. Thanks.

I would like gratefully to acknowledge the following authors and publishers for permission to reprint materials from their works:

From 'Nonsense' by A.C. Baier. Excerpted by permission of Macmillan Publishing Company, a Division of Macmillan, Inc., from *The Encyclopedia of Philosophy*, Paul Edwards, Editor-in-Chief. Vol. 5, 520–2. Copyright © 1967 by Macmillan Inc.

Selections from 'Semblance' and 'The Objects of Meaning' are reprinted from Charles Bernstein, *Content's Dream: Essays 1975–1984* (Los Angeles: Sun & Moon Press, 1986), 34, 35, 182. © Charles Bernstein, 1986. Reprinted with the permission of the publisher.

Quotations from *The L=A=N=G=U=A=G=E Book*, edited by Charles Bernstein and Bruce Andrews (Carbondale: Southern Illinois University Press, 1984). Reprinted with permission of the editors.

Selections from 'My Poetry' are reprinted from David Bromige's *My Poetry* (Berkeley: The Figures, 1980). © David Bromige, 1980. Reprinted with the permission of the publisher.

Selections from 'Ted Hughes's Concept of Language: Beyond Inscription' by Jamie Bush are reprinted with permission of the author.

Selections from John Cage's *Empty Words*, copyright 1979 by John Cage. Wesleyan University by permission of University Press of New England.

Jeremy's Constellation, 1979 and *Silverbirchmorse, 1979* by Paula Claire from 'The Notation of My Sound Poetry' are reprinted with permission of the author.

'oilfish' to *'old chap'* for *'c'* is reprinted from Tina Darragh's *on the corner to off the corner* (College Park, MD: Sun & Moon Press, 1981). © Tina Darragh, 1981. Reprinted with the permission of the publisher.

Selections from *The Logic of Sense* by Gilles Deleuze, translated by Mark Lester and Charles Stivale 1990. © Columbia University Press, New York. Reprinted with the permission of the publisher.

Selections from Donald J. Gray's *Alice in Wonderland* are reprinted by permission of W.W. Norton & Company, Inc., copyright © 1971 by W.W. Norton & Company.

Selections from *My Life* are reprinted from Lyn Hejinian's *My Life* (Los Angeles: Sun & Moon Press, 1987), 7, 8, 11, 13, 14, 15, 16, 17, 25, 29, 33, 39, 42, 43, 47, 48, 52, 53, 55, 57, 62, 64, 65, 67, 68, 70, 77, 79, 82, 85, 86, 89, 96, 113. © Lyn Hejinian, 1987, 1980. Reprinted with the permission of the publisher.

Selections from *Spelt from Sibyl's Leaves* and *The Windhover* by Gerard Manley Hopkins courtesy of Oxford University Press.

Selections from *Defenestration of Prague* are reprinted from Susan Howe, *The Europe of Trusts*, p. 101 (Sun & Moon Press, 1990), © Susan Howe, 1983, 1990. Reprinted with the permission of the publisher.

Selections from 'On Contemporary Poetry' and 'The Burial Mound of Sviatagor' are reprinted by permission of the publishers from *Collected Works of Velimir Khlebnikov*, Volume I, translated by Paul Schmidt and edited by Charlotte Douglas, Cambridge, Mass.: Harvard University Press, copyright © 1987 by the Dia Art Foundation.

Selections from *Incantation by Laughter* and 'To the Artists of the World' and from Charlotte Douglas's introduction and commentaries are reprinted by permission of the publishers from Velimir Khlebnikov, *The King of Time: Poems, Fictions, Visions of the Future*, translated by Paul Schmidt and edited by Charlotte Douglas, Cambridge, Mass.: Harvard University Press, copyright © 1985 by the Dia Art Foundation.

Selections from *The Jungle Book* by Rudyard Kipling courtesy of Penguin Books.

Selections from *Desire in Language: A Semiotic Approach to Literature and Art* by Julia Kristeva, edited by Leon S. Roudiez and translated by Thomas Gora, Alice Jardin, and Leon S. Roudiez, 1980, © Columbia University Press, New York. Reprinted with the permission of the publisher.

Selections from Ron Silliman's *Ketjak* are reprinted with the permission of the author and publisher.

Selections from Ron Silliman's *The New Sentence*, copyright © 1987. Reprinted with the permission of Roof Books.

Selections from Edith Sitwell's *Collected Poems*, copyright © 1957, reprinted with the permission of David Higham Associates Ltd.

Selections from A.C.H. Smith's *Orghast at Persepolis*, copyright © 1972, reprinted with the permission of the author.

Selections from Gertrude Stein's *Tender Buttons* in *Selected Writings of Gertrude Stein*, edited by Carl Van Vechten, copyright © 1962, reprinted with the permission of Random House.

from Throgmoggle & Engestchin: a relationship in Colleen Thibaudeau's *The Artemesia Book*, copyright © 1991 Colleen Thibaudeau, reprinted with the permission of Brick Books.

Selections from Dylan Thomas's *Fern Hill, Altarwise by Owl-light*, and 'Notes on the Art of Poetry' reprinted with the permission of New Directions Publishing Corporation and David Higham Associates Ltd.

Selections from *Mots d'Heures: Gousses, Rames* by Luis D'Antin Van Rooten © 1967 by Courtland H.K. Van Rooten. Used by permission of Viking Penguin, a division of Penguin Books USA Inc.

Privet and selections from *I's* (pronounced 'eyes') in Louis Zukofsky's *Complete Short Poetry*, copyright © 1991, reprinted with permission of Johns Hopkins University Press.

Figure 1 is from Lewis Carroll's *Through the Looking-Glass*, reprinted with the permission of W.W. Norton and Company; figures 2, 5, and 6 are from Edward Lear's *Nonsense Botany*, and figures 7, 8, 9, 10, and 16 from his *A Book of Nonsense*, all reprinted courtesy of Faber and Faber Ltd.; figure 11 is from John Cage's *Empty Words*, reprinted with the permission of Wesleyan University Press by permission of University Press of New England; figure 12 is from bp Nichol's *The Martyrology Book 5*, reprinted with the permission of Coach House Press and the estate of bp Nichol; figure 13 is from Paula Claire's 'The Notation of My Sound Poetry,' reprinted with the permission of the author; figure 14 is from Steve McCaffery and bp Nichol's *Sound Poetry: A Catalogue*, reprinted with the permission of Steve McCaffery and the estate of bp Nichol; figure 15 is from bp Nichol's *The Aleph Beth Book*, reprinted with the permission of Oberon Press.

My aim is: to teach you to pass from a piece of disguised nonsense to something that is patent nonsense.
– Ludwig Wittgenstein, *Philosophical Investigations*

The soul of man is Humpty-dumpty; its coherence is not simply deferred;
it is superceded. There are many languages: some are eccentric, others only tan-
gent, some of them speak of other languages which they do not touch at all.
Someday we may learn the grammars but for the present we hear a music and
play it by ear.
– Don Byrd, 'The Poetry of Production'

Preface

'No room! No room!':
Guest List for a New Mad Tea-Party

———◆◆———

'At any rate I'll never go *there* again!' said Alice, as she picked her way
through the wood. 'It's the stupidest tea-party I ever was at in all my life!'
    – Lewis Carroll, *Alice's Adventures in Wonderland*

The stupidest tea-party Alice ever attended is one of the seminal
instances of Nonsense in English literature, rife with the sort of
linguistic pratfalls that make the whole genre so marvellously and
multiply miscommunicative. Puns, riddles, literalistic wrenching of
words and of logic, alliteration, and various other types of sound
play, non sequitur, parody – each of these literary devices makes an
appearance at Carroll's party. The actual guests at the party are few,
and are themselves literal jokes. The Mad Hatter and the March Hare
are personifications of colloquial expressions; the never wakeful
Dormouse is an exaggerated etymological exercise – its name comes
from the Latin *dormire*, to sleep (Gardner 1970, 94). Alice crashes the
party.
    Who would be invited if one were planning another sort of Mad
Tea-party, one for the inventors, not the inventions, of Nonsense?
Carroll, of course. And Edward Lear. Some lists might expand to
include A.A. Milne, Mervyn Peake, and Christian Morgenstern; the
Marx Brothers and Monty Python; or John Lennon, whose books of
Nonsense verse *In His Own Write* and *A Spaniard in the Works* were
published in the mid-sixties. Not a long list – unless one were to
reconsider the genre from a theoretical perspective and to examine
what it has to offer the reading of other types of literature, especially
avant-garde and contemporary poetry.

My purpose is not to hand out free passes to a hypothetical tea-party, or to make Nonsense writers out of authors clearly not working within the genre. Rather, it is to reconsider the relationships between generic Nonsense, language, and poetry, to locate points of linguistic crossover between them that will expand the possibilities for reading both Nonsense and poetry. If the result of this reconsideration is that categories broaden, that unexpected guests arrive, so much the better.

I use upper and lower case *n*s to differentiate between the literary genre (Nonsense) and the linguistic or philosophical disruption (nonsense): the genre is an outgrowth of, and capitalizes on, the disruption, so the two are intimately connected. So too is the genre connected with poetry per se, but I make a distinction throughout this book between them; Nonsense is a specialized form of writing, whether poetry or prose, whose characteristics will be mapped out in the taxonomy of Nonsense criticism that comprises Part One of this study. Poetry encompasses Nonsense verse, of course, but is used here to designate a wider category often and wrongly considered more 'serious' verse.

Linguistic nonsense, because of its symbiotic relationship with sense, has long been the concern of philosophy; in fact it lies at the heart of much philosophical questioning. Yet it is not in a philosophical way that I intend to consider nonsense. While I touch very briefly on philosophical thought concerning nonsense in Part One, and make use there and elsewhere of the writings of French philosopher and nonsense theorist Gilles Deleuze, I make no attempt to discuss either the linguistic disruption or the genre as a philosophical construct.

There is, I believe, a fundamental difference in philosophical and literary approaches to the topic; for the former nonsense is central and a potentially crippling error in thought, while for the latter it is marginal but (in my view) a playful indicator of language's ability to make meaning in many ways. When I engage aspects of philosophical argument they should be recognized as existing at a considerable and inevitable distance from literary perspectives on nonsense.

'The future of poetry lies in the exploitation of non-meaningful levels of language,' writes Veronica Forrest-Thomson in her posthumously published *Poetic Artifice* (1978, xiv). These levels establish poetry as a form of discourse that must be read as entirely separate from normal, communicative language, read with its materiality, its artifice, in mind; it is, according to Forrest-Thomson, a form of discourse that borrows and 'subordinates' other languages (1978, 3). Years later, Brian McHale connected Forrest-Thomson's work with what he terms the '(non)sense of postmodernism' (1992, 6), but neither he nor any other critics of nonsense (whose number continues to grow) have made much of an attempt to extend systematically this notion of nonsense's involvement with nonmeaningful levels of language in poetry. Susan Stewart's work on the genre, certainly the most far-reaching to date, is little concerned with poetry; Alison Rieke's study, to my knowledge the most recent available, does a lovely job of connecting Joyce, Stein, and Zukofsky to a Nonsense sensibility without tackling nonsense in a sustained theoretical way.

It remains, then, to reconcile nonsense theory and poetry, to explore the points of intersection and similarity between generic Nonsense and other forms of poetic writing in order to better understand how each entertains language(s). Nonsense is nothing if not artificial, I concur with Forrest-Thomson and urge a recognition of its materiality as well. But, more important, I urge a recognition of the sympathy between nonsensical and poetic strategies, and of the simple fact that becoming more aware of how nonsense disrupts language with its multiplicity of ways for making new sense (nuisance) may well make one a fuller, more engaged, reader of other types of poetry.

The second part of this book is an exploration of various aspects of Nonsense's relationship with poetic language and of how that relationship might facilitate a reading of poetry. There are sample readings of selected poems in each chapter, but my general thrust is not one of practical application. In an effort to address this imbalance between theory and practice, to disrupt the generally communicative momentum established by the chapters – *Touch Monkeys* is, after all, concerned with a linguistically and structurally disruptive phenomena, so a little structural disruption is not out of place – I have included six 'interchapters.' These offer practical applications of some of the principles discussed in the chapters they surround. They are also dramatic examples of my own belief that literary theory needs to have (at least) double vision; it must focus on its own 'genre' of thought without losing sight of the texts to which it is intimately tied.

A nonsense style of reading may not lend itself to all types of poetry, but it does accommodate a wide range of writing. The poets and poems in these interchapters have been selected to reflect the extent of that range, the flexibility of the approach.

There was a table set out under a tree in front of the house, and the March Hare and the Hatter were having tea at it: a Dormouse was sitting between them, fast asleep ...

The table was a large one, but the three were all crowded together at one corner of it. 'No room! No room!' they cried out when they saw Alice coming. 'There's *plenty* of room!' said Alice indignantly, and she sat down in a large arm-chair at one end of the table. (Carroll 1971, 74–5)

Being of the critical 'camp,' which tends to have little sympathy for Alice, I rarely agree with her take on what happens in Wonderland. But this once she may be right. When one reconstrues nonsense, when one recognizes its value as a tool for analysing experimental poetry and acknowledges its affinities with and potential for modifying contemporary literary theories, one soon realizes there may indeed be '*plenty* of room' at the tea-party table.

London, Ontario, 1992

PART ONE

'Loppleton Leery'

———◆◆———

The first three lines or 'argument' in Colleen Thibaudeau's *from Throgmoggle & Engestchin: A relationship* (1991, 151–2) contain its only English sentence, or its only *sensible* English sentence:

> Inwhich you meet Throgmoggle and Engestchin and you
> may feel that the latter is not a fully developed
> character and you are probably right.

The rest of the poem is a phonic romp through the nonsensical potentialities of language. Thibaudeau doesn't write 'standard' English in her poem; but she does make 'words' that are phonetically possible in English by bringing together phonemes utilizing the standard sound conjunctions of the language. As well, she plays with some standard ordering principles of English – grammar, punctuation, capitalization, and typography. Those first three lines, along with the presence in the poem's latter portion of capitals and commas, elicit expectations (which will later be undone) of conventional and coherent meaning and so lure the reader unsuspectingly into a semantic morass:

> Throgmoggle Fordful
> manty overgoo
> bog manty gong goppling
> rill cum nack throggins.
>
> *Choomin:*
> Chillchinchar Engestchin

chanty chopcharchill
chorey chopcharchill chooley
chingle choon chingley
choodle.

Throgmoggle Fordful?
Chillchinchar Engestchin?

Fulford mog-gle throg
Throggins
Besaboom
Besaboom
Throggins
Manty choon Manty
chorey manky
manky minsteven
Besaboom chorey
Choodle chin chin char
Gundalling tandy
Upert bee neery
Upert a choodle,
Laddledy leery
Upert a choodle
Nin Nin Nin
Besaboom chorey.
Powdler
Blanko
Upert a choodle
Nin Nin Nin
Manky Minsteven
   loppleton leery
   laveling,
   limpeling,
   leddledy lumpoling ...

Fordful moggle
chorey chumbles
dipdum danker.
Engestchin chuh
chuh

ch
h
*

Para pom
tandle:
Chillchinchar Engestchin
chanty chop charchill
chorey chop charchill
chingle chun chingley
choodle
    ooldum.
Throgmoggle Fordful
manty overgoo
rhinger minsteven
bog manty gong goppling
rill cum nack throggins.

Para pom tandle.

In his essay 'Dante,' T.S. Eliot claims 'genuine poetry can communicate before it is understood' (1951, 238); such is certainly the case with this poem. The 'argument' and ordering conventions, conspicuous because of Thibaudeau's unremitting phonemic anarchy, help make *from Throgmoggle* successful as generic Nonsense and as nonsensical poetry, for they communicate a type of, or possibility for, meaning despite her linguistic inaccessibility.[1] Characters are buried somewhere under the apparent gibberish, although one's a bit famished literarily. So a meaning-seeking mind sets to work.

The poem's more rounded character, if a reader can assume the argument suggests only one is not fully developed, is immediately introduced: Throgmoggle Fordful (Fordful – her/his/its last name?). Tentatively Throgmoggle can be called 'he' and Engestchin 'she' – the sounds of Throgmoggle's name are harder, more stereotypically masculine than those of 'Engestchin.' And the latter's ending recalls the Germanic feminine and diminutive suffix *-in*. The repetition of 'manty,' with its implication of reiterated meaning, encourages a reader to use repetition as a key to break Thibaudeau's 'code.' Other words at first seem to be English – 'bog,' 'gong,' 'rill' – but their context makes them nonsensical despite suggestions, especially from 'bog' and 'rill,' of landscape or setting. 'Overgoo' at the end of the second line combines 'over' with the colloquialism 'goo,' pushing its energy across the line break (the open *oo* sound slips more vigorously out of the mouth than any other sound ending words in this stanza) and spilling into 'bog' – an appropriate slide since 'goo' might be thought to have much to do with bogdom. But the connection is tenuous and offers no reliable means for deciphering the stanza.

Sound patterns give more plausible results. Though none of the lines rhyme overtly, a complex network of sound and rhyme, of assonance and alliteration, resonates among the syllables: 'throg,' 'mog,' 'bog'; 'goo,' 'gong,' 'gop.' The final word of the first stanza, 'throggins,' circles back to echo the first syllable of Throgmoggle, and the predominance of *og/go* rhymes suggests that many other words grow out of that name. The stanza offers a quite thorough 'throggin' of its first word, each rhyme or permutation an aspect of the rounding of Throgmoggle. 'Rill' is a partial rhyme with the end of 'Fordful,' so the character is given back to front and front to back. All Throgmoggle's sonal corners are covered.

Stanza two raises another problem in the search for the poem's 'meaning.' Which words are Throgmoggle's, which Engestchin's? (Or has Thibaudeau introduced an entirely new character – Choomin; the *in* ending may suggest, as it seems to in Engestchin, a proper noun. The first word of the stanza could then be read as an indication that Choomin speaks now.) The insistent repetition of *ch* makes the stanza choom along at a staccato pace implying that the discussion may be less than pleasant, and that the relationship mentioned in the poem's title is perhaps not blissful. As well, the repetition of words ('chop-charchill') and syllables ('chill,' 'chin,' 'char,' 'choo') develop a chattering cacophony, a nagging insistence, which cuts short and intrudes upon the silence following the colon of the first line. 'Chillchinchar' is placed as if part of Engestchin's name, though one might argue its role is adjectival, and Fordful's adverbial. Thibaudeau's use of capitals here is no firm clue since throughout the poem there seems no comprehensibly consistent approach to their use, except for the continual capitalization of 'Throgmoggle,' 'Fordful,' 'Engestchin,' and 'Chillchinchar.' Reading the last as part of Engestchin's name allows the stanza's syllabic distortions of 'Chillchinchar' and its alliterative *ch* pattern to be viewed as more raucous name play in the spirit of the first stanza. Here, however, the containment or cyclical completion of the previous stanza is lacking, and 'choodle,' far from being a pull back into Engestchin's name (or her adjective), seems the stanza's strongest movement away from it.

Because two variations of typeface (italic and roman) are used, this 'excerpt' (the title indicates it is part of a whole, although this is the complete text of the poem as published) unfolds like a dialogue between the two characters, with one typeface attributed to each character; when Thibaudeau reads the poem publicly, she uses three 'voices' – one narrator and two characters. If the poem's argument can be trusted (and why not try?) one character is underdeveloped; I'm inclined to think it's Engestchin because the rhyming associated with her name doesn't round her out in the way that associated with Throgmoggle does. And if character is partially developed through 'speech,' one clue for attributing voice would be the sheer number of lines given each style. Maybe this underdeveloped character has little to say for herself. Since the roman face has had more to 'say,' and since the phonic play on Throgmoggle's name is more sustained than that on Engestchin's, perhaps Throgmoggle should be associated with roman, the more sustained typeface, and Engestchin with italic.

But the next stanza puts a slight crimp into this:

Throgmoggle Fordful?
Chillchinchar Engestchin?

There are two possible directions for identification to take here. Either one uses this stanza as a means of equating the characters with the typeface they are named in, and thereby confirms the suspicions above about which 'part' each character has. Or, maintaining the poem's sense of dialogue, one reads the stanza as vocative, a tentative naming or recognition – as in, 'Hey Throgmoggle Fordful! Is that *really* you?' – or a query like 'Are you fordful today, Throgmoggle?' (That's assuming, of course, that the possibility of Throgmoggle and Engestchin questioning themselves is ruled out: 'Are you feeling Chillchinchar today, self?' 'Am I really Throgmoggle Fordful?')

This is the poem's smallest, most perfectly balanced, most hesitant stanza; tenuous not only in its slightness and tone, but in its placement as well. This stillness in the sprightliness of dialogue seems nonetheless to participate in that dialogue, indeed to help *indicate* the structure of that dialogue. And the structure overrides earlier suspicions; it suggests that Throgmoggle's 'part' is in italic and Engestchin's in roman. Following the implication of the stanza's questions, one realizes that Engestchin may have much more to say for and about herself than Throgmoggle.

The poem's longest stanza follows, alternating styles of typeface antiphonally, conversationally. The inverting, asserting of names and identity begins again; this time turning Fordful and Throgmoggle inside out and upside down – a frolicking that Throgmoggle interrupts with a bullfroggish chorus (*'Throggins / Besaboom / Besaboom / Throggins'*). This repeats the final 'throggins' of stanza one, while *'Besaboom'* rhymes with the initial *'Choomin'* of stanza two, so this stanza is connected with earlier ones. The stanza continues with its phonic play, here slightly more lilting (because of alliterating *m*s and *l*s) than in earlier stanzas, with the strains of *'Besaboom'* intermingling occasionally. Ironically, Throgmoggle's last word in this stanza (and for some time to come) is *'Blanko,'* a word which, although not English, has some quite specific semantic connotations for English readers. And soon Engestchin will be reduced to speaking a blank of a different sort. Before this 'reduction' of Engestchin, however, there are her loppeling lines, which trail off in a quite individual and non-nominal way. Many of these words are participial, active words that strike out in a grammatically and phonically new direction. Only one of these words, 'leery,' and few of the sounds (*op, um*) have been used so far. In a poem governed almost entirely by verbal and phonic repetition, this is a noteworthy shift away from the norm and one that Engestchin seems not to be able to maintain or resolve; the stanza ends in ellipsis, with an unexpected lack of energy – unexpected especially because Engestchin has never yet seemed at a loss for words.

She regains her voice in the name play of the next stanza, however. What is interesting here is not so much the introduction of new words ('dipdum,' 'danker') despite her earlier slip into silence, but the reduction of her own name to sputtering sounds and then, again, to silence. 'Chuh' is the sounding out of the phonic unit that appears most commonly when Engestchin's name is played with. This is collapsed into the phoneme itself ('ch'), and then collapsed to 'h,' an aspirant, a silent breathing, and then to the silence of blank space and the asterisk. Her name reduced to air, her 'self' dismantled, transmogrified to a concrete mark rather than a deferred and deferring letter: Engestchin (the name itself sounds reminiscent of 'anguishing'), again left silent.

The rest of the poem can be read as a unit. The phrasing of 'Para pom / tandle' – first with a line break, then without – mirrors the reunification offered, in this reprise with variations, of the initial name and sound play on both Throgmoggle Fordful and Chill-chinchar Engestchin. Such thoroughgoing play on the names has not yet occurred in the same stanza. But this union is qualified by the division of a word that was not originally divided – 'chop charchill' – and, perhaps not surprisingly, that has thus far been associated with Engestchin's name. The second last stanza offers a resolution, an amalgamation that at once counters and contains the previous stanza's movement. A solution to Throgmoggle and Engestchin's mutual silence, succinctly put in the isolation of 'Para pom tandle.'

This is a brief, so partial, and necessarily uncertain reading of some of the elements in Thibaudeau's poem, but it illustrates, at least, the delicious give and take of her language. *from Throgmoggle & Engestchin: A relationship* works as poem and as Nonsense because it 'loppleton leery'-s along the border between meaning and meaninglessness. Each reading offers the possibility of a new sense, a new scenario. Is this a relationship in decay (marital? parental?) making a (last ditch) effort at reunion? Is Engestchin, despite 'her' verbosity, feeling her identity squelched and distorted, her individuality sapped of energy? Are the two characters blithely going about their lives, effortlessly making room for each other? Is this just the empty chatter of a cocktail party? I have an urge to imagine Engestchin cleaning kitchen cupboards and talking to herself, while Throgmoggle leans in the door from the living-room with an occasional comment. Any and all of these suggestions fit the poem's teasing possibilities.

While no one of my suggestions for reading the poem can *definitively* translate the Throgmogglian dialect (who would want to, since such translation would inevitably squelch Thibaudeau's lively, witty poem?), each reveals meaningful structures underpinning the seemingly garbled words, and dramatizes the poem's movements towards and away from sense. As in the analysis of more conventional poetry, one can find alternative systems operating to create alternative ways of meaning. What at first appears to be utter gibberish has the potential for types of meaning (most notably sound as sense) quite different from what many readers have been taught to expect. But meaning nonetheless.

ONE

Runcible Relations:

A Taxonomy of Nonsense
Criticism and Theory

When Uncle Sam
Became a Ham
We did not care to carve him up:
He struggled so;
We let him go
And gave him to the pup.
  – Mervyn Peake, from *Uncles and Aunts*

A casual read through *The Artemesia Book* doesn't prepare one for *from Throgmoggle & Engestchin*, even if Thibaudeau's occasional portmanteau-esque and abbreviated words in other poems (for instance, *'anyfool wd know it wd have to be | a muchlessfargone Head'* in *St. Thomas: the Great Heat Wave of '36* [1991, 118]) have registered themselves as more than rare forays into linguistic invention. Thibaudeau, an undeservedly unsung poet who has published five books and two chap-books in a career spanning more than forty-five years, is something of a chameleon, trying on poetic forms and styles – lyric, narrative, concrete, sound and prose, among others – with eccentric inventiveness while never losing her regional Ontario grounding. Despite the quirky originality of her style, most of Thibaudeau's other poetry seems to ground a reader in a fairly trustworthy framework of meaning. But *from Throgmoggle* with its radically undercut gestures towards meaning is, some might argue dismissively, gibberish, sheer nonsense.

Well, is it? Implicit in my analysis of Thibaudeau's poem is an understanding of Nonsense as a positive linguistic venture. But what assumptions underlie that statement? Is 'nonsense' more than a derogatory term for 'garbled' language? This chapter provides a taxonomy, a survey of the widely various responses to nonsense and the adjacent literary genre, Nonsense. In it, I carve out a sense of the two by plotting them roughly on a literary and linguistic map, while allowing my own sense of nonsense (the basis for the theory I elaborate in Part Two of this book) to evolve from an interplay with these other critical positions and definitions.

Deciding what constitutes either sort of nonsense is not simple. Emile Cammaerts writes in *The Poetry of Nonsense*, the genre's first extended treatment, 'It is far easier to say what is *not* nonsense than to say what is' (1925, 8), and Myra Cohn Livingston insists that 'nonsense, like poetry, eludes definition' (1981, 123). Even a cursory glance at critics and reference sources illustrates just how slippery the concept 'nonsense' is and how divided its critics can be.

The *Oxford English Dictionary* defines nonsense as 'That which is not sense; spoken or written words which make no sense or convey absurd ideas.' On the other hand, Susan Stewart argues throughout *Nonsense: Aspects of Intertextuality in Folklore and Literature* (1978) that nonsense is symbiotic with common sense. And A.C. Baier in the *Encyclopedia of Philosophy* writes, 'Nonsense is parasitic upon sense and never departs so far from sense that it ceases to be part of some language, to the minimal extent of sharing its alphabet with that language' (1967, 5:521). According to Lionel Trilling, nonsense, 'when it succeeds, ... makes more than sense' (quoted in Bloom 1987, 4). Dutch Nonsense specialist Wim Tigges adopts Frye's 'basic types of *melos* and *opsis*, of babble and doodle ... respectively the charm and the riddle,' characterizing it as 'charm and riddle at the same time' (1987, 41). And Richard Gott, in a review of *The Chatto Book of Nonsense Poetry*, attributes to nonsense a Britishness akin to 'cricket and Marmite': 'Silly, usually unpleasant and meaningless, often racist and mysogynist [*sic*], nonsense poetry is to British imperialism what Donald Duck is to the American variety' (1988, 37).

These sample definitions slide between nonsense as a linguistic venture and Nonsense as a genre; a sliding endemic to the subject because the two feed each other, inform their respective definitions. Their relationship grows out of a shared approach to language, and to language's principles of order and meaning. Writing within the Nonsense genre is comprised of works, either fictive or poetical, which use nonsense language as a focal point and a fundamental stylistic principle. Both manipulate language (although it may be argued that nonsense doesn't always do so intentionally); both, consequently, frustrate one's comfortably staid certainties about the way in which language transmits or, as is more to the point, *makes* meaning. The growing interest in nonsense language, indicated by studies like Lecercle's (1985), Tigges's (1987, 1988) and Rieke's (1992), is in part due to an increased awareness of its literary uses and of how such uses reflect a changing understanding of the role language plays in the formation of individual and society.

While critics continue to disagree about what nonsense is, the definitions above demonstrate that most critics isolate the 'sense' within the 'non.' With the exception of Gott's (which defines Non-sense as a manifestation of the British Raj mentality) and Tigges's (one of his few 'characterizations' of it that doesn't include sense), every quotation or reference above describes nonsense and Nonsense in terms of their relationship with sense. And that seems reasonable; for how can one classify something that, by its very nature, makes suspect the language with which and the systems of thought by which one attempts to classify it? How describe the limits of a con-cept questioning the reliability of such limits? The answer: one doesn't. Rather, the word or concept is described with other words, despite the fact that such description, instead of 'explaining' or 'clari-fying' the word, pushes it deeper into language, further towards abstraction. Definition and classification are actually attempts to broaden the linguistic bases of a concept, to tie it more firmly to a series of abstractions. A definition may be thought of as literal, but it is actually literary – this is just what Alice's experiences with Looking-Glass Insects and Lear's Nonsense Botany demonstrate (see figures 1 and 2).[1] When Lewis Carroll and Edward Lear take defi-nitions and classifications literally, Nonsense is the 'predictable' result.

Not long before her visit with the Looking-Glass Insects, Alice has an exchange with the Red Queen which makes suspect, as well, that compendium of definition, the dictionary. When Alice charges that the Queen's boast '*I* could show you hills, in comparison with which you'd call that [hill] a valley' is nonsense, the Red Queen shakes her head and replies, 'You may call it "nonsense" if you like ... but *I've* heard nonsense, compared with which that would be as sensible as a dictionary!' (Carroll [1872] 1971, 125).[2] Ironically, the Queen's claim is true; her nonsensical statement is as sensible as the dictionary, for

"Well, there's the Horse-fly," Alice began, counting off the names on her fingers.

"All right," said the Gnat. "Half way up that bush, you'll see a Rocking-horse-fly, if you look. It's made entirely of wood, and gets about by swinging itself from branch to branch."

"What does it live on?" Alice asked, with great curiosity.

"Sap and sawdust," said the Gnat. "Go on with the list."

Alice looked at the Rocking-horse-fly with great interest, and made up her mind that it must have been just repainted, it looked so bright and sticky; and then she went on.

"And there's the Dragon-fly."

"Look on the branch above your head," said the Gnat, "and there you'll find a Snap-dragon-fly. Its body is made of plum-pudding, its wings of holly-leaves, and its head is a raisin burning in brandy."

Figure 1 Looking-Glass Land Insects from Lewis Carroll *Through the Looking-Glass*

the dictionary (as much as it purports to contain the many 'senses' of words) is highly nonsensical. Stewart writes that because 'they reduce the world to discourse ... there is nothing that is so nonsensical as the dictionary, the telephone book, or the encyclopedia' (1978, 190–1). With definitions, then, one is between a rock and a hardly existent place. Taken literally definitions can result in nonsensical incongruity; taken literarily definitions create a Nonsensical and hermetic world of words.[3]

Phattfacia Stupenda

Manypeeplia Upsidownia

Figure 2 From Edward Lear *Nonsense Botany*

In *The Field of Nonsense*, Elizabeth Sewell points out that Humpty Dumpty, the only character in Carroll who pontificates on language and meaning, sits high atop a wall in a very precarious position (1952, 122). This position is shared by those who try to define anything succinctly, especially nonsense. That being the case, I won't manufacture my own definition. Wittgenstein's characterization, in *Philosophical Investigations* ([1953] 1958), of meaning as use is handier in this situation than standard ways of defining. Rather than having an isolatable substantive definition, words – for Wittgenstein – evolve a meaning over an extended period of use; meaning becomes allied with context. I'll take my cue from Wittgenstein and from Gilles Deleuze, who suggests that 'meaning is not an entity but a relation' (quoted in Baum 1987, 69) – as the 'definitions' above (for the most part unwittingly) show. What follows is an attempt to let an understanding of the terms 'nonsense' and 'Nonsense' evolve out of their relationships with other concepts, and is an exploration of how the terms relate to linguistic and (to a lesser extent) psychic distortions in these categories or contexts: madness, anarchy, meaninglessness, dreams, play, philosophy, and linguistic operations. This exploration will facilitate an organizing of, and an accounting for, the often conflicting critical responses to both types of nonsense. These groupings seem naturally relevant to nonsense, but others could be suggested, for instance, relations with the Absurd, the grotesque, the nursery rhyme; many of these categories stretch to include other tangentially related topics as well.

Such contexts are not meant to offer an exhaustive reading of the area, but rather to provide a convenient way to synthesize some of the varied tacks people take when writing about nonsense and Nonsense. No one entirely excludes an other. As M.R. Haight writes: 'Nonsense shades gradually, in various directions, into pure fantasy, pure farce, the grotesque, the Surrealist, and so on' (1971, 255). This shading is true of nonsense taken relationally as well as generically. Most critics blend at least two of the groups considered below: the self-contradiction that can result seems particularly appropriate.

What strings these categories together is language. For nonsense is at the heart of language; and Nonsense creates a world of words (Sewell 1952, 17). Both types of nonsense, therefore, have much to do with semiotics, the study of sign systems – especially with linguistic semiotics, although Nonsense's close ties with illustration indicate it is also important to visual semiotics.[4] By stretching conventional attitudes about language, by playing with words as if they were things, these two types of nonsense draw attention to, and help a reader question, the way words mean, the way they relate to each other and to the things they refer to in any context.

While it would have been possible to avoid the continual interweaving of associative phenomena (dreams, madness, games, carnivals, etc.) and the logical and linguistic properties of nonsense, such interweaving demonstrates that nonsense can best be dealt with in the context of a lingually constructed reality; because one relates to the world through language, and because nonsense is at all times inherent in language, it is an inescapable 'presence' within all aspects of reality – social, psychological, historical, literary, political. The very pliable groupings used in this chapter indicate, as well, that my focus is not so much on Nonsense as a genre (though of course that will come into play) as on the act of reading and what one can bring from a reading experience of Nonsense to the reading of other, supposedly 'sensical,' writings.

Orchestrating opinions whose variations are sometimes great, sometimes a mere splitting of hairs, can make for a gangly and graceless dance, a pas-de-deux in hip-waders. But looking at nonsense in these ways will facilitate a slightly different approach to the works of Carroll and Lear, whose writing will be frequently used as examples; more important, these ways of looking at nonsense will introduce its wide range of associations, and a few of the other writers who, it is claimed, belong to the Nonsense family. Aristophanes, Rabelais, Shakespeare, Jarry, Stein, Joyce, the Marx Brothers, and Flannery O'Connor, according to some genealogies, are members; according to others, this family emerged only with the rise of Victorian England and is very much a nuclear one (Tigges 1988, 138–9).

Looking through Dark Glasses:
Nonsense and the Language of Madness

Framing this discussion of runcible relations with madness and linguistic operations has a certain propriety, for much of the language theory employed in the later parts of this study uses madness as a means of explicating some of the ways language functions. Foucault, in *Madness and Civilization*, writes: '*Language is the first and last structure of madness*, its constituent form; on language are based all the cycles in which madness articulates its nature' (1961, 100). He uses the term 'language' broadly, speaking of the language with which 'the mind speaks to itself,' as well as of the body's 'visible articulation' (Foucault 1961, 100). Such structures of discourse can be used to define madness, Foucault hazards, since one form the intimacy between language and madness takes is a nonsensical linguistic disruption unifying the body and language. Discourse on the edge of madness: Nonsense.

Madness leaps immediately to mind when considering *Alice's*

Adventures in Wonderland. This leaping may be the result of the presence of the Mad Hatter (deranged by the mercury he used in making hats), the March Hare (crazed with spring and the need to mate), or the Cheshire-Cat who, in a notorious passage, tells Alice: 'we're all mad here. I'm mad. You're mad' (Carroll [1865] 1971, 72). Such a ready association with madness is suggested perhaps by the fact that all three crazed characters are turns of phrase turned to life, or perhaps (and more likely) by the dementia of the place itself. The uncontainable forces of change and contradiction, the variations and vanishings in Wonderland leave even Alice's, that most stubborn and staid of minds, reeling; in fact, Peter Heath argues that Alice's sanity is almost undermined (1987, 52).[5]

The connection between Nonsense and madness, however, goes back much further than to Carroll's novels. In 1711 Addison, writing for *The Spectator*, deemed Nonsense the daughter of Falsehood and the mother of Frenzy (who eventually married one of the daughters of Folly) (Ross 1982, 336), thereby placing Nonsense precariously between madness and unreality. Addison's designation also relates Nonsense, if only by marriage, with the tradition of folly and fools.[6] This is a relationship confessed (with clearly differing sentiments) by such critics as G.K. Chesterton (1953b, 112), Alison Rae Rieke (1984, 11),[7] and Hugh Haughton (1988, 9).

But even if in this regard Nonsense walks a precarious edge, with a certain vigour in arm waving, balance may be struck; madness, however, is more often than not excessive. The two differ in both the degree and the intent of their linguistic disturbances. In his study of the relationship between language, nonsense, and desire, *Philosophy through the Looking Glass*, Jean-Jacques Lecercle argues that, far from being monozygotic twins or even blood-brothers, Nonsense and madness are at best cousins-once-removed. He uses *'délire'* as a point of connection, something he describes as

a form of discourse, which questions our most common conceptions about *language* (whether expressed by linguists or by philosophers), where the old philosophical question of the emergence of sense out of *nonsense* receives a new formulation, where the material side of language, its origin in the human body and *desire*, are no longer eclipsed by its abstract aspect (as an instrument of communication or expression). (1985, 6)

Délire is language 'tainted by desire, by the actions and passions of our body, by its instinctual drives' (Lecercle 1985, 7); it is the language of madness itself. This definition connects with Foucault's reading of classical madness, which posits 'a delirious discourse' affected by the movement, bearing, and conduct of the body (1961, 99).

Lecercle's characterization of *délire* does not agree with most readings of Nonsense, however, which deem absolutely essential to the genre a complementary tension, the delicate joining of seeming opposites.[8] He allows that Nonsense is a very mild form of *délire* since it admits the incomprehensible into language and so treads on language's frontiers, but simultaneously dismisses it (especially in Carroll's works) as 'a pedagogic trick ... to teach children their way into communicative language' (1985, 79). The dismissive attitude he adopts from Gilles Deleuze, who, along with Felix Guattari in their jointly written *Anti-Oedipus*, dubs Carroll 'the coward of belles-lettres' (1972, 135). More important, he also borrows from *The Logic of Sense*, an earlier work by Deleuze, antithetical structures that underscore his argument: surface language (equated with Carroll's work) and depth language (their example is Artaud) (1985, 41).

Deleuze argues, in *The Logic of Sense*, that there are three types of nonsense. One of the surface, which never fully engages the potential risks of language and which is therefore inextricably allied to the production of 'sense'; this, he claims, is the nonsense of Lewis Carroll. The other two kinds of nonsense are of the body, the schizophrenic body, and experience language as physical assault; these are the nonsenses of the depths and have nothing to do with sense – such is the nonsense of a writer like Antonin Artaud. The relationship that various types of nonsense have with madness may be radically different, and their degree of involvement with the body may vary, yet I suggest that at no point can language be wholly divorced from the libidinal drives of the body that produces it. The psychic landscape that allows for such an interrelationship is of no real interest to Deleuze because he is dealing with nonsense from a very different perspective than the one which I use. Here, where a continuum between surface and depth is denied, I part company with Deleuze; however, his ideas remain of interest and several aspects of his theory can be set to work and subverted in my admittedly different context.

Deleuze arrives at the distinction between these nonsenses, between surface and depth, through contemplation of Stoic causality, and its implications for understanding how sense resides within a proposition. He reconstrues Stoic causality in such a way that it seems to anticipate Husserl (1969, 20–1). The connection between cause and effect, between depth and surface, is split apart; causes are on one side of an unbreachable barrier, effects on another, although some initial cause must first have generated an effect. After this initial split, effects generate other surface-effects, which are in no way related to causes, to depths. This 'causality,' Deleuze implies, is almost phenomenological (1969, 21).

According to Ronald Bogue, sense for Deleuze is simply the product of language, 'a mere linguistic result or after-effect,' although it is always supposed to precede language – to be the cause rather than the effect of a statement (1989, 70). Deleuze isolates three basic relations within a proposition: denotation (the association of words with the particular things that they are said to represent), manifestation (which relates the proposition to its speaker and so 'manifests' the speaker's desires and beliefs), and signification (the word's relation to 'universal or general concepts' and 'the syntactic connections to the implications of the concept' [1969, 14]). But, for Deleuze, sense itself can reside in none of these relations since, as Bogue explains, each of these '[presupposes] one another' and all three assume an already existing framework of meaning (1989, 70). Consequently Deleuze proposes that sense be counted as a fourth relation within any given proposition. It is 'the expressed of the proposition ... an incorporeal, complex, and irreducible entity, at the surface of things, a pure event which inheres or subsists in the proposition' and is 'neutral' (Deleuze 1969, 19).

What is commonly referred to as sense is 'common sense' or 'good sense' (Bogue 1989, 74). Deleuze construes sense as not meaning per se, but an 'expression' or flow growing out of, but separable from, the tripartite structure of any given proposition or word. The sense of the word 'table' is not the four-legged object to which I point; nor is it that particular table that I, in writing the word, intend or believe I am referring to; again, it is not the general concept of 'table' – a flat-topped construction of variable size, propped up by legs. Deleuze insists that these linguistic functions, which are often deemed to constitute meaning and as interchangeable with the sense of a word, are not sense. Rather sense is the fluid border 'between propositions and things' (1969, 22). 'It seems,' as Bogue explains, 'to inhere in language, but to appear in things ... to be an event that is spatially and temporally "there," yet always somewhere else, always already over and about to be' (1989, 73). The sense of the word 'table,' then, is at once 'a simulacrum, a paradoxical, contradictory entity that defies common sense' (1989, 73) and an attribute of the object itself (1989, 72).

Deleuze puts it this way: 'Sense is never only one of the two terms of the duality which contrasts things and propositions, substantives and verbs, denotations and expressions, it is also the frontier, the cutting edge, or the articulation of the difference between the two terms' (1969, 28). Sense, the boundary, the intermediary, between things and propositions, is relegated to the *surface*, a realm of effects and quasi-causes, a name Deleuze gives to effects that generate other effects. It cannot be a 'cause' or an unprecedented point of origin. True causes, or 'bodies' and 'states-of-affairs,' belong to depths from which sense and the surface are cut off, excluded, because, having left these depths (1969, 24), their natures are irrevocably altered.[9]

Sense is copresent with nonsense, or with 'surface nonsense' of the sort that Deleuze says Carroll writes (1969, 68). Nonsense means *itself* and so has no sense of its own, no need of mediation between thing and proposition; but it does generate the possibility for sense. It 'donates' sense to its linguistic context, actively promoting the production of sense even if it has no sense itself. It is, he writes, 'opposed to the absence of sense' (1969, 71). But Deleuze 'understands' by 'nonsense,' as well, the existence of two other types of nonsense, which are not surface-related but schizophrenic. These are the language of the fragmenting body, of Artaud's body without organs, and have nothing to do with the production of sense or the surface. They are akin to the type of language Artaud sought for his theatre of cruelty, a 'new physical language based on signs' (Artaud quoted in Hayman 1977, 77), and to the type of language he strove for in his poetry. Precisely because of their relationship with depth, Deleuze privileges these types of nonsense over the surface nonsense he attributes to Carroll.

'Schizophrenics experience words as devouring, lacerating, or jubilant physical entities within a teeming plenum of matter,' writes Bogue.

They have two fundamental intuitions of the body: as a collection of dissociated body parts, dismembered, interpenetrating and mutually devouring; and as a miraculously solidified 'body without organs' ... For schizophrenics, words either enter the dismembered body as exploded words, wounding, rending phonetic elements devoid of meaning, or issue forth from the body without organs as glorious unarticulated sonic blocks. (1989, 74–5)

Nonsense experienced as depth, as lingual assault on the schizophrenic body, is the nonsense of the fractured word, of the body scream, of Lecercle's *délire*, not of the Jabberwock or the Queen of Hearts. Or so Deleuze and Lecercle contend. This nonsense, they say, is the result of a schizophrenic subjecting herself not merely to linguistic disruption but to a bombardment of words and sounds that devastates the 'self.' While Carroll's language remains situated at the 'surface,' which sense dominates, for the schizophrenic no retreat to the surface is possible; language is experienced bodily.

Following Deleuze's differentiation between surface and depth nonsense, Lecercle suggests that Carroll and Artaud (and so Nonsense and *délire*) offer different responses to the question raised by Humpty Dumpty – 'which is to be master?' (Carroll [1872] 1971, 163) – raised, that is, by the Humpty Dumpty who, not long after asserting his superiority over language, is made subject to the language of the nursery rhyme that plots his fate. Lecercle concludes that the dream framework of Carroll's novels detracts from his commitment to risk the physical experience of language, to suffer the painful link between body and word (1985, 32), and so effectively keeps his Nonsense on the safe side of madness.

Nonsense and *délire* do confront Humpty Dumpty's question differently. Early in his study, Lecercle defines *délire* as that state in which the question of mastery (if not completely resolved) leans heavily in favour of language; in *délire*, language is master (1985, 9). This is a paradoxical contention, given that the body, in the delirious speech of which Lecercle and Deleuze write, overwhelms language. Schizophrenics may react to language as to physical assault, may believe that words, indeed, *can* hurt them, but their subsequent self-protective disfiguring of language often results in the body's 'triumphing' over the articulable sense traditionally associated with language.

What better way to illustrate this difference between Nonsense and *délire* than that Lecercle chooses – comparing Carroll's *Jabberwocky* with Artaud's translation of it?

> 'Twas brillig, and the slithy toves
> Did gyre and gimble in the wabe:

All mimsy were the borogoves,
And the mome raths outgrabe.
([1872] 1971, 164)

Il était Roparant, et les vliqueux tarands
Allaient en gibroyant et en brimbulkdriquant
Jusque là où la rourghe est à rouarghe à rangmbde
et rangmbde à rouarghambde
Tous les falomitards étaient les chats-huants
Et les Ghoré Uk'hatis dans le GRABUGEUMENT.
(quoted in Lecercle 1985, 34)

A friend once used *Jabberwocky* as a parsing exercise; a glance at the
first stanza shows how successful that could be. One way Carroll
balances sense and senselessness is by preserving syntactical form
despite his introduction of neologisms and 'noncontent.' Neither
Carroll's early etymology (created for his brothers and sisters when
a version of this first stanza was still just a send-up of Anglo-Saxon
verse) nor Humpty Dumpty's 'masterful' interpretation can push the
verse into the realm of definitive and definable meaning. Yet the
nonsense words don't push syntax over the edge of meaninglessness
either; syntactical meaning is not disrupted, so the poem confirms
one sort of meaning while undermining another.

Artaud's version could probably be used for a similar parsing
exercise. He keeps 'rational' connectives and a fairly conventional, if
unpunctuated, sentence structure. That is as it should be, though;
certainly in Nonsense, words themselves are violated much more
frequently than syntax (Stewart 1978, 34).[10] Can one possibly imagine
an asyntactical language? Even seemingly asyntactical compositions,
like concrete poetry, usually elicit from the reader a syntactical
impulse, the ordering inherent in the act of reading. Nevertheless
language in Artaud's translation does seem to be breeding itself –
both the extra, longer lines and the hyper-sense of his portmanteaux.
These are, if anything, more potent than Joyce's neologisms in *Finnegans Wake* – so much packed into one word that the suitcase pops
open en route and one barely knows how to repack, how to begin
sifting for meaning. Artaud offers excess where Carroll shows
restraint. This guttural excess Lecercle connects with the schizophrenic body, indicative, he suggests, of bestial grunts and screams
(1985, 35).

Lecercle, too, is guilty of an Artaudian excess when he contends that Artaud's portmanteaux go so *far* beyond the rules of language creation, rely so heavily on the 'instinctive working' of language that they prove uncontestably that language, if 'left to itself,' 'screams' in meaningless or seemingly meaningless paroxysms (1985, 35). He ignores the presence of discernible, or almost discernible, words in Artaud's translation. What about 'chat-huants,' for instance? It isn't entirely translatable, but one can certainly make a beginning on it, as one can make a beginning on 'borogoves'; the same is true of the stranger, more stuffed words like 'rouarghambde.' Even when one can't pin a word down to five or six meanings or cognates, there is always the affective meaning derived from the sounds and shapes of the words themselves. Moreover, is it at all conceivable that language could be 'left to itself'? Surely Artaud's translation isn't an example of automatic writing; and even that is controlled, conceivably, by something – be it the unconscious, the spirit, god.

Artaud challenges conventional notions of what a word is, but the stretch is not always to a breaking thinness; indeed often the stretch is little, the word 'thick' with potential meaning. Nor do those long, drawn-out cascades of consonants and vowels preclude meaning, as Lecercle suggests; if at times Artaud's language screams, it may still evoke some meaning in the scream, and consequently never completely evades the possibility of sensical interpretation.[11] A mad, psychotic, excessive language rules in Artaud's 'translation,' but it is not without its affinities to Carroll's quieter, more controlled yelps, his more balanced Nonsense. Nor does its excess demand that Carroll's work, and Nonsense generally, be construed as milquetoast pieces of frivolity.[12]

Foucault offers a lovely image for classical unreason, which, when elucidated, may provide a metaphor for nonsense's connection to and divergence from madness:

reason dazzled.
Dazzlement is night in broad daylight, the darkness that rules at the very heart of what is excessive in light's radiance. Dazzled reason opens its eyes upon the sun and sees *nothing*, that is, *does not see*. (1961, 108)

Foucault's image appeals, in part, because it conveys the idea of madness's having access to secret truth (the sun as light, as knowledge), but also because it can be aptly turned to apply to Nonsense and so respond to Lecercle and Deleuze. If classical unreason is reason dazzled, then Nonsense is reason in dark glasses, looking into the eclipse of language and sometimes risking a slip of the glasses, a flash of exposure, a glimpse of solar disruption. An optician would tell anyone that staring directly into a solar eclipse is madness; she would insist as well that risking even one slip of the glasses is courting blindness.

Nonsense maintains the tension that madness forsakes. When a writer of schizophrenic nonsense stares wide-eyed into the eclipse of language, one is well aware of what will happen; suffering is palpable in her words. But when a Nonsense writer peeks momentarily above the glasses, a reader doesn't know what the result will be. *This* is the risk in Nonsense – not of utter blindness (or total blindness to socially accepted reason) – but the risk of not knowing, and ultimately of never knowing if the Nonsense is finely constructed. Wendy Steiner contends that in *Alice's Adventures in Wonderland* '[all] the nonsense interruptions, all the spatial discontinuities and logical leaps of the book are signs of this struggle between the knower and his undoing' (1982, 131). The struggle is never won; the knower is never wholly undone, but neither is she ever entirely successful. She remains suspended in the half-light of 'negative capability,' the discomfort and delight of uncertainty.

Loosing the Straitjacket:
Nonsense, Anarchy, and Carnival

If nonsense is not linguistic madness, is it perhaps linguistic subversion? Is Nonsense verse, as Roger Henkle would have it, 'rigidly controlled anarchy, in a straitjacket of conventional verse forms and rhyme schemes' (1973, 116)? Henkle's image appears to entertain the paradoxical nature essential to Nonsense, but it denies Nonsense any freedom of movement, any chance for risk. Once again Nonsense is deemed to be playing it safe.

Lear's limericks succeed precisely because they balance a tight rhyme scheme, rigid metrics, and incongruous words and behaviour. He has tailored the limerick, adjusting the traditional five-line, *aabba* limerick form to four lines with an *aaba* rhyme. The resulting *b* line contains an internal rhyme; in order to find the traditional limerick rhyme scheme, Lear's reader must turn inward to the line's centre. Much as he does in a smaller way by collapsing the third and fourth rhyme, Lear forces the energy of the whole in upon itself. This turning back occurs not because of the final rhyme echoing the first two lines, but because of Lear's refusal to allow a linear progression or climax (Ede 1975, 22). Rarely in Lear's most successful limericks do his final lines stand as more than mild alterations of his first. An adjective (generally misused or purely invented) changes slightly the subject – be it 'That lively Old Person of Ischia,' 'That intrinsic Old Man of Peru,' or 'That ombliferous person of Crete.' The result is the sugar-coated entropy typical of Nonsense as both Ede and Stewart understand it, with its 'impossibility ... to go anywhere, to proceed in a straight line towards a "purpose at hand" ' (Stewart 1978, 71).

To counter Henkle's strait-jacket image, then, there is Ede's insightful observation that the limerick's emphasis on sound over sense, while requiring tough metrical regulations, and a rigorous adherence to certain rules of sound play, flies in the face of ordinary sense and allows one to fiddle with both language and reality (1975, 27). The controlling form, which Henkle implies structures anarchy, is itself unstructuring. Lear *restructures* the limerick form to facilitate the breaking down of sense, and the forcing of both the poem and the reading process back in upon themselves. By working against diachronic unfolding in the poem, Lear creates the static world typical of Nonsense, a world constantly in process but in which nothing happens.

If one were to accept Lecercle's nonsense of the schizophrenic body, where 'disorder reigns' (1985, 36), as an example of linguistic anarchy (something I'm not willing to do), then there would be less reason to relate Nonsense and anarchy. Unlike the writers of 'schizophrenic nonsense,' classical Nonsense writers do not, as a rule, do violence to or through language. A major constituent of the genre, violence is present thematically, passively.[13]

Nonsense employs a subversive, evasive language, but its subversion is more peaceable and playful than violently anarchic, closer to the pleasurable upheaval found in carnival, as Mikhail Bakhtin defines it in *Rabelais and His World*. There, carnival is almost synonymous with excess, transgression, and spirited revelry; its foremost historical exemplar, medieval carnival, began as a poke in the eye of authority. Playfully inverting the rituals and symbols of religious feast-days, it offered the folk population a release of tension and pent-up energy before the seriousness and religiosity of sanctioned holy times like Lent. According to Bakhtin, carnival is a celebration of 'temporary liberation from the prevailing truth and from the established order' (1968, 10), a 'dynamic expression' whose symbols are 'filled with the pathos of change and renewal,' and which exhibits a topsy-turvy logic of protean twists, turns, and inversions (1968, 11). Though one might argue against 'dynamic' as an adjective suitable to Nonsense, for which a state of 'static' process has already been claimed, this description seems applicable to both nonsense and Nonsense. For one ingredient essential to carnival, the tone of its laughter, turns precisely upon the balance so necessary to successful Nonsense. Carnivalesque laughter is 'complex.' A 'festive laughter,' 'it is universal in scope ... directed at all and everyone, including the carnival's participants.' And it is 'ambivalent: it is gay, triumphant, and at the same time mocking, deriding. It asserts and denies, it buries and revives' (1968, 11–12).

But carnival, despite its participants' tendency to engage in self-parody, lacks Nonsense's rigorous self-awareness. Nonsensical self-reflexivity lends itself as much to infinitely regressive questioning and threats of stagnation as to dancing in the street. Nonsense is at heart a more serious offshoot of the folk tradition – John Cleese to carnival's Benny Hill – profaning similar sacred traditions, although with more telling means.

In 'Word, Dialogue and Novel,' Kristeva follows Bahktin, defining the carnivalesque text, and carnivalesque discourse, in terms that can be applied almost wholesale to the *Alice* books. 'A carnival partici-pant,' she writes, 'is both actor and spectator; he loses his sense of individuality, passes through a zero point of carnivalesque activity and splits into a subject of the spectacle and an object of the game' (1980, 78). For both Alice and the reader, loss of identity becomes a crucial theme from the moment Alice decides she must have turned into Mabel (Carroll [1865] 1971, 29). Both are objects, observers, and unwitting players of Carroll's game; and since the game is one in which the limitations of our logic, our language, and our way of making sense of the world are exposed, ultimately the limitations of the very foundations of our identities are exposed, as Lisa Ede argues so well (1975, 93). The many different sizes Alice becomes, the roles she plays, the many cases of mistaken identity she experiences – with such a long neck she *must* be a serpent, insists the pigeon who shoos Alice away from her nest (Carroll [1865] 1971, 61–2) – all fracture her assumed unity of being.

Kristeva continues, emphasizing that carnival brings to the fore both literary production and unconscious structures: 'sexuality and death' (1980, 78). All three are foregrounded in Carroll's *Alice* books. *Alice's Adventures in Wonderland* is infamously framed by its dreamy book-ends. Such framing adds to metafictionality, to self-referentiality, Stewart argues in her discussion of the technique (1978, 21–7). This literary reflectiveness is emphasized in the book's prefatory poem, *All in the Golden Afternoon* (which in maudlin verse describes the original telling of 'Alice's Adventures Underground'), and in the book's final episode. In the latter, Alice's elder sister has an equally maudlin 'dream' of young Alice, Wonderland, and Alice grown to womanhood. Carroll makes Wonderland the core of a telling-sequence. He tells the story; Alice tells it to her sister; her sister imagines Alice telling it to her own children. Within the story itself, many other stories are told and retold: for instance, the mouse's tale (Carroll [1865] 1971, 40) and the story of the Mock Turtle ([1865] 1971, 102–5), and Alice's twisted attempts to recite famous poems, such as *How Doth the Little Crocodile* ([1865] 1971, 29) and *You Are Old, Father William* ([1865] 1971, 56–7). All of these emphasize the act of telling, and the extent to which context affects the tale told or verse recited. Alice's recitations and the other characters' stories are framed by Wonderland, as Wonderland is framed by dream, as dream is framed by earlier and later tellings. Story is continually being recontextualized and so reconfiguring itself within the paradigm of its telling.

Quasi-Freudian readings are too frequent for the unconscious sexuality of the work to need much explanation; whether or not one chooses to see the rabbit hole and tunnel as a vagina and birth canal, the pool of tears as amniotic fluid, and Alice's physical fluctuations as pubescent, the presence of sex in the book need not be dwelt upon for long. But it is worth noting that none of these sexual elements is overt; in this instance, Carroll diverges from the carnivalesque model that Bakhtin and Kristeva present.

Nor is death a hidden component. The Queen of Hearts is continually and loudly threatening death to anyone who disturbs her. And Alice, when shrinking in the first chapter of the book, contemplates being reduced to nothing ([1865] 1971, 23). No one dies in the book, of course, because that would move the zone of action away from linguistic threats and threats to language and into a realm of physical and material danger, out of Nonsense, where seemingly senseless language creates a reality, and into the senseless reality of Absurdism (Tigges 1988, 128).

When Kristeva moves on to '[figures] germane to carnivalesque language,' such as 'repetition, "inconsequent" statements ... and nonexclusive opposition' (1980, 79), the reader of *Alice* is surely on home ground. The Mad Tea-Party (Carroll [1865] 1971, 74–84) is replete with inconsequence, repetitions abound throughout the text, and 'nonexclusive opposition' is another way of naming that complementary tension that lies at the heart of Nonsense. Kristeva's insistence that 'drama becomes located in language ... [that] parodies and relativizes itself, repudiating its role of representation' (1980, 79) is almost a synopsis of the tale's procedures.

Although self-referentiality seems a departure from Rabelaisian carnival (more a product of the '*interior infinite*' Bakhtin locates in the melancholy leanings of Romanticism [1968, 44] than the fruit of unadulterated carnival joy), this strand of Kristeva's description is so popularly and so aptly applied to Nonsense that it deserves a passing glance.[14] Susan Stewart suggests that nonsense's self-reflexivity ultimately undermines the common sense with which it is symbiotic. For her, Nonsense is 'an untouched surface of meaning whose every gesture is reflexive' (1978, 4). Each gesture is a 'split in consciousness ... [that] breaks open the pervasiveness of common sense' and reveals that it is both ideologically and culturally bound (1978, 49). Nonsense, by undoing what it relies upon, is always in danger of undoing itself; by assaulting and exposing the common sense integral to it, simultaneously assaults and exposes itself. One is reminded of Hamlet's crippling self-reflexivity, and it comes as no surprise that Stewart comments upon nonsense's entropy. Such hyperconsciousness makes each word the site of struggle and upheaval. Pure nonsense is, in Stewart's words, 'the most impossibly social gesture' (1978, 22). It is ' "good for nothing" ' (1978, 119).

The Cadence of Meaning:
Meaninglessness Intruding on Meaning

Plotting Nonsense on a linguistic map, Cammaerts wrote: 'It lies in the somewhat inaccessible region where the human tongue loses all meaning' (1925, 51). His point is one with which almost all other critics of Nonsense agree to disagree. Even Susan Vigeurs, in her lively 'dialogue' with Foss, Edward Lear's cat, will 'allow' Foss – Nonsense's champion against an alliance with poetry – to go no further than to assert that Nonsense has 'the cadence of meaning without the content' (1983, 139). If 'meaning is not an entity but a relation' – the underlying premise and motivating structural principle of this chapter – then cadence may have as much to do with meaning as content does; a seeming lack of lexical sense does not exclude all types of meaning.

Substantive meaning, pitted against its copresent meaninglessness, saves Nonsense from the absurdity that Heath ascribes to the *Alice* books' stringent logic (see note 5). While Carroll's Nonsense does follow a rigour of logic that may seem 'absurd,' it never creates Absurdism's meaningless or senseless reality. Nonsense presents both meaning and meaninglessness at once, the symbiosis of sense and senselessness. To insist that Carroll doesn't write Nonsense because he writes logically is wrong-headed. His work illustrates potential for senselessness within seemingly rigid constructions of meaning, without denying the presence of, or scorning the possibility of, sense.

Nonsense questions meaning by allowing meaninglessness to intrude upon it, and (as Stewart's discussion of intertextuality indicates) questions meaninglessness by disputing the meaning on which it depends. How meaninglessness is allowed to intrude into meaning is an issue over which critics are split into two fairly clear camps: those who see Nonsense as reducing meaning to a minimum and those who see it as reproducing meaning ad infinitum. Lecercle (1985), Holquist (1969–70), and Sewell (1952) are among the minimalist contingent. For them Nonsense's language is constrained and literalist; much Nonsense derives its initial effect from just such literal readings.

Taking literally statements like Lear's about the Jumblies – 'They went to sea in a Sieve, they did,' (1947, 71) – or the following passage from 'The Story of the Four Little Children Who Went Round the World,' is a great part of the fun of Nonsense:

At this time, an elderly Fly said it was the hour for the Eveningsong to be sung; and on a signal being given all the Blue-Bottle-Flies began to buzz at once in a sumptuous and sonorous manner, the melodious and mucilaginous sounds echoing all over the waters, resounding across the tumultuous tops of the transitory Titmice upon the intervening and verdant mountains, with a serene and sickly suavity only known to the truly virtuous. The Moon was shining slobaciously from the star-bespringled sky, while her light irrigated the smooth and shiny sides and wings and backs of the Blue-Bottle-Flies with a peculiar and trivial splendour, while all nature cheerfully responded to the cerulaean and conspicuous circumstances. (1947, 100)

Attributing just one meaning to each word results in the continual qualification, contradiction, and confusion so typical of Lear's work – oxymorons abound, adjectives and adverbs constantly undercut each other or the words they modify: 'trivial splendour,' 'sickly suavity,' 'shining slobaciously.' Here is a mild version of Stewart's self-negating Nonsense text (1978, 72).

But, an advocate of meaning's multiplicity in nonsense, I suggest that the assonance and sibilance (this is possibly the most sibilant passage Lear ever wrote) get up a buzz like that of the Flies' Eveningsong, one almost 'mucilaginous'; the sound itself is another form of sense. The lexical meanings of the words are nearly drowned out by the possibilities of phonic meanings in Lear's language, from which they, the words, cannot be wholly separated. And what does one do with a word like 'slobaciously'? Although it's composed of recognizable morphemes and has an identifiable syntactical role, this neologism cannot be read *just* literally; it has no readily definable lexical meaning, only echoes of other words (slob, slobber, gracious, tenacious?). 'Slobaciously' becomes the final conduit for those other forms of sense (the rip in the screen where the fly gets in) and encourages one's mind to root around for different ways in which these words can mean.

Lear was an inveterate user of neologisms, and Carroll, with the publication of *Through the Looking-Glass* ([1872] 1971), revealed a similar passion (Partridge 1950, 179). Sewell says Carroll's neologisms 'can scarcely be said to be words, since words should have reference but these have none' (1952, 115); but clearly she is working with a limited definition of 'word' – one that demands that a word be wholly a unit of definable *lexical* sense. What then of the words in Thibaudeau's poem, in Velimir Khlebnikov's *zaum'* writings,[15] or in James Joyce's *Finnegans Wake*? These works employ lingual units evocative of sense, but not entirely recognizable. Thibaudeau's poem is not meaningless, though one would be hard pressed to tie its meaning down. And even the most nonsensical (and longest) word in all of Joyce's 'epic'('bababadalgharaghtakamminarronnkonnbronn-tonnerronntuonnthunntrovarrhounawnskawntoohoohoordenenthur-nuk!' [[1939] 1976, 3]) is replete with meanings, being a macaronic-portmanteau-compendium of 'thunder' and packed full of social, theological, and parodic 'senses' as well.

Joyce's neologisms, and portmanteau words generally, provide a convenient point from which to look more closely at the arguments for and against multiplicity. Those who consider Joyce a nonsense writer, or a writer of partial nonsense at least, use him as a prime example of the multiplicity of nonsensical meaning.[16] Lecercle, however, classes Joyce among the writers who '[rely] heavily on [the] dark side of language' (1985, 65) or *délire*; and it is true Joyce writes not classical Nonsense per se, but rather a flowing, flowering nonsense, fecund beyond pruned reason. Joyce's hyper-portmanteaux ('crogmagnom,' 'reversogassed,' 'expectungpelick' [(1939) 1976, 20]), in their excess, stretch the portmanteaux of Carroll's works, which Humpty Dumpty describes as 'like two meanings packed into one word' ([1872] 1971, 164). In his 1876 preface to *The Hunting of the Snark*, Carroll corroborates, albeit somewhat tentatively, Humpty Dumpty's explanation ('seems ... like the right explanation for all [of them]' [(1876) 1971, 215]) and extends it by attributing the ability to speak in portmanteaux to those blessed with 'the rarest of gifts, a perfectly balanced mind' ([1876] 1971, 216). Perhaps this explains Lecercle's characterization of portmanteau words as attempts 'to control language' (1985, 35).

There are a few problems with Humpty Dumpty's account of portmanteau words. My initial instinct, despite Carroll's assent, is to distrust his attempts at definition. This is an egg, after all, heading for a great fall, a fall at the hands of language. How much 'control' does Humpty Dumpty have over the language he uses? How much understanding of the way it works? His conversation is opaque at best, his explication of *Jabberwocky* of little use in making sense of the poem; if language is a tool for communicating, Humpty Dumpty is not a very skilful user of that tool.[17] Perhaps Humpty Dumpty is too entertaining and attractive a character, for he has always been taken quite readily as the authority he claims to be. Why trust him any more than the proprietor of the Sheep Shop, Tweedledum and Tweedledee, or the Walrus and the Carpenter?

Because of Carroll's sanction. Interestingly enough, Carroll's first etymology and explanation of the same stanza of *Jabberwocky* – then titled *Stanza of Anglo-Saxon Poetry* – contained definitions different from those of Humpty Dumpty. 'Tove,' for instance, was initially defined as 'a species of Badger. They had smooth white hair, long hind legs, and short horns like a stag. lived [*sic*] chiefly on cheese' (quoted in Huxley 1976, 63). Humpty Dumpty describes 'toves' as 'something like badgers – they're something like lizards – and they're something like corkscrews ... also they make their nests under sundials – also they live on cheese' (Carroll [1872] 1971, 164). 'Mimsy' is first just 'unhappy' (Huxley 1976, 63) and then both 'flimsy and miserable' (Carroll [1872] 1971, 165). If he seriously intended to corroborate Humpty Dumpty's explanation of portmanteaux, Carroll could not claim a 'perfectly balanced mind' since the meanings of his portmanteau words and other neologisms shifted. Moreover, one of the words that Humpty Dumpty glosses as a portmanteau word is an actual, albeit obscure, English word: 'Slithey' (which he, and Carroll before him, calls a conflation of 'lithe' and 'slimy') is a slightly modified form of the verb 'to slithe,' an early medieval variant of 'to slide.' In at least this one instance, Humpty Dumpty either speaks tongue in cheek or with egg on his face.

Looking back at Carroll's discussion of such words reveals that he is talking about the words that go into *making* a portmanteau, not about the potential resonances such combinations can spawn. That he discusses only the method of arriving at portmanteaux does not mean he denies the new word any generative powers. Portmanteau words and neologisms in Carroll's Nonsense are not 'overloaded' with meaning as Joyce's and Artaud's are, but neither are they as closed and confining as some critics make them out to be. Rather they indicate the ability of the word to mean beyond literalism.

Deleuze's explanation of portmanteau words offers another, and perhaps more useful, way of understanding this linguistic phenomenon. The successful portmanteau is not merely the joining or contracting of two words with a resulting proliferation of meaning (1969, 45). And it is not just the connotation of 'two heterogeneous series' (1969, 45), though this latter function of connotation is important. By fusing two separate series, two different albeit related orders of meaning, the portmanteau anticipates one of the ways in which I understand nonsense itself to be formed: the joining with each other or superimposing upon each other of two (or more) separate sign systems. Moreover, a portmanteau word of the first order, according to Deleuze, has a content that 'coincides with its function'; for example, 'jabberwocky,' composed (claims Carroll) of 'jabber' and 'wocer' or 'wocor' meaning 'offspring or fruit,' denotes not only an imaginary animal but also a 'voluble, animated, or chattering discussion,' that is 'a series of verbal proliferation of expressible senses' (1969, 45).

Arguing from Carroll's suggestion that the portmanteau word is evidence of a 'perfectly balanced mind,' Deleuze contends that this verbal form is 'grounded upon a strict disjunctive synthesis' (1969, 46); he explains, using Carroll's example word 'frumious,' that 'the necessary disjunction is not between fuming and furious, for one may indeed be both at once; rather, it is between fuming-and-furious on one hand and furious-and-fuming on the other. In this sense, the function of the portmanteau word always consists in the ramification of the series into which it is inserted' (1969, 46–7).

Portmanteaux initiate an endless branching off of potential meaning, and attempt to entertain all or many of those meanings simultaneously.[18] The attempt to balance meanings, which Deleuze emphasizes, is of central importance to an understanding of nonsense as it will be construed in this study, and significantly extends Carroll's explanation of portmanteau words' structure.

There are other arguments for Nonsense's multiplicity of meaning. Puns and double entendre, techniques typical of the genre and of nonsensical writing generally, also generate more meaning than is literally evident in a word. According to Stewart, puns generate ulterior texts as well by splitting the movement of reading into several directions – one to follow each connotation of the pun simultaneously (1978, 162). Given Stewart's assumptions about nonsense's self-reflexivity, even the most 'literal' words should be seen as able to appeal to another side of language – each word in nonsense is a trying on and a sending up of at least two language systems and so inherently contains more than one meaning.

If anyone comes close to resolving the split between minimalists and pluralists in Nonsense criticism, it is Stewart, when she argues that 'nonsense, fettered mainly by its own ongoing, self-perpetuating context, becomes perhaps the most multiply-meaningful of fictions, while, at the same time, it becomes the least meaningful of fictions in everyday life terms' (1978, 36).

Nonsense and Dream:
'Things flow about so here!'

That's Alice's plaintive cry in the Sheep Shop of *Through the Looking-Glass* (Carroll [1872] 1971, 154), and it's certainly an accurate assessment of a trying situation. With the mere crossing of a brook (represented in the text by a pattern of asterisks) the White Queen has turned into a sheep who is knitting incessantly. And though the Sheep continually takes up and uses more knitting needles so that, as Alice notes to herself, 'She gets more and more like a porcupine every minute!' ([1872] 1971, 155), the shop itself is stranger still:

The shop seemed to be full of all manner of curious things – but the oddest part of it all was that, whenever she looked hard at any shelf, to make out exactly what it had on it, that particular shelf was always quite empty, though the others round it were crowded as full as they could hold. ([1872] 1971, 154)

Things even float through the ceiling to get away from Alice's gaze. And then, of course, the shop turns into a boat, with Alice at the oars.

This passage is perhaps the most dramatically dreamlike in the *Alice* books. It may trace its roots back to the transformations of theatrical pantomime (Carroll [1872] 1971, 153n), but it slides easily into Carroll's Nonsense world, which is replete with transformations and physical changes. Because such a passage feels organic with the rest of the work, a closer relationship between dream and Nonsense than the opposition Sewell argues for seems probable. For the passage above is not Sewell's 'concrete, clear and wholly comprehensible' Nonsense (1952, 23).

Much of Sewell's *The Field of Nonsense* is devoted to breaking down the relationship between dream and Nonsense, which critics like Cammaerts (1925, 32) and Chesterton (1913, 447) established. She argues against the synthesis typical, for her, of dream and poetry (1952, 23) and characterizes Nonsense as dealing with '[smallness], ordinariness, artificiality, distinctness of units and a tendency to concentrate on the part rather than the whole' (1952, 101). Nonsense, a product of 'the mind's force towards order' (1952, 44), is intimately related to reason and logic (1952, 5). Its world is 'carefully limited,' 'controlled and directed by reason'; Nonsense itself is 'a construction subject to its own laws' (1952, 5).

One would be foolish indeed to argue against the presence of logic in Nonsense – looking to Carroll gives ample evidence of its importance. What undermines the strictness of Sewell's argument, however, is (ironically enough) a tendency towards inconsistency. Tigges (1988, 13) notices her shift from the early statement that 'Nonsense verse is too precise to be akin to poetry. It seems much nearer logic than dream' (1952, 23) – which she has already equated with poetry. Midway through her argument, Sewell says that 'Nonsense adds to poetry's precision an element of incongruity' (1952, 102). Suddenly poetry is on the side of logic, and Nonsense nearer to dream.

More disturbing, because more subtle, is Sewell's failure to recognize order, which characterizes her Nonsense world, as a synthesizing principle. She rejects unity in favour of Nonsense's 'universe in which everything goes along serially, by one and one' (1952, 56), yet order, by its very nature, contains and holds together all parts into a whole, and connects them into a system that usually fails to acknowledge its own existence. During her entire argument against 'an underlying and occult unity among phenomena, created by a multiplicity of irrational relations and perceived by the dream faculty of the mind' (1952, 112), she seems oblivious to the fact that such 'occult' unities do not merely connect but, like metaphor, implicitly highlight the *disjunction* between combined elements. Irrational synthesis, especially as Nonsense entertains it, never loses sight of the tenuousness of combination; rather than affirming unity, it illustrates the delicate and hesitant relations between parts of any whole – even between the parts of an ordered whole.

By determining Nonsense to be 'a construction subject to its own laws' (1952, 5), Sewell implies that the ramifications of those laws don't apply to her argument. Unlike Stewart, who recognizes nonsense's symbiotic relation with common sense and its connection to the very process of her study, Sewell fails to recognize that nonsense spills over into and comments upon her own systems of thought. Because of this failure, she feels confident in declaring order a sure winner in the nonsensical contest between the irrational and logic; she implies that ultimately the tension between order and disorder, logic and dream, which motivates Nonsense, is resolved, and so disturbs the delicate balance essential to Nonsense.[19]

In *The Interpretation of Dreams*, Freud connects dreams and language by analysing the process of reduction and disguise through which dreams represent and through which language further tangles and articulates unconscious desires. He suggests dreams have a latent content, a hidden meaning made inaccessible by the unconscious's principles of distortion – for instance, condensation, displacement, and simultaneity. These processes can also be found in language. 'A word,' writes Freud, 'as the point of junction of a number of ideas, possesses, as it were, a predestined ambiguity, and the neuroses (obsessions, phobias) take advantage of the opportunities for condensation and disguise afforded by words quite as eagerly as do dreams' (1900, 230).

Language can become the seat of dream-work, then, of condensation, displacement, and simultaneity; and when it does, one form of sense is obscured by the manufacture of the unconscious's latent sense. Freud locates much of a verbal expression of the unconscious, very much like its expression in dream-work, in jokes (1905, 61), but the same techniques are found in nonsense's dislocations, non sequitur, puns, and portmanteaux.

One of the most important connections between dreams and nonsense is that the language of each employs similar devices for the production of latent meaning. In fact, writing of the Dadaists' nonsensical exploits with language, John D. Erickson refers to 'the *poem-work*' and explicitly connects these linguistic experiments with Freudian dream-work (1984, 80). If, as the Surrealists believed, 'Freud's most important discovery ... had been that "it is impossible really to talk nonsense"' (Young 1981, 113), then nonsensical poetry is also always open to meaningful scrutiny; Freud's pursuit of the unconscious speaks to my pursuit of nonsense as well.

Freud removed dreams from the realm of prophecy and deigned them a secular form of revelation, yet dreams and prophecy of a religious nature also have their affinities with Nonsense.[20] While religious nonsense is comparable to classical Nonsense, however, it is not a part of this tradition. The point of religious nonsense is not to unite sense and nonsense but to reach a transcendental sense through nonsense; nonsense becomes a tool, a means to an end, as in Buddhist koans, and that end is considered far more important than the nonsensical process used in getting there. Moreover, Nonsense toys with sense in order to question sense and, implicitly, itself; religious nonsense may question systems of secular sense, but it certainly does not doubt its own religious sense.

But two common elements of religion, the charm (a magical incantation whose words are believed to hold special efficacy) and the riddle (a cryptic naming and teaching game that is meant to reveal some hidden knowledge [Welsh 1978, 26]), do have closer affinities with nonsense. Tigges's claim that nonsense is 'charm and riddle at the same time' (1987, 41) has already been noted. While his contention may be slightly extreme, both charm and riddle have their function in the creation of nonsense.

Andrew Welsh, in *Roots of Lyric*, quotes Valéry's discussion of charms (1978, 149–50) in which a musical meaning that lies beyond the semantic is described, something sounding very like Tigges's 'communication without communicating' (1988, 248), or Eliot's genuinely good poem, which 'can communicate before it is understood' (1951, 238). It is a meaning which, like that in Thibaudeau's poem, defies lexical norms by establishing meaningful cadences, part of whose efficacy resides precisely in its opposition to traditional sense.

Hugo Ball even more tellingly connects charm with his linguistic experiment; in a journal entry of 15 June 1916, he wrote: 'To be precise: two-thirds of the wonderfully plaintive words that no human mind can resist come from ancient magical texts. The use of "grammologues," of magical floating words and resonant sounds characterizes the way we both write (1927, 66–7). And later, he claims that he and the other Dadaists have 'rediscovered' the word as 'a magical complex image' (1927, 68). While Ball had definitely the most religious leanings of the Dadaists,[21] his connection of Dadaist nonsense to ancient civilizations' understanding of the immense material power of words is an important comment on the group as a whole. Far from being nihilistic (as they are often presented), the Dadaists engaged in 'a metadiscourse, a discourse upon the reductionist, negative discourse of traditional Western art and modes of thinking' according to Erickson (1984, n.p.). This turn to the engendering power of words is evidence of the Dadaist commitment to life, and to reperceiving the world and its objects as purified of the twisted logic of the Western world, as essence (Erickson 1984, 13).

Nonsense's affinity with riddles comes in quite another, and initially awkward, guise. The emphasis often placed on the riddle's teaching function doesn't argue strongly for a relationship with nonsense, unless one accepts Chukovsky's theory that Nonsense is a game intended to reinforce a child's knowledge of the world. Chukovsky is not entirely wrong; a healthy knowledge of how the world works does help highlight the nonsensicalness of Nonsense, though it isn't essential to the enjoyment of nonsense's rhythms and sounds. But his version makes the genre too practical, too directed a pursuit. Nonsense ultimately exists for its own sake.

Alice's Adventures in Wonderland is infamous for its 'unsolvable' riddle: 'Why is a raven like a writing-desk?' (Carroll [1865] 1971, 75). Unsolvable? Not quite. Huxley quotes Carroll's Preface to the 1896 edition of *Alice*: 'Enquiries have been so often addressed to me, as to whether any answer to the Hatter's Riddle can be imagined, that I may as well put on record here what seems to me to be a fairly appropriate answer, viz. "Because it can produce a few notes, though they are *very* flat; and it is never put with the wrong end in front!"' This, however, is merely an afterthought: the Riddle, as originally invented, had no answer at all' (1976, 21). Certainly not the greatest of Carroll's thoughts, fore or aft. But Huxley also provides other attempts at a solution: 'Because Poe wrote on both'; 'Because the notes for which they are noted are not noted to be musical notes'; 'Because it slopes with a flap'; 'Because "Each" begins with an E' (1976, 22). Here is the quintessential Nonsense riddle – one that originally had no answer, no sense, proving to have more senses than it can hope to (or might want to) contain.

Welsh suggests that 'a riddle is not simply the "answer" but the process, a way of seeing that creates a space for fuller knowing' (1978, 77). Nonsense, then, could be considered a never-ending, multiply-opening riddle; the reader is thrown the tricks and game of language and joins in a 'riddling' process about as accommodating as the Hatter's riddle. Getting away from answers is the point of the *Alice* books (if they can be said to have anything so definitive as a point), for answers dictate resolution, necessitate a loss of tension. If these riddles teach, they teach the reader to question. But if, as Frye contends in *Anatomy of Criticism*, riddles are part of the process of reducing language to a visible form (1957, 280), Nonsense is part of an inverse process, reducing visible forms – both dreams and reality – to language.

'Alice soon came to the conclusion that it was a very difficult game indeed': *The Element of Play in Nonsense*

On an obvious level, Carroll's Nonsense is play. Both *Alice* books include games: a card-game and croquet, and a game of chess. Games are incidental to *Alice's Adventures in Wonderland*; that is, they provide actual events in the plot. But they are also structural to a degree, since many of the characters are cards. The overriding structure of the 'card' section is, oddly enough, a nursery rhyme – or the imagined results of one. When Carroll wrote the second *Alice* book, he seems to have taken up where the first left off in more than one way: where the first has but one nursery rhyme, the second has many; and where games are present in the first, they predominate in the second. He even includes a play-by-play diagram of the chess game structure of *Through the Looking-Glass* ([1872] 1971, 104), and has the Red Queen explain the principles of the game to Alice ([1872] 1971, 126–8).

But nonsense and Nonsense have stronger genetic ties with play than these samples of Carroll's borrowings from organized games. In *Homo Ludens: A Study of the Play Element in Culture*, Johan Huizinga lists, among others, these characteristics of play: a voluntary participation ([1950] 1955, 7), a separation from ordinary life ([1950] 1955, 8), a limitedness in terms of time and space ([1950] 1955, 9), the creation of order and a tension or uncertainty about play's ultimate outcome ([1950] 1955, 10). At one time or another each of these features has been attributed to classical Nonsense.

Tigges, for instance, suggests that Nonsense adheres voluntarily to 'its self-appointed rules' (1988, 54), but adds that these rules are both present and absent, for constant and ironclad rules would almost by definition demand meaning and a determinable terminus point, and consequently would cramp Nonsense's self-negating style. Sewell's view of the closed field of Nonsense entertains Huizinga's second characteristic, but so too does Stewart's contention that the self-reflexivity of nonsense is language at the furthest remove from ordinary common sense. The third characteristic, however, doesn't fit with Stewart's understanding of nonsense since, despite its distance from ordinary life, she believes that nonsense remains symbiotic with common sense and so inversely permeates all sense-related activities. Sewell, as has already been mentioned, calls Nonsense a product of 'the mind's force towards order' (1952, 44), and Lecercle insists it is a 'meaning-preserving activity' (1985, 140) implicitly contingent upon order as an underlying principle. Nonsense creates a new order by creating a new reality and may be allied with order as with common sense. But it is not synonymous with order as Huizinga suggests play is, and as Sewell and Lecercle ultimately claim, because it must simultaneously entertain disorder. There is tension in play as in Nonsense, but in play that tension ultimately finds a resolution with one player winning, unless, as occasionally happens, the game ends in a draw.

Nonsense *always* ends in a draw unless its game is rejected, violated in some way – as Alice violates it at the end of both of Carroll's books by diminishing its other players: ' "Who cares for *you*?" said Alice ... "You're nothing but a pack of cards!" ' ([1865] 1971, 129).

These are the words of a spoilsport, of someone unwilling to play the game, as she has been unwilling to play the games of the Mad Tea-Party: ' "It's the stupidest tea-party I ever was at in all my life!" ' ([1865] 1971, 83).

Too often Alice's unwillingness is attributed to Carroll as well (as in Lecercle and Deleuze); too often his Nonsense is diminished, called the game of a spoilsport. But as Ede cogently argues (for what follows I'm indebted to her), Alice is not Carroll's mouthpiece, nor is she held up as an archetypal and most perfect participant. Alice's character is replete with quirky problems for those who are used to considering her the sweet Disneyesque dream-child of animation. Both Carroll's and Tenniel's illustrations (the latter submitted to Carroll's very fastidious eye before being accepted for publication) depict an often harsh and quite unattractive girl. Alice's behaviour tends to be smug and unthinking; she is utterly unquestioning about the rightness of her own world and its conventions, not unlike the stereotypical North American or English tourist abroad. And she brings up subjects that cause no end of distress to the inhabitants of Wonderland; for instance, she insists on telling the mouse in 'The Pool of Tears' about her cat, Dinah, and then about a little terrier she knows, both of whom are terrific mousers ([1865] 1971, 33–4).

And what does one say of a girl who unconsciously turns almost every poem she recites into a textbook case of the violence of a capitalist society motivated by survival of the fittest? 'How doth the little busy bee' suddenly becomes, in Alice's mouth, 'How doth the little crocodile' – a fittingly ironic evolution since she thinks her world beyond reproach or savagery. The change is most explicitly *not* attributable to the mood of Wonderland; its inhabitants, the Mock Turtle and the Gryphon, turn the violence and didacticism of Mary Howell's *The Spider and the Fly* into the lovely, cooperatively lunatic 'Lobster-Quadrille.' 'For in spite, or perhaps because of its anarchism,' writes Ede, 'Wonderland is able to convert a poem of entrapment and violence (Victorian social Darwinism?) to a comic celebration of social harmony' (1975, 87).

Alice's is ultimately not an affirmable vision or version of the world, not an ideal way to play any game, especially not one as extreme and bizarre as Wonderland's. Alice, as game player, is not to be imitated. Nor does Carroll urge us to accept readily her version of 'fair play.' As Ede remarks, by rejecting the Queen of Hearts and her court as 'nothing but a pack of cards,' Alice 'escapes the burden of knowledge. As she has all along, she uses a mad concept of language [mad because illogical and ultimately not founded on reason] to protect both her ego and her imagination from risking an encounter with the chaos that lies outside her narrow world of social rules' (1975, 111).

The play that Alice rejects is really just the play of a lively and illogical language. Carroll, by having the Wonderland characters seem to represent logic, puts Alice in the position of having to make her own language logical and so see how untenable is her belief that language and life are coherent and 'inherently meaningful,' (Ede 1975, 89).

When Language Goes on Holiday:
Philosophy's Nonsense

Wittgenstein, one of this century's most influential thinkers about nonsense, was not writing about Carroll's 'fairy tales' when he noted in his *Philosophical Investigations* that 'philosophical problems arise when language *goes on holiday*' ([1953] 1958, I.38), though he could well have been. This comment about the difficulties of philosophical language aptly summarizes the crux of Alice's problems, especially in Wonderland. And while Wittgenstein and Carroll had very different responses to nonsense generally,[22] there are important similarities between the intensely serious philosopher and the writer of Nonsense/logician, and a connection between literary nonsense and philosophy, which need to be examined.

This connection, however, is a loose one, and if not allowed to remain so can lead to misinterpretations; literary nonsense engages in many of the linguistic activities that result in philosophical nonsense, but engages in them for different reasons and to different degrees. Works of Nonsense are not easily placed within the traditional divisions of nonsense set out by philosophers because they never wholly embrace those categories. Carroll's work, for instance, follows logic to its illogical ends, and employs what A.C. Baier calls 'nonsense vocabulary'; it uses, too, obvious falsehoods and semantic nonsense – all traditional types of philosophical nonsense. But it also engages language at a more material level with portmanteaux, puns, and personifications of words. In philosophical nonsense, disruptions tend to effect a very specific type of sense, that necessary for the communication of a precise, definable linguistic meaning. In literary nonsense, while such disruptions of communicative sense are absolutely essential, disruptions may also promote the establishment of more material forms of sense, related to the senses for instance, which may interfere with the communication of sense. Literary nonsense, then, is not so much the interruption of sense as the multiplication of sensical possibilities, the emphasizing of *other* ways to manufacture meaning. The connection between philosophical and literary nonsense is tenuous, at best, but it may be useful to gain a general understanding of what philosophical nonsense *is*, if only to help determine what literary nonsense is *not*.

In Section I.7 of *Philosophical Investigations* ([1953] 1958), Wittgenstein talks of 'language-games'; his simile suggests that learning the meaning and function of a word is like learning a move in a game. Carroll may never have articulated this concept, but he did present language as a game of another sort.[23] Many of Carroll's language puzzles have a didactic air to them, which may have contributed to Lecercle's claim (quoted above) that Carroll's Nonsense is that of a pedant. Heath too argues that *Alice's Adventures in Wonderland* was meant to '[make] little logicians' of children (1987, 51), that it was perceived by Carroll as a 'work of instruction and profit for the infant reader' and as such failed miserably since children invariablymiss its point (1987, 50). Two things are striking about Heath's view of the tale: he is not entirely wrong about Carroll, and he unconsciously implies one of the connections between Carroll and Wittgenstein.

Heath is on the right track about Carroll's work, but he's wrong about the *Alice* books. The *Sylvie and Bruno* books are the clear example of Carroll trying to use fiction as a forum for preaching logic, among other things. The latter present their logical play inside a framework of didacticism so unmitigated as to be embarrassing to Carroll's devoted followers. Their twists of language and logic never challenge such fundamental issues as the tie between individual identity, society, and language; never question the foundation of logic and of sense; never expose the capitalist climate of Victorian England (whose logic and values Heath claims Carroll is trying to instil in young people) as cruel, exploitative, or even limited, as the *Alice* books do. Rather the distortions (so effective, so delightful, in the early novels) become, in the *Sylvie and Bruno* books, saccharine attempts to sweeten an over-long fable brimming with the sentiments of High Victorianism and High Anglicanism. Even their prefaces are pulpits for Carroll's concerns – the need to expurgate the Bible for children, to do up Shakespeare properly for young girls (Bowdler's version being far too indecent) (preface to *Sylvie and Bruno* [1889] 1976, 280–2) and to put an end to the cruelties of 'sport' (the hunting, baiting, and fighting of animals) (preface to *Sylvie and Bruno Concluded* [1893] 1976, 516–7).

For all that, however, the *Sylvie and Bruno* books employ nonsense in much the way Wittgenstein does in *Philosophical Investigations* (the comparison isn't meant to reflect badly on Wittgenstein). *If* Carroll is trying to teach children how to avoid nonsensical errors, his method, though fictive as opposed to meditative, is closely allied to Wittgenstein's: to teach through example, to cure through inoculation and wit (Pitcher 1965, 592). As Pitcher argues, 'the very same confusions with which Wittgenstein charges philosophers were deliberately employed by Carroll for comic effects.' And some of the same philosophical doctrines are ridiculed (1965, 593).[24]

But how exactly does Wittgenstein define nonsense? For the Wittgenstein of the *Tractatus*, nonsense is an arrangement of words (a proposition) that could not possibly fit within an imagined reality. His ideal language or naming corresponds absolutely to Reality, is a diagram of its functioning; nonsense is an incomprehensible glitch in the diagram – not only is it not true, it is not even false.

Later, Wittgenstein moved away from this systematization of language towards a view of it as a deed, a gesture that evolves through use and in a specific context. Philosophical nonsense, in this scenario, is language decontextualized, language that has been mishandled, wrested from specific contexts where it is serving, gesturally, to communicate. This definition is closely related to Nonsense, in which language as a meaningful structure is destabilized, in part because of the misuse of words. As in Lear's limerick:

> There was an Old Man who supposed,
> That the street door was partially closed;
> But some very large rats, ate his coats and his hats,
> While that futile old gentleman dozed.
> (1947, 16)

Why 'futile' instead of, say, 'misinformed' or 'deluded,' or even more appropriately 'stupid,' since the partially closed door in the accompanying illustration offers no protection? By using the adjective 'futile' in what seems to be a sensically inappropriate manner, Lear recontextualizes it and so illustrates how much one's experience of meaning depends on the context, the use of a word. He also encourages the reader to look back and manufacture a new meaning appropriate to this new use. Lear's misuse of the word 'futile' draws attention to the intertextual possibilities of every word in the rhyme; each word has other meanings and contexts that resonate behind current contextual usage. And each word has the potential to generate awkward sense if displaced. By forcing 'futile' to stretch its range of meanings in order to accommodate the verse's 'sense,' one admits into the 'background' of the limerick, as well, the possible range of meanings for its other words. Those meanings don't inundate and eradicate the sense of the poem; they are constrained, just barely, for the present moment of each word's use.

Another example of meaning affected by context is Carroll's word 'Snark.' One of its accepted functions is now a noun denoting 'an imaginary animal.' However, far from having created a neologism to name the elusive object of the Baker's search, it is highly possible that Carroll merely borrowed an English dialect term: 'snark' – an intransitive verb meaning 'to snore, snort'; a transitive verb meaning 'to find fault with, nag.' If this is the case, then Carroll, by giving a rare but existing word a new nonsensical use, gave it an entirely new context and initiated a transformation of meaning and function within sentence structure. This transformation or extension of meaning was completed when Carroll's 'definition' of 'snark' became included in that social institution, the dictionary.

Wittgenstein doesn't provide the sole philosophical account of nonsense, of course. A quick and general look at the six types of nonsense listed by A.C. Baier in the *Encyclopedia of Philosophy* (1967) may help extend one's understanding of how philosophical nonsense works. Examples of most of these categories can be found in Nonsense, but neither the genre nor the linguistic disruption (as a literary occurrence) are limited to these types. Baier explains the types by placing them within a hierarchical paradigm – the first type distorts sense minimally and is comprised of the most recognizably English words and structures. As one goes through the list, she claims, nonsensical disruption enters on a progressively larger scale by assaulting progressively smaller units of sense; it moves from sentence in context (the equivalent of literary nonsense's text or paragraph) to sentence itself, to phrase, to word.

Baier begins with 'obvious falsehood' (1967, 5:520), a statement that is clearly contradicted by the circumstances under which it is stated. If, for instance, at the Queen's croquet match, Alice had told the Cheshire-Cat: 'Everyone's getting along oh-so-well, and hedgehogs are wonderfully accurate croquet balls,' she would have been guilty of type one nonsense. Watching the game for a moment would reveal to anyone that the hedgehogs in Wonderland were hopelessly useless as croquet balls and that there was considerable dis-ease among all of the players.

'Semantic nonsense' is the second type Baier lists; here 'the rules or conventions violated are those tying [a] well-formed sentence to certain nonlinguistic contexts' (1967, 5:520). An example might be using 'goodbye' as a greeting; Marx Brothers' movies are replete with such semantic nonsense.

Baier lists 'category mistakes' or 'semi-sentences' next. In this third type of nonsense, a generally well-formed sentence includes a predicate that is not suitable for its subject. She admits that figurative language can break this rule without producing nonsense; 'the kettle is boiling' is metonymic, not nonsensical, although it is physically impossible for a *kettle* to boil (1967, 5:520).[25] Baier acknowledges that this type of 'mistake' is frequently found in Nonsense. Take, for instance, this extended category mistake in Lear's description of the Co-operative Cauliflower in 'The Story of Four Little Children Who Went Round the World': 'they soon found that what they had taken for an immense wig was in reality the top of the cauliflower, and that he had no feet at all, being able to walk tolerably well with a fluctuating and graceful movement on a single cabbage stalk, an accomplishment which naturally saved him the expense of stockings and shoes' (1947, 102–3). This example is more evidence of the fineness of Lear's lexical discriminations and of language's inherently nonsensical nature, the 'mistake' being an extended pun on 'stalk' – as the stem of a plant or a manner of walking.

'Nonsense strings' are another form of nonsense that Baier notes. This type is made up of 'strings of familiar words lacking, to a greater or lesser extent, the syntactic structure of the paradigms of sense or any syntax translatable into the familiar' (1967, 5:521). Such strings are related to the nearly impossible asyntactical language posited earlier, and are examples of Chomsky's ungrammatical 'sentence.' Baier's sample – 'Jumps digestible indicators the under'

(1967, 5:521) – is reminiscent of work by the more radical of the
'L=A=N=G=U=A=G=E' poets.

The next type, 'vocabulary nonsense,' is a common, almost an
essential, element of Nonsense. 'Utterances which have enough familiar elements to enable us to discern a familiar syntax, but whose
vocabulary, or a crucial part of it, is unfamiliar, and untranslatable
into the familiar vocabulary' (1967, 5:521) make up vocabulary nonsense. Lear's toeless pobble and his luminous-nosed dong, Carroll's
jabberwock and boojum, and Dennis Lee's silver honkabeest are
included in this category; there are many examples in Joyce's *Finnegans Wake*, Thibaudeau's *from Throgmoggle*, and Artaud's 'translation' of *Jabberwocky* as well.

Baier's sixth and final type of nonsense is pure gibberish. '[Neither]
familiar syntax nor familiar vocabulary, still less familiar category
divisions or semantic appropriateness' (1967, 5:521) can be found in
such specimens of nonsense. Baier asserts that such nonsense continues to be a 'part of some language, to the minimal extent of sharing its alphabet with that language' (1967, 5:521).

I quote this statement again (it was included in the initial survey
of definitions) because of the importance of its claim that nonsense
is never outside of language as it is broadly conceived. Because
Wittgenstein's idea of meaning is inextricable from process, even the
gibberish of type six nonsense may have a potential for lexical meaning. Since the meanings and limits of language contract and expand
over time, it is at least conceivable (although currently improbable)
that at some time 'vokalupeist' might be a meaningful English word.
And if it *is* conceivable, one has to admit that gibberish can never be
entirely excluded from the possibility of making sense.[26]

Note, however, that 'vokalupeist' cannot be made a meaningful
word by my use of it; though it does have, as a result of my use, a
second order meaning – 'vokalupeist' is an example of a word that
cannot be made meaningful by my use of it. Language is saved from
Humpty Dumpty–ism by the public element of Wittgenstein's definition; words don't mean according to *individual* use. In fact, Pitcher
believes that Wittgensteinian philosophy, with its insistence on the
distinction between 'definition' and 'the mental activity of *meaning*'
(Wittgenstein [1953] 1958, I.665), can successfully silence Humpty
Dumpty (1965, 603). Wittgenstein argues: 'But – can't I say "By 'abra-
cadabra' I mean toothache?" Of course I can; but this is a definition;
not a description of what goes on in me [i.e., the mental process of

meaning] when I utter the word' ([1953] 1958, I.665). When Humpty Dumpty defines 'toves,' the word doesn't necessarily mean in that way for him; he has stipulated a definition that is probably utterly irrelevant to the question of what is meant.

'You've no idea how confusing it is all the things being alive':
Linguistic Materiality, Reference, and Innuendo

For Wittgenstein, the nonsense of language on holiday is language decontextualized; for Carroll, it steps outside the system of what common sense deems acceptable, exposing common sense for what it is – a constraint upon an inherently illogical and lively language. In Wonderland, and in Nonsense, language is alive. Ede offers a twist on Alice's complaint to the Cheshire-Cat – 'you've no idea how confusing it is all the things being alive' (Carroll [1865] 1971, 92); she notes that the words themselves are alive though Alice fails to see this, fails to realize how her limited view of language tries to 'deaden,' limit, and classify all the wonder in Wonderland (1975, 111). Part of that wonder, as has already been pointed out, results from the fact that turns of phrase ('mad as a hatter,' 'mad as a march hare') become flesh and blood.

Nonsense is a world of words (Sewell 1952, 17), and demonstrates that language is 'built up,' according to Haughton, 'between babble and Babel' (1988, 5). Not only does it disorder reference, as Sewell claims (1952, 38), but also it questions the reliability, the possibility of a reference that is not arbitrary. As such Nonsense is also frequently construed as metalinguistic (1952, 18, 20), as using language to talk about itself (Sutherland 1970, 119). An obvious and obfuscating example of this is Alice's conversation with the White Knight in *Through the Looking-Glass*:

'The name of the song is called "*Haddocks' Eyes*." '
'Oh, that's the name of the song, is it?' Alice said, trying to feel interested.
'No, you don't understand,' the Knight said, looking a little vexed. 'That's what the name is *called*. The name really *is* "*The Aged Aged Man*." '
'Then I ought to have said "That's what the *song* is called"?' Alice corrected herself.
'No, you oughtn't: that's quite another thing! The *song* is called "*Ways and Means*": but that's only what it's *called*, you know!'

'Well, what *is* the song then?' said Alice, who was by this time completely bewildered.
'I was coming to that,' the Knight said. 'The song really *is* "*A-sitting On A Gate*": and the tune's my own invention.' (Carroll [1872] 1971, 186–7)

Alice's confusion, and the reader's, arises from a failure to distinguish (as Carroll via the White Knight does) 'among things, the names of things, and the names of names of things' (Gardner 1970, 306). Nonsense requires that one do just that, however; to survive in a nonsensical world one needs to recognize the separateness of thing and word, of referent, sign, and signifier. Such acute awareness of language as language, and of its naming function, often leads to the inability to communicate, which is rampant in nonsense.

Foss the cat, Susan Vigeurs's Nonsensical sparring partner, follows Humpty Dumpty's lead (perhaps this should warn of a potential problem), and says that words in Nonsense have 'an independence that begins in their failure to communicate meaning and ends in [their] having no representative or symbolic function at all. Language becomes material' (Vigeurs 1983, 141–2). Linguistic materiality in Nonsense will be explored in detail in the second part of this book, but Foss's reasoning in his discussion of materiality needs to be considered here. Vigeurs counters Foss with a telling point, one that, although only slightly askew from Foss's contention, provides a better way of viewing Nonsense's materiality. 'Words in nonsense,' she argues, 'have an independent life. They are not responsible for meaning' (1983, 142). Not being responsible for meaning is not the same as not having meaning. Rather it suggests that nonsensical words do not themselves strongly suggest a context of meaning – as 'slobaciously' does not, as 'borogoves' does not. And that the act of meaning as it is traditionally conceived is not their sole function.

But often language that challenges the traditional conception of meaning often doesn't filter and make reality containable either. When nonsense occurs, language and reality fail to coincide (Steiner 1982, 107). This sounds a bit like the early Wittgenstein unless it is extended – language and the illusion of an Absolute Reality fail to coincide. Far from being a screen protecting one from reality, language reveals itself as a factor in the creation of realities.

Nonsense language often involves a type of 'double-talk' (Sonstroem 1967, 198) akin to Kristeva's variations on carnivalesque or poetic language, language that is always read as at least double

(1980, 66, 69). In a letter to 'the Lowrie children,' Carroll explains: 'As to the meaning of the Snark? I'm very much afraid I didn't mean anything but nonsense! Still, you know, words mean more than we mean to express when we use them: so a whole book ought to mean a great deal more than the writer meant' (Cohen 1979, 548).

By admitting the protean power of words, Carroll unwittingly replies to minimalists like Sewell, some of whose views have been mentioned above, or Holquist, who claims Nonsense words have only one meaning (1969–70, 151). A literal reading of language invariably leads to miscommunication, something in which Carroll himself was so interested he used it as a working principle for much of his Nonsense.

Part of this doubleness, this excess of innuendo, and so potential failure to communicate (can this be read as a possibility of communicating too much?), involves the desire that is in and beneath language. Lecercle may attribute this desire to *délire* only, but Kristeva points out that it functions at some level in all language. As Alwin Baum argues in 'The Semiotics of Paradox,' Humpty Dumpty's language is 'the looking-glass reflection of social discourse – its alter-ego, the subconscious. It is precisely the anarchy of association which social language must attempt to repress, since language is the primary vehicle through which pre-conscious desire may articulate itself' (1987, 78). The difference is not the presence of desire, but the degree to which that desire is suppressed. In 'social' or common sense language, desire is suppressed as firmly as possible. *Délire* lets desire run rampant – no repression here. But nonsense both represses and indulges, structures and releases, desire. My discussion of desire and language, of how desire can be seen as a ground for my ideas about nonsense and as a link between Nonsense and poetic language, however, will be saved for Part Two.

'Nobody'

—◆◆—

'I see nobody on the road,' said Alice.
'I only wish *I* had such eyes,' the King remarked in a fretful tone. 'To be able to see Nobody! And at that distance too!'
  – Lewis Carroll, *Through the Looking-Glass*

The White King's astonishment at Alice's ability to see Nobody, and from such a great distance, is another proof that the Nonsense universe is composed of words, and that its pratfalls are linguistic. The King thinks that Alice really *can* see Nobody, that 'nobody' has an existence, a status similar to that of somebody, anybody, everybody else, in Looking-Glassland. Carroll is exemplifying not only the miscommunication so common in his Nonsense, but also the personification or objectification that marks one aspect of nonsense language.

This playful use of pronouns is not limited to Nonsense; in fact, e.e. cummings, one of the most 'nonsensical' poets of the twentieth century, recasts pronouns as what might be called 'pro(per)nouns.' In *anyone lived in a pretty how town*, cummings generates a multiple function for 'anyone' and 'noone'; they are simultaneously characters in a story and indefinite pronouns dramatizing their own grammatical function.[1]

In this interchapter I will briefly compare the use of pronouns in cummings's poem with their use in Carroll's *Verses from the Trial of the Knave of Hearts*. The approach will be quite different from that of my other interchapters; rather than offering a close reading of these poems, I use one aspect of each to illustrate an important difference between the genre Nonsense and other types of poetry: Nonsense generally maintains its balance between meaning and meaninglessness; many other poetries entertain both of these elements, but often have at least one undefeatable movement towards meaning.

Discussing cummings's poem solely in terms of its pronominal use may seem limiting, especially since the poem contains many other, much more disruptive linguistic and grammatical innovations. Indeed, this discussion assumes – perhaps unfairly – that a reader recognizes within the poem such linguistic tricks as syntactical inversions; the changing of a word's grammatical function from, for instance, verb to noun, conjunction to adjective; and semantic distortion. I concentrate on what seems to be one of cummings's least radical linguistic moves in this poem because it provides one of the poem's strongest gestures towards meaning. While all of his disruptive turns of phrase help cummings to undermine and challenge normal sensical structures, his 'pro(per)nouns' root the poem in a sensical tradition somewhat removed from generic Nonsense.

cummings's poem requires one to read 'anyone' as a character's name or proper noun in order to make grammatical sense of it. As James Paul Gee points out, the first line seems like a fairly regular sentence if 'anyone' is read in this way (1983, 125). Since one *does* take 'anyone' this way, and the poem clearly suggests that a reader should do so, what develops is a linguistic love story. The relationship between 'anyone' and 'noone' is sketched out in the verse, although it is not clear from the poem if 'anyone' ever notices 'noone' or is aware of her love for him.

There is another aspect to the love story 'told' in the poem – a negative aspect. The 'someones' and 'everyones' 'in the pretty how town' are indicative of an apathy underscoring the 'relationship' between 'anyone' and 'noone.' These adults '[care] for anyone not at all' (l.6) and never notice that 'noone' loves 'anyone.' Some of the children in the poem, however, guess 'that noone loved him [anyone] more by more' (l.12). Reading this line with the indefinite pronouns functioning in their *normal* grammatical roles further emphasizes the countermovement of cummings's poem; Gee suggests that, 'Taking "anyone" and "noone" as pronouns, they [the children] have also guessed that people are beginning to love one another less and less' (1983, 133). 'Noone''s love for 'anyone,' then, is offset by the under-

standing that noone loves anyone anymore, a reality clearly demon-
strated by the poem's 'someones' and 'everyones.'

But this narrative of love is also the personification (almost) of a
grammatical rule. The close union between the characters 'anyone'
and 'noone' is very much like the relationship between the pronouns
'anyone' and 'noone.' ' "Any," ' Gee points out, 'is what Otto Jes-
persen has called a "pronoun of indifference." ... We can say, then,
in a somewhat oversimplified way, that *any* basically occurs in two
environments, *negative* environments and *conditional* environments ...
It is excluded from other environments, those basically involving
simple positive (non-negative) assertions of fact' (1983, 125–7). So
'noone,' as 'a negative element in language,' creates the sort of environment in which 'anyone,' character *and* pronoun, can function
happily and effectively (Gee 1983, 127). Despite his frequent abuses
of grammar, and his reliance upon what Chomsky would call semigrammaticality, cummings *animates* this grammatical principle. He
has stretched the categorical function of these pronouns, in part, so
that he can vivify their traditional function; simultaneously he
unmakes and makes grammatical meaning.

The indefiniteness of cummings's pronouns allows the poem to be
read in at least two ways – as a love story proper that is set in the
context of human apathy, and as the dramatization of a grammatical
rule. While these pronouns can't be pinned down to a single referential capacity, the result is that the poem has several possible ways
of sustaining meaning throughout its entirety. I have explained Gee's
argument so thoroughly precisely because when Carroll plays with
pronouns in *Verses from the Trial of the Knave of Hearts* ([1865] 1971,
126–7), such is not the case.

The most important technical difference between the two poems,
at least in terms of this discussion, is that cummings experiments
with indefinite pronouns, Carroll with personal pronouns. Whenever
cummings uses personal pronouns in 'anyone lived,' there are clearly
identifiable antecedents that, even if these *are* indefinite pronouns, fit
into the sensical patterns of the poem. Moreover, both the indefinite
and the personal pronouns help to stabilize the sense of the poem;
once the stretch to 'pro(per)noun' is made, no matter how complex
cummings's linguistic play may be, the sense of the poem falls fairly
easily into place. Carroll creates most of his lexical disruption with
personal pronouns, which, if they have any antecedents at all, point
back to other (unstable) personal pronouns. Consequently, an abso-

lute meaning, or the locating of meaning in some solid object, is continually deferred.

The King of Hearts uses this poem as evidence to convict the Knave of Hearts, since he contends that it's about the treachery surrounding the Knave's theft of tarts; *Verses* would thereby be a gloss on another, much more sensical, poem – 'The Queen of Hearts / She made some tarts' (Baring-Gould [1962] 1967, 152). The possible referents for most of Carroll's pronouns (and these are *possible* as opposed to *probable* since there is nothing in the poem to support the connections made) lie outside the text of Carroll's poem, and in the Mother Goose rhyme whose characters animate Carroll's story. 'He' may be thought to refer to the Knave, and 'She' to the Queen of Hearts, but even so the sense of Carroll's poem is not clarified by these antecedents since, despite the King's rather creative attempts at rendering such an interpretation feasible ([1865] 1971, 127–8), the rest of the poem doesn't conform to the theft/trial scenario.

The absence of antecedents for the personal pronouns isn't the sole disruption of sense in Carroll's poem, however. The sheer number of these pronouns – forty-two in twenty-four lines – help to muddle meaning. This kind of limited excess is typical of Nonsense; Carroll not only demonstrates how tenuously sense is tied to grammatical and linguistic rules, but also revels in this tenuousness. It is not enough to demonstrate this connection; Nonsense nearly always inundates a reader with it. What might have been a minor disturbance to sense becomes a major upheaval.

The scarcity of nouns (only nine in the whole poem) adds to its lack of concrete sense. Almost all of them refer to an abstract notion or category rather than to an actual, and well-defined, thing: 'character,' 'word,' 'matter,' 'affair,' 'notion,' 'fit,' 'obstacle,' 'secret,' 'rest.' Even these more concrete grammatical forms are vague and obscure in their reference. Nothing in this poem points to much of anything.

Given Carroll's quite serious disruption of referential sense, it's interesting that he has created *no* syntactical disruptions at all. All of the lines in the poem are grammatically correct; the stanzas are too, though sometimes their grammatically sensical sentences don't fit together in a completely sensical way. For instance, in stanza one, the first two lines go well together, as do the last two lines, but the join between them, while grammatically possible, is less sensically comfortable than that between either of the two smaller groupings. As well, the stanzas have no clear relation to each other, apart from the fact they are in the same poem and deal with pronouns in a similarly cavalier manner.

What Carroll has done is disrupt language at a level analogous to that of coreference, *between* lines or propositions, rather than, as cummings does, *within* them. He gives a reader minute structures, nuggets of sense but no sustained framework within which to place them. The poem's 'logic' does hold, even if its overarching meaning is indecipherable. Unlike cummings's poem, in which several possible themes can be found, *Verses* has none. It creates sense on a small, rather than a large, scale. cummings does the opposite – he assaults minutiae in a syntax much more complicated than Carroll's, but never eradicates the possibility of a sensical interpretation of his poem. Both poems, to put the distinction another way, establish the balance between meaninglessness and meaning, which Chapter One suggests is central to Nonsense, but by eschewing a larger framework of sense for his poem, Carroll maintains that balance. cummings does not.

These two poems, of course, illustrate the difference between Nonsense and poetry, which uses nonsensical language, a difference not always so readily discernible, not always discernible in this way. Sometimes Nonsense verse exemplifies less well the type of relationship with sense found in Carroll's poem, a particularly fine example of the genre. And much poetry is not as nonsensical as cummings's 'anyone lived,' though that, as shall be seen, is nowhere near the disruptive extreme. Rather than providing any absolute measure, however, the distance between these poems suggests possibilities for measure; their difference highlights some of the characteristics of their respective forms. The second part of this book is concerned with the *similarities* between Nonsense and nonsensical writing, or, rather, with the ways in which those similarities show the usefulness of a grasp of Nonsense strategies in the reading of poetry.

PART TWO

TWO

'Touch Monkeys':

A Semanalytic Approach to Nonsense

Writing, like all the languages in the world, was invented, according to the ancient Egyptians, by the god Thoth, the Ibis. Scribes were represented as writing while squatting in front of an image of Thoth's sacred animal, the baboon.
– Julia Kristeva, *Language: The Unknown*

> – That kid, banderlog singing.
> 'I think, madam, you can hardly
> Be aware that your child's song
> Is a cause of annoyance to the rest of us'
> (The writer not what he says but whispers, like
> Brother Harry) 'Let me impress upon you ..
> One word you must inscribe upon your banner
> .. *Loneliness.*'
> – Ha-ha the monkey of it.
> – Louis Zukofsky, *A-13*

Generic Nonsense is a family tree threatening to branch out in almost any direction for just about any length of time. Such expansive rooting and offshooting of relations seems overwhelming. Indeed it leads one to suspect that nonsense inheres in all language. But let's shelve such suspicions for the time being, as things are 'shelved' in Carroll's Sheep Shop (where they linger, tantalizing, on the periphery of vision); whatever those larger implications may be, my focus is on a highly specialized type of language – 'poetic language.' I use the term as Julia Kristeva does: as applying to language that is more consciously full of meaning than the communicative language of everyday use (Lechte 1990, 35). Nonsense and poetic language engage the same sorts of material practices in their linguistic play – condensation, rhyme, rhythm, repetition, and other melodic devices. In fact, the two meet within this material side of language, within what I call nonsensical language. This meeting is manifold – a rich mingling of languages and forms of articulation. Kristeva's argument that poetic language is the scene of desirous eruptions into convention-bound language provides a model that can serve as both an analogy and ground for the theory of nonsense language developed in this section; in the course of using Kristeva, I will go through her theory, and out the other side.

A Slithy Slobacious Semiotic:
Julia Kristeva Meets Nonsense

Kristeva's theory grows out of French Freudian psychoanalyst Jacques Lacan's view that the unconscious is both structured like language and subject to the pressures of 'desire.' For Lacan, this 'desire' is the result of the repression of drives and wishes, and unconscious signification; it is a marrow-deep yearning for the m/other, who has been separated from the child not so much at birth (in the child's perception) as at what Freud identifies as the Oedipal phase, the moment at which the child is also, according to Lacan, reborn into language. In *Revolution in Poetic Language* (1974b), Kristeva alters and combines this notion of desire with, among other things, Saussurean linguistics and Derridian grammatology. Because Kristeva's provocative theory provides a model for my own theory of nonsense language, it's necessary to lay out her rather complex, and densely articulated, ideas.

In the Nonsensical spirit of definitive deferral, in whose wordly world one word always reaches back to another, I root my theory and my theoretical analogy in a literary one: a monkey chain of analogues. Entering Kristeva through Rudyard Kipling's writing is admittedly oblique, and might surprise Richard Gott, who sees Nonsense as very much of one blood with Kipling's rigid colonialism but, one assumes, absolutely separate from Kristeva's (and his own) Marxism (1988, 37) and from her conception of a socio-historically revolutionary language. It would surprise Kipling, whose satiric 'intent' and meaning will be wrenched open in the entering, as well.[1] It might even come as a surprise to Kristeva, whose theory analyses avant-garde writing, which attacks the very notions of the stable sense of self and society implicit in Kipling's writing. His story 'Kaa's Hunting,' from *The Jungle Book*, involves a society, the rules and exceptions in its formulation, and its efforts at communication, while Kristeva's theory concerns the psychic and linguistic development of the individual. A link between the two is apparent only when Kipling is turned inside out.

In 'Kaa's Hunting,' Mowgli the Man-Cub encounters the *Bandar-log*, Monkey-Folk, who 'play all day' ([1894] 1987, 40). Mowgli's teacher, Baloo the bear, describes the *Bandar-log* as outcasts, who 'have no speech of their own, but use the stolen words which they overhear when they listen, and peep, and wait up above in the branches ... They boast and chatter and pretend that they are a great people about to do great affairs in the Jungle, but the falling of a nut turns their minds to laughter and all is forgotten' ([1894] 1987, 40). These Monkey-Folk, 'howl[ing] and shriek[ing] senseless songs' ([1894] 1987, 41), lawless, playful, and ultimately destructive, are animate versions of Kristeva's idiosyncratic 'semiotic.'

'By *semiotic*,' Kristeva writes, 'I mean the primary organization (in Freudian terms) of drives by rhythms, intonations and primary processes (displacement, slippage, condensation)' (1985, 216). Her semiotic is markedly different from the word's usual use (semiotics as a science of signs) encountered in Part One; it is comprised of unconscious forces, drives, and 'instincts,' which, moving through the subject's body, are bounded by social and familial constraint. These drives – she calls them ' "energy" charges' (1974b, 25) – exist before and outside of 'meaning' (1974b, 36), before the subject (an entity always in the process of becoming whose development is connected to the regulation of a societal or 'symbolic' order [1974b, 37]) is even posited by the recognition (Lacan's 'mirror stage') of its separateness from other bodies. Within this constrained situation, semiotic drives 'articulate' what Kristeva calls a '*chora*,' a signifying node where the linguistic sign does not yet speak of separation or lack, doesn't express the absence of the Other, and consequently doesn't distinguish between the real and the symbolic (1974b, 25–6).

Like Kipling's *Bandar-log*, then, Kristeva's semiotic exists outside the Law of the 'Jungle,' outside of signification and the Other, of the symbolic that controls and orders the world in a supposedly unified and unbreakable way. It stands as a 0 to the symbolic's 1 – 'linguistic, psychic, and social "prohibition" ... (God, Law, Definition)' (1980, 70). It takes and twists the speech of the Other; 'nonexpressive' (1974b, 40) and existing before language, it can 'speak' itself only by breaking into and deranging the speech of the symbolic mode.

The presence of the semiotic makes 'communicative' language uneasy. But in poetic language the semiotic erupts; it ruptures the 'thetic' border that separates it from the symbolic (Kristeva 1974b, 62) and so '[prevents] ... the thetic from hiding the semiotic process that produces it' (1974b, 58). Susan Stewart says that Nonsense glosses common sense; in much the same way, the semiotic's volcanic laving of poetic language calls attention both to itself and to symbolic language, and points to its more staid and quieter presence in 'rational' discourse. Again Kipling supplies an image that may serve to flesh out Kristeva's abstraction.

A hostage of the *Bandar-log*, Mowgli travels with them to the Cold Lairs, the ruins of an ancient human civilization. He sees them there, attempting to use the court and buildings, but with no idea *how* these places were meant to be used: 'They would sit in circles on the hall of the king's council chamber and scratch for fleas and pretend to be men; or they would run in and out of the roofless houses and collect pieces of plaster and old bricks in a corner, and forget where they had hidden them, and fight and cry in scuffling crowds' ([1894] 1987, 53).

The monkeys' high jinks are a vivid image of the working of poetic language – they are playing at civilization, at humanness. They run about on the remains of some very fundamental structures, the architecture of a whole society, and make a mockery of that society. In much the same way, the semiotic element of poetic language runs unrestrained *under* the architecture of our civilizing language – lightly under syntax, but more significantly, with a heavier tread, under semantics. Unabashedly physical in the face of a threatened, rigid culture, the semiotic borrows the communicative tools of language and uses them (as the Monkey-Folk use the king's hall) in the 'wrong' way.

The *Bandar-log's* nonsensical society lacks Nonsense's self-referentiality, but it does carnivalize civilization, and its gestures and articulations hold both the thing parodied and the act of parody within a basic nihilism. Similary poetic language is, essentially, a nonsensical utterance that entertains Nonsense's self-referentiality, and undermines both denotation '(the positing of the object)' and meaning '(the positing of the enunciating subject)' (Kristeva 1974b, 58) within the framework of the very meaning it assaults.

The semiotic attacks the language through which it articulates itself; conversely, the semiotic is the origin of that symbolic language. The vulnerability of linguistic structures, which seem so strong, so unified and unbreakable, is a central tenet of Kristeva's theory. Engaged in a dialectical process, poetic language encounters its origins and passes beyond them. By passing back through the 0 of semiotics, poetic language achieves what Kristeva calls a '0–2' interval – continuum and multiplicity – rather than its highly symbolic '0–1' dichotomy of unicity and Law (see 1980, 70). Language no longer stops at solidity and single-mindedness; its architecture has been broken down, its meaning broken into an unending polyphony, manyness.

Yet all these energies, all these drives, lead essentially to nothing. Kristeva's *chora* is engaged in a process of 'negativity'; it 'is no more than the place where the subject is both generated and negated, the place where his unity succumbs before the process of charge and stases that produces him' (1974b, 28). Kristeva holds both language and the 'subject' or concept of the self to be composed of several heterogeneous regions, which Lechte says are 'disruptive of each other because there is no communicative link between them' (1990, 75). Like language, this subject is always 'in process/on trial,' always fluctuating, never stable and solidified, never consistent. The subject, and the language that articulates it, is constituted by desire, torn between the social and the stable realm of the symbolic (God/Law/Order) and the negativity of pre-Oedipal desires, the musicalized movement of origins: the pull is irresolvable.

Nonsense holds in flux seemingly opposing states, too, but even while it allows these states to exist within a larger continuum, nonsense language serves as the point at which they meet – it both bridges and contains antithetical elements. Nonsense, as a place of merger, is quite different from what Kristeva names the thetic phase, the point at which the semiotic and the symbolic (if imagined spatially) touch, the 'threshold' (1974b, 48) between the two. And it is here, paradoxically, at the point of merger that nonsense and Kristevan poetic language diverge; where Kristeva's poetic language involves the *in*habitation of the symbolic by the semiotic, nonsensical language requires *co*habitation, and not just of the semiotic and the symbolic, but of several orders more multiple than those in Kristeva's model.

In Kristeva's model, meaning resides in the identification of self and other, in the split inherent in the signifier/signified relationship, and becomes possible during the thetic phase in which the Other is symbolized. It produces a '*transformation* {from drive to signifier}' indicated by syntactical divisions (1974b, 55). 'All enunciation, whether of a word or of a sentence,' she argues, 'is thetic. It requires an identification; in other words, the subject must separate from and through his image, from and through his objects. This image and objects must first be posited in a space that becomes symbolic because it connects the two separated positions, recording them or redistributing them in an open combinatorial system' (1974b, 43).

In order to communicate in a directed way, to make a request or state a desire, a child must recognize and acknowledge the difference between herself and the person with whom she wants to communicate, between herself and the object about which she wants to communicate. My daughter can't ask her father for her stuffed bear, Edna, if she doesn't realize that her father and the bear exist apart from herself; or, at the very least, if she cannot conceive of them as very distanced parts of herself. One's sense of wholeness must be fragmented, or stretched to breaking, if articulation is to occur.[2]

The child's recognition that she is not connected inextricably with the rest of the world, the awareness of her own separateness, informs the thetic phase; it initiates language and, implicitly, lack. Signification marks the loss of semiotic wholeness, of a quasi-Edenic unity, and marks as well a movement into the need to symbolize, to represent the self in terms of language's structures – as the 'signifier' rather than as what is being signified (Kristeva 1974b, 48), rather than simply as being. This act of symbolization attempts to suppress and regulate the semiotic, a precondition of its very existence.[3]

Desire buckles against such suppression. This desire is for the 'wholeness' lost with the recognition of other bodies, for a return to a state that can be acknowledged only after it has been left. This act of desiring requires a subject who experiences lack, who already exists outside of the semiotic to which it longs to return (1974b, 131). Here is a double-bind that makes the fulfilment of desire impossible: the needs of a desiring subject can be met only semiotically, but they can be articulated only within, and directed only towards, a symbolic structure.[4]

Kristeva remarks that '[because] the subject is always *both* semiotic *and* symbolic, no signifying system he produces can be either "exclusively" semiotic or "exclusively" symbolic, and is instead necessarily marked by an indebtedness to both' (1974b, 24). The *chora* may exist before the subject, and so exist before the symbolic's attempted repression of the semiotic, but ironically it is accessible only within a signifying process, articulable only in its fusion with the symbolic. One is made aware of the *chora* only as it is incorporated within some system of meaning. Like the *Bandar-log*, the semiotic *chora* must steal an Other's words.

In her theoretical model, then, Kristeva offers a seemingly dual model, whose semiotic/symbolic interchange might look like this:

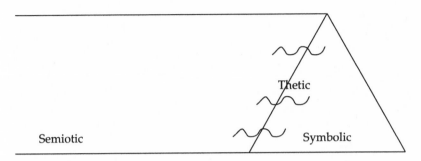

Figure 3

It could be argued that the thetic stands as a third element in Kristeva's system; if that is so the thetic (located about where I've put the slash, and taking a form similar to a slash) is a silent term. It is a holding in, a separating of, the semiotic and the symbolic. Lechte explains, 'The thetic is also the precondition of the difference between signifier and signified, denotation and connotation, language and referent; in effect it is the basis of all theses and antitheses, of all oppositions' (1990, 135). It is a place of severance, not merger. But the semiotic is intensely slippery, not easily withheld. Poetic language occurs in a Kristevan framework when that third element, the thetic, is breached, when an abundance of the semiotic spills over into the realm of signification.

The poetic text, Kristeva says, presents the dichotomy between *chora* and 'code' in its genotext and phenotext: the former is 'a *process*, which tends to articulate structures that are ephemeral (unstable, threatened by drive charges ...) and nonsignifying' (1974b, 86); the latter is not process but 'structure,' 'language that serves to communicate' (1974b, 87). Every text contains both genotext and phenotext, but in varying degrees. The more disrupted the language of the text, the greater the genotext; for, Kristeva argues, the continued influx of semiotic drives 'produces a catastrophe in the space of symbolic reference' (1985, 218). It initiates the '[recreation] in ... speech [of] this pre-sentence-making disposition to rhythm, intonation, nonsense; makes nonsense abound within sense' (1974a, 29–30). This catastrophe shows itself in the integration of 'primary processes' – most noticeably perhaps condensation – within the order of syntax and word division, causing 'the unity of morphemes' to break down. And, she continues, 'the most striking example of this process (which is only a simplification of the complex semiotic/symbolic relationship) can be found in Lewis Carroll' (1985, 218) – in the explanation of portmanteau words that he gives in the preface to *The Hunting of the Snark*.

If the resonances between Kristeva's theory of poetic language and nonsense, which I've been attempting to illuminate, have remained unclear at this point, Kristeva's single, brief gesture towards Carroll's work certainly establishes the potential for connection. But resonance is ultimately where the connection remains. While Kristeva supplies a useful model of language disrupted by an/other, and while the manifestations of that disruption are similar in both poetic and nonsensical language, nonsense parts company with the Kristevan paradigm's adherence to a seemingly dual system.

Nonsense, as I view it, has a different three-termed system: Meaninglessness, Meaninglessness/Meaning (or meaning-*full*ness, the domain of nonsense), and Meaning. The system might look like this:

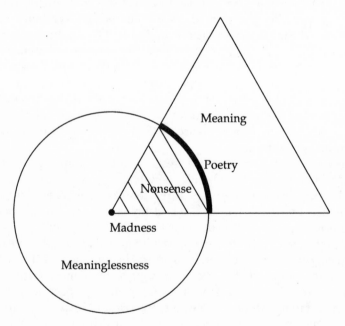

Figure 4

Meaning here is like the equilateral triangle of Kristeva's symbolic, but, as in Lacan's rendering of the unary signifier (see note 3), it blends with Meaninglessness (what Lacan calls Being). This blending results in nonsense, a meaning-full, never demeaning, parody of the symbolic triangle whose one side bulges out in wilful mockery. That bulge, at once the side of the smaller triangle and the arc of the circle, is the line poetry treads. The point at which the last vestiges of sense appear in meaninglessness is the point of traditionally conceived madness.

And if the spatial version of nonsense and poetic language differs, so does the source of disruption. Desire, the workings of the 'primal' *chora*, musses up Kristeva's poetic language, but while the energies and movements of the body certainly instigate nonsensical behaviour in language, they are not, as I construe such language, solely responsible for it. Kristeva finds portmanteau words exemplary; I turn to Carroll's hybrid words, but for different reasons and with different results.

Nonsense functions, I suggest, as the articulation or transliteration of one sign system within another. The suggestion translates Deleuze's ideas about portmanteau words (discussed in Part One) to a larger scale. Nonsense, like the portmanteau word that hosts two linguistic series, is created by the merger of two, three, four, possibly more, separate sign systems. Not the merger of codes, dialects, or national languages – of literary and legal language, of French and English, or any other subcategory of a verbal system – these create a form of 'secondary' nonsense; but the blending of different *ways* of meaning: musical, linguistical, visual, physical, one or more transliterated into another.

Each system or way of meaning – at least some of them would qualify as 'desirous' in Kristeva's thinking – is suspended in a state of partial alienation: music that has adopted the terms of a verbal alphabet but not given itself over to the meanings of wholly composed words; words that have moved towards articulating the body without relinquishing their usual verbal habits. The result is the excess of sense(s), the stretching of meaning spoken of in Part One, or what Forrest-Thomson calls 'the re-creation of the old orders, primarily through non-semantic levels' (1978, 161). Nonsense does far more than stabilize sense; it pluralizes sense, leaving no *one* sense, no *way* of establishing sense, stable. In it one finds layered systems of meaning, alternative systems of meaning, surfaces beneath surfaces, and so at times finds surfaces to be depths, interiors. The implicit hierarchy in Deleuze's distinction between surface and schizoid nonsense may be questioned when various systems of meaning merge, when the verbal surface of sense dissolves into another sensical 'surface,' and one mode of being breaches the 'boundary' separating it from another mode of being.

Nonsense language is like poetic language then – a speaking with, and through, and under, an/other language. Yet other languages reach beyond psychic desire and the unconscious to other disciplines and forms of meaningfulness. Nonsense is truly interdisciplinary, truly multiple, using seeming disorder or confusion to explore relations between orders, to discover new orders. Kipling's *Bandar-log* provide a useful analogy for Kristevan semanalysis, but they offer an even more cogent one for nonsense language: their parody and play, whether intended or not, animate the spirit of nonsensical language and nonsensical reading (minus the self-consciousness, of course).

Birth of the *Bandar*-logician:
Nonsensical Readings of Poetry

I don't intend to equate generic Nonsense with other forms of poetry here; rather my point is to *relate* nonsensical language and poetic language, and to find ways in which reading Nonsense can serve the understanding of poetry, to encourage readers to be *Bandar*-logicians who hunt out the '*Bandar*-logos' in poetry, who (as David Byrne says in the Talking Heads film *Stop Making Sense*) 'touch monkeys.'

Neither do I intend to produce critical Nonsense, although there are examples of that form of criticism; for instance, Frances Huxley's *The Raven and The Writing Desk* (1976) and Judith Crewes's 'Plain Superficiality' (1987). Both approach Carroll's works 'with a wry seriousness' (Huxley 1976, 8) and a wonderfully wingy logic (à la Carroll) that has the reader panting to keep pace with the mental aerobics. Huxley and Crewes' works are spirited and exciting, but not really in the realm of the *Bandar*-logician.

Numerous critics have noted a relationship of some sort between Nonsense and poetry since both play with language. A common crossover point is the recognition of poetry as a game.[5] But poetry has a more important connection with Nonsense, another shared quality that makes the application of 'nonsensical' reading techniques seem appropriate. While poetry almost always makes an undefeatable gesture towards meaning (even if that meaning must be read as limited by the system of thought that produced it, as Derrida would insist), that gesture is not, especially in twentieth-century poetry, limited to thematic or sententious meaningfulness. In *Modern Poetry and the Idea of Language* (1974), G.L. Bruns quotes Valéry: 'if anyone wonders ... what I "wanted to say" in a certain poem, I reply that I did not *want* to *say* but *wanted to make*, and that it was the intention of *making* which wanted what I said.' Bruns concludes that 'poetry in this sense literally ceases to be an act of meaning, insofar as the intentionality of the utterance is so thoroughly of a technical order' (1974, 87). Poetry can mean, or *intend*, without containing a definitive statement. Michael Riffaterre argues in *Semiotics of Poetry* that 'by saying something literature can say nothing' ([1978] 1984, 17). And Canadian poet Don McKay relocates the stress in Auden's comment in 'In Memory of W.B. Yeats' that 'poetry makes nothing happen' (1979, 82) to insist that 'poetry makes nothing *happen*' (1989, 208). Rather than being powerless, having no 'social' purpose, poetry is an energizer, an activator of 'nothing.' Whether or not poetry engages social issues, whether or not it has a political point, it still can embrace the negativity inherent in signification, can in fact be *more* political, *more* active, by disrupting the language in which social structures are defined. The nothing that poetry makes happen is potent indeed.

Poetry may well share Nonsense's dynamic stasis, its determined waffling over meaning and sense, or at least a portion thereof. It is this point of kinship, more than the ludic spirit of both poetry and nonsense, more than any other element connecting the two, which makes Nonsense a useful tool for reading poetry. To make nothing *happen*, to make it happen even while seeming to say *something* – this is the quality of poetry that attracts the *Bandar*-logician. Let's try a looking-glass inversion. Reading two pieces of Nonsense (by Carroll and Lear) in terms of their use of poetic language, and two poems (by Gerard Manley Hopkins and Dylan Thomas) with *Bandar*-logical eyes should demonstrate both the interpenetration between and the individuality of these two sources of analysis.

The most 'logical' piece of Nonsense to return to is *Jabberwocky*, the poem in which Carroll began using the portmanteau words (like 'mimsy') that Kristeva finds such apt examples of her description of poetic language's functioning. Looking at the first and most difficult stanza suggests how genotext (the material aspects of language) and phenotext (the communicative level of language) are interacting.

> 'Twas brillig and the slithy toves
> Did gyre and gimble in the wabe:
> All mimsy were the borogoves,
> And the mome raths outgrabe.
> ([1872] 1971, 164)

As has been argued before, syntactical structure, the positioning essential for communicating, is reasonably intact here. So the phenotext, though not unscathed, is certainly discernible. Kristeva would probably argue that the portmanteaux demonstrate how, in some places, the syntactical divisions of the lines *have* collapsed – hence the condensation, for example, of 'flimsy' and 'miserable' (if Humpty Dumpty's word is taken on this) into 'mimsy.' Perhaps 'brillig' is a word collapsing in on itself; Humpty Dumpty's glossing of it, read in a Kristevan framework, seems to imply as much. While one can still figure out which words function as nouns, which as verbs, there is a decided weakening of morphemic divisions.

Of course another way the symbolic organizes language into a stable system is by linking it (even if arbitrarily) to a referent: 'this' means 'that.' In this respect, the semiotic creates numerous catastrophes. Words like 'brillig,' 'toves,' 'wabe,' and 'borogoves' assault the denotative functioning of language; what, Alice and the reader ask, do such 'words' refer to? And because in Kristeva's system meaning is achieved through the process of establishing a 'self' within a dichotomous flux, because that self is asserted through discourse, the reader may be led to wonder not only about the sense of the word but also about the state of the subject. These words are not merely flippant coinages; they animate a tussle between the semiotic and the symbolic – a tussle the semiotic is momentarily winning. They are language in its '0–2' dimension, its carnivalized aspect, and show, despite Humpty's attempts to ground them in definition, the potential for an unruly multiplicity. Meaning, and so the self, is split by this semiotic infusion. Language, likened to a body, wrenches itself apart.

Equally important, this stanza illustrates how the semiotic and the symbolic can coexist, as they must in poetic language. Because Carroll's meaning doesn't fully dissolve, the ecstacy of *jouissance* doesn't completely destroy meaning. It never can. The symbolic mode is always needed to articulate that ecstatic drive. That is why the logical structure of *Jabberwocky* is so important; the symbolic gives form to the movement of desire. And that is why even Artaud doesn't lose touch with form, though his translation of *Jabberwocky* is more desirous, less constrained, than Carroll's original.

One way of describing the genotext, according to Kristeva, is as 'language's underlying foundation' (1974b, 87). Part of that foundation is phonic – so patterned sounds indicate a mixture of semiotic and symbolic. Lecercle insists that the phonetic laws of *délire* overcome phonotactics (1985, 35), and that Artaud is a dramatic example of this overcoming. An even more dramatic example of sound rising up against meaning is found in the sound poetry considered in chapter four. But all poetry weaves sound patterns with or against (in Nonsense more usually against) its sense. The stanza from *Jabberwocky* is no exception.

Its quite cacophonous balance of sounds is anticipated in the first word, ''Twas.' A flexibility of tongue and lip is required to start a word with *tw*, with its dramatic balancing of hard and soft sounds. That same dramatic balancing carries over into the *b, g*, and *t/ m, s*, and *w* opposition that marks this stanza. And neither hard nor soft can ultimately be declared winner – an equality in struggle central to Nonsense. However, the sound patterns in this stanza produce a culturally determined, affective meaning – as they do in Thibaudeau's *from Throgmoggle & Engestchin*. 'Slithy' may be said to sound slippery and slick, even if one doesn't know its archaic meaning; 'brillig' harsh and curt. The sound pluralizes an already split meaning; not only is meaning wrenched apart by the introduction of indefinable words, it is also multiplied by the connotations of sound patterning.

The genotext shows itself as well in such melodic devices as the regular and distracting rhythm of poetic language. In this stanza each of the first three lines is fairly regular iambic tetrameter. This bouncing rhythm leaves problematic words in its wake as the reader leaps along over pockets of unmeaning. The fourth line changes, though, seems initially to fall short. Scanned xx // x/, this line undercuts the predominance of the iambic tetrameter by substituting a trimeter, which never settles into a dominant pattern. The stanza's central rhythmic organizing principle (rhythm, being a semiotic device, promotes an alternative organization, an other order) is upset, but not entirely deposed in this final line. Here the semiotic plays hell with the order of metre, first submitting to structure, then toppling it, and finally allowing it momentarily to reemerge.

When I discussed the passage from Edward Lear's 'The Story of the Four Little Children Who Went Round the World,' I argued that its 'mucilaginous'-ness, its buzzing intensity, was the push of a multiple and polyphonic language trying to break open unified signification. Kristeva offers a theoretical basis for just such a description; her diagnosis would be similar, her terminology different. The sound rush is not mucilaginous but semiotic; and the primacy of this pattern, in which alliteration and assonance seem to dictate word choice over and above meaning, shows how, in Lear's crisply structured passage, the genotext asserts itself. The 'tops' of his 'transitory' 'Titmice' are probably 'tumultuous,' not because Titmice's tops tend towards tumult, but because alliteration demands it. In fact, how *can* the top of a Titmouse be tumultuous? The influx of sound is such that either one's sense of the real or one's understanding of the meanings of words must give. Again a death drive presents itself in the form of phonic play; by undermining one's notion of stable symbolic meaning, these excesses of sound undermine the stability of identity.

Of course there are far fewer examples here than in Carroll's *Jabberwocky* of the collapse of morphemes and the challenging of syntactic order. 'Slobaciously' is the only instance of a visible break in syntactical divisions. However, Lear's oxymoronic use of adjectives and adverbs puts a strain upon syntax as a relational construct. If the symbolic maintains its grasp on the world by relating one word to another based on a very fixed notion of what each word denotes and on what terms it can relate to the words around it, then Lear's semiotic impulse negates that ordering by inserting contradiction into the relational process. How *can* 'splendour' be 'trivial'?

To look to the other side of the inversion. David Sonstroem, in 'Making Earnest of the Game,' contends that reading Hopkins in terms of nonsense is very revealing, though his definition of nonsense is quite different from mine. He suggests that Hopkins's seriousness is qualified by what seems playful and points to the sadness inherent in Lear's playfulness (1967, 192–3). Both writers exhibit a childlike element in their work; but, he adds, 'the greatest similarity between the two is simply in the texture and flow of their lines' (1967, 193). He goes on to list the many stylistic (nonsensical) elements that shape the flow of Hopkins's lines.

Sonstroem notices that Hopkins uses portmanteau words, and runs other words together – 'Amansstrength,' 'churlsgrace' – and calls the technique a variant on portmanteaux. Hopkins also pulls words together by hyphenating them – 'dappled-with-damson,' 'seraph-arrival,' 'Never-eldering.' In *Spring and Fall: To a Young Child*, the first four lines are themselves a nonsense jungle. And what is nonsensical about a word like 'unleaving' (which seems only a short jaunt from the 'legitimate' unleafing) is not just its morphemic upheaval but also its palimpsestic functioning. It conflates the forms of verb and noun, holds activity and stasis together in one nonsensical word. The roots of this neologism are clear. 'Unleaving' is itself, but it is also 'leaf'/'leaves' and 'to leave.' Theologically this functions as an incarnation of the active verbal, the divine union of speech and act linked to creation in Genesis. It also creates a union of the temporal (active) and the eternal (static).

Hopkins uses sound, especially alliteration, to connect disparate words and establish a musical subtext. This line from *The Windhover* shows how one alliterative pattern slides into another: 'I caught this morning morning's minion, king- / dom of daylight's dauphin, dapple-dawn-drawn Falcon, in his riding.' Internal rhyme – 'Fall, gall themselves, and gash gold-vermillion' (*The Windhover*); 'Stones ring; like each tucked string tells, each hung bell's' (*As kingfishers catch fire*) – offers another, sometimes conflicting, pattern of sound to augment the alliteration. End rhyme is often forced (Sonstroem 1967, 193); words are split 'at the end of a line for an unusual rhyme' (1967, 194). Lists (usually adjectival) are common (1967, 194), as in: 'Off her once skeined stained veined variety upon, all on two spools; part, pen, pack' (*Spelt from Sibyl's Leaves*).

After remarking upon the similarity of techniques used by Lear and Hopkins, Sonstroem entertains their differences: 'Whereas the conventional poet's practice is first to make sense and yet have it come out rhyme, and the nonsense poet's practice is first to make rhyme and have it come out to the embarrassment of sense, Hopkins's practice is first to make rhyme and yet have it come out sense' (1967, 200).

The emphasis on rhyme can be traced to Sonstroem's insistence upon rhyme's primacy in nonsense (1967, 198). And, while clearly his distinction is not mine, it is of some use here. In Kristevan terms the quotation above might read as follows: conventional poetry aims at sense and communication (phenotext) but lets in moderate amounts of sound play (desire/genotext); Nonsense overwhelmingly lets in desirous and other languages until it inundates and embarrasses the symbolic, without ever eradicating the phenotext; Hopkins starts with desire (genotext) as a motivating principle, but uses it to bolster the phenotext. Such a 'translation' is not just a handy way to work in some thick terminology; it widens considerably the implications of Sonstroem's distinctions. There is no denying that Hopkins is a poet of sense, of theological sense; but, like Buddhist koans, his poems use nonsense to reach that sense.

Two elements of Hopkins's poetic – 'sprung rhythm' and 'inscape' – add to this nonsensicality. In his 'Author's Preface' of 1883, Hopkins calls sprung rhythm the rhythm of common speech, of written prose, of music, and of nursery rhyme (1970, 49). In it, he says, the first syllable of every foot is always stressed, and can be followed by slack syllables (in number ranging from none to three). The length of feet is not fixed, but varies from the monosyllabic to the tetrasyllabic. What is related to the establishment of a genotext is not only the lilting rhythm such scanning results in, but also its tendency to 'rove over' (1970, 48); in this method of scanning, the line breaks are discounted, feet can uninterruptedly span the end and beginnings of lines. So the rhythm, the arrangement of the sound, works against the more formal line breaks. Paradoxically, the movement of common speech, or Hopkins's version thereof, undermines its more structured and conventional poetic equivalent.

Inscape, Hopkins's belief in the 'thisness' of a thing, the presence of its being, seems at first an odd inclusion in the list of nonsense techniques and principles. But, while Hopkins clearly is working with a divine sense of being, quite alien to Kristeva's notion of the beingness of semiotic presence or to Lacan's concept of being, inscape does motivate for Hopkins the linguistic distortions that Kristeva attributes to the semiotic. Desire is not unlike a frustrated need to 'be' in language, to fulfil the demands of an overwrought 'being' in terms of representation. Within a very different framework, Hopkins seems to have isolated a similar problem: the split between being and language. Where Hopkins differs most is his eventual attribution of inscape to language, to every word, so that – even as it seeks to express the inscape of various things linguistically – language 'becomes a counterpart of reality, not because it imitates some object, but because it acquires an inscape of its own, a self-sustaining individuality that distinguishes it from all other realities' (Korg 1979, 15).

By granting language an inscape, and so removing it from the realm of mere representation, mere symbol, Hopkins's theory of inscape in effect resolves Kristeva's dichotomy theologically. In Kristevan terms, it allows the semiotic a recognized status within language; desire is satisfied, the thetic is rendered unnecessary because the split between signifier and signified is resolved, theoretically at least, by inscape. Rather than breaking the Kristevan diagram down further, as nonsense theory does, Hopkins unifies the elements of the diagram and intermingles Meaning and Being; God, Law, and Desire. He reads divinity as the cure, not the cause, of division. His mixture doesn't debase theology and order, though it wrenches language; rather, in theory, it theologizes language, according it the greater authority of concrete existence.

A brief look at *Spelt from Sibyl's Leaves* will illustrate some of these principles more thoroughly. The poem follows the Italian sonnet form: the octave centres on the evening, as it 'strains to be time's vast, womb-of-all, home-of-all, hearse-of-all night' (l.2), and as the speaker anticipates its descent apocalyptically as death and judgment (or in the guise of despair). The sestet warns that dualities alone exist, that one must choose between 'two flocks, two folds – black, white; right, wrong' (l.12); its world is perilous and bleak.

This is a difficult poem with many long, alliterative, and assonantal words, often piled on top of each other. 'Earnest, earthless, equal, attuneable, vaulty, voluminous, ... stupendous' – this first line not only establishes three assonantal and alliterative groups (*e*, *v*, *s*) but also, with its ellipsis, keeps one in awe, in anticipation, as the final *s* pattern (a secondary theme in each of the first) is confirmed. And the turn from a pattern of assonantal *e*s to alliterative *v*s is set up to work against itself initially. The breaking point is 'attuneable' – meaning to be harmonious, equal; but phonic equivalency (alliteration/assonance) is shifted to another (albeit related) phoneme. Only after ellipsis, after a further break, are the patterns made harmonious, strung together by their alliterated *s*s.

Alliteration and assonance are dominant motivating principles in every line of this poem: 'But these two; ware of a world where but these two tell'; 'Where, selfwrung, selfstrung, sheathe- and shelterless, thoughts against thoughts in groans grind' (ll.13, 14). Sound overwhelms sense here; the thickly woven patterns eventually achieve the harmonizing effect of night, as all sounds are muffled and fade into, merge with, one another. The individuality of the poem, of its words, faces the same threat of extinction that the speaker fears from overwhelming night. He moves to accomplish linguistically the very death that he dreads, the equalizing and evening out that cause his despair. Thus the poem is a capsule of dread and desire.

The frequent hyphenating of words initiates the collapse, which the tone of this poem so eloquently presses: 'Fire-featuring,' 'tool-smooth,' 'womb-of-all, home-of-all, hearse-of-all.'[6] This last example has also an incremental power that, because of the common denominator ('of-all'), implicitly joins 'womb'/'home'/'hearse' and so runs the course of human life. Other words are run together, more solidly joined: 'beakleaved,' 'selfwrung,' 'selfstrung.' And the dialect word 'throughther' stands as a portmanteau, as two words welded together almost indistinguishably.

Other elements of the genotext lead one to perceive, beneath these tones of despair, a self-negating welcome. Words are repeated throughout the poem in various contexts – 'black' and 'all,' for example. The constant repetition, or rather near repetition, of words and phrases in the same line is also another mark of materiality. One of the clearest examples is 'her earliest stars, earlstars' (l.4), where repetition breaks down syntactic divisions, and the component parts of the first blend in the second. One sees, in this near repetition, a phrase falling in upon itself, the way night works. Other partial repetitions give a sense of peering through a darkness in which words maintain only the faintest outlines of their uniqueness: 'self-wrung, selfstrung' (l.14); 'But these two; ware of a world where but these two tell, each off the other' (l.13); 'Her fond yellow hornlight ... her wild hollow hoarlight' (l.3; ironically it is the 'hornlight'/'hoarlight' that is most deeply immersed in the darkness of echoic play). Besides Hopkins's overt gesture of interior doubleness ('off' as opposed to 'of'), this second example engages exact repetition and homonymic repetition: that is, rhyme – which Sonstroem calls Nonsense's reason for being, and which Barthes considers a 'structural scandal' (1964, 87).

Rhyming is another way Hopkins blends the poem into a homogeneous mass. The poem follows the rigorous rhyme scheme of its sonnet form (*abbaabbacdcdcd*), which, despite rhyme's relationship with the semiotic, gives some order to the poem but is counteracted by more determined half-rhymes and internal rhymes.[7] Hopkins's reader is constantly shifted away from the poem's forward movement and back into the morass of the lines themselves. The prevalence of half-rhymes, like 'Earnest,' 'earthless,' 'earliest,' 'earlstars,' and 'earth,' depicts a coming together across numerous lines, and not just a turning back in towards the centre of individual lines. The tentative ordering of formal rhyme is greatly shaken by internal rhyme as, once again, words fold back into one another. Perhaps it comes as no surprise that Sonstroem likens Hopkins's poetry to a word game similar to Carroll's Doublets, which works on the principle that one word contains many (all?) others (1967, 200).

The splitting of 'astray' in lines 5/6 is another example of structure favouring materiality over semantic value – the rhyme scheme demands that the word break (as/tray) in order to rhyme with 'stupendous' and 'us.' But this disruption seems even more dramatic than that caused by the internal rhyming and alliteration because, while all other elements of the semiotic and nonsensical intervention have tended to bleed things together, this one breaks them apart. The breaking open of any word inside a poetic which, because it sees a relation between the Divine Word and the poetically inscaped word, regards each word as a unique and vital thing in itself, is a serious matter. The wholeness of the word is split open; Kristeva might argue that the self is shown to be fractured and her 'diagnosis' would not be wholly misapplied.

In the midst of its speaker's fear of death and torment, this poem animates just such a loss of individuality. Language is so distorted by this excess of inscape that, ironically, its own principle of uniqueness is undermined. All the phonic examples of life's manyness, its continual interconnectedness lead to uniformity – except in the one instance (dramatic in its very isolation) when one word is broken into parts. The reader is left, linguistically, with two poles: the choice between 'two flocks, two folds,' between the immersing or the fracturing of identity. Either all words become one word, in which case their uniqueness, their being-ness is lost, or each word becomes more than one word (and this is possibly another way to read the rhyming and blending of words), in which case, again, uniqueness is lost.

For the *Bandar*-logician this poem courts union with that which it tells its reader to avoid. It is both a warning about the horrors of death, night and judgment, and a linguistic invitation to enter into them. As the speaker holds black and white to be the only alternatives, the only 'choices,' as he paints a chilling picture of this blackness, his language blackens itself. The beauty of this linguistic blackness further subverts the seeming direction of the poem. Hopkins uses many typically poetic conventions – rhyme, rhythm, alliteration, repetition – but uses them with an extravagance akin to nonsense. What is most important to this reading is that he does so to the partial contradiction of his 'sense.' The meaning of the poem is not destroyed, but it is pluralized and relativized as it entertains its own contradiction.

Bringing a nonsensical point of view to Dylan Thomas's poems seems almost redundant, for he stands as a poetic *homo ludens*. His work is full of jarring juxtapositions that make sense uncertain and difficult. Connections are far from obvious. Thomas claimed to use 'old tricks, new tricks, puns, portmanteau-words, paradox, allusion, paronomasia, paragram, catachresis, slang, assonantal rhymes, vowel rhymes, [and] sprung rhythm' (1965, 189) in his writing – almost all of which are to be found in Nonsense's own bag of tricks.

His poetry finds one of its strongest voicings in the musical elements and qualities that make up the latter part of this 'list.' His love of nursery rhymes, poems that he claims seduced him with their emphasis on language as sound, is a focal point in his poetic:

The first poems I knew were nursery rhymes, and before I could read them for myself I had come to love just the words of them, the words alone. What the words stood for, symbolised, or meant, was of very secondary importance. What mattered was the *sound* of them as I heard them for the first time on the lips of the remote and incomprehensible grown-ups who seemed, for some reason, to be living in my world. And these words were, to me, as the notes of bells, the sounds of musical instruments, the noises of wind, sea, and rain, the rattle of milkcarts, the clopping of hooves on cobbles, the fingering of branches on a window pane, might be to someone, deaf from birth, who has miraculously found his hearing. I did not care what the words said, overmuch, nor what happened to Jack and Jill and the Mother Goose rest of them; I cared for the shapes of sound that their names, and the words describing their actions, made in my ears ... Out of them came the gusts and grunts and hiccups and heehaws of the common fun of the earth; and though what the words meant was, in its own way, often deliciously funny enough, so much funnier seemed to me, at that almost forgotten time, the shape and shade and size and noise of the words as they hummed, strummed, jugged and galloped along. (1965, 185–6)

This love of 'the shape and shade and size and noise of ... words' is carried over into his own densely musical lines.

Such phonic play is augmented by other, equally nonsensical tactics: his gentle bending of syntactic rules, his metaphorical and metonymic word replacements, his sensitive exploitation of line breaks, his linking of constructive and destructive elements in single image-complexes, and his use of connotation to emphasize the reverberations occasioned by his juxtaposition of seemingly disparate matter.

Susan Vigeurs points to *Fern Hill* as an example of the apparent nonsense in Thomas's work: 'rules of grammar are being ignored – and those rules aren't arbitrary, but have to do with the way we order the world. Words have been jolted out of their normal relationship with each other' (1983, 143). Vigeurs seems to be using 'grammar' in an extremely prescriptive and narrow sense. Thomas may be quite associative in his linking of words, but he has not disrupted, in any major way, the structural integrity of his sentences; his sentences are always, at the very least, semigrammatical, more often fully so. However, she is right in commenting on the nonsensicalness of his work – a nonsensicalness achieved lexically more often than syntactically. Even the simple substitution of 'sun' for 'day,' quite a practical sort of metonymic twist, begins to take meaning in a non-communicative direction, to require a different sort of attentive engagement with the words and a questioning of their referential function.

All the sun long it was running, it was lovely, the hay
Fields high as the house, the tunes from the chimneys, it was air
   And playing, lovely and watery
    And fire green as grass.
   (ll.19–22)

Such metonymic substitution, like sound play, is central to Thomas's ludic writing.

Thomas describes his process of writing in terms that could have been lifted right out of my earlier taxonomy of Nonsense. He claims for his work a dialectic that 'breeds' contradictory images, each containing the potential for its own destruction and so uniting destructive and constructive energies simultaneously (see Treece 1956, 37n). Though one might question the presence of a rigid dialectic in his work, it's interesting that Thomas believes his images work this way. It may be more to the point to call his a poetic of noncontra-dictory opposition that revels in the fullness of meaning. Such an opposition, a 'creative destruction, destructive creation,' is what he required of fellow poet Vernon Watkins (Watkins 1957, 38). To borrow Pound's phrase, Thomas's poetry is 'charged with meaning,' with the multiplicity of meaning such critics as Rieke and Stewart relate to nonsense.

Thomas relies a great deal on connotation, on what Barthes calls 'the development of a system of second-order meanings, which are so to speak parasitic on the language proper' (1964, 30), in attempting to achieve this language.[8] Discussing Thomas's reliance on connotation in his notes to *Altarwise by owl-light*, which is arguably Thomas's most nonsensical piece, Daniel Jones suggests that the sequence is held together not by the common logic of reason but by 'the logic of a common relationship' (Thomas 1971, 263). But such a suggestion seems limited, for the workings of connotation, of the plurality of Thomas's references and interconnections argue for many relationships. These may be held communally, but they certainly (to read another sense of 'common' into Jones's comment) are not ordinary. The continual sliding of images, of relations and so of sense, works dramatically against the stability of communication that Kristeva makes requisite in the symbolic dimension and that would necessarily, one assumes, be found underlying 'the logic of a common relationship.' Jones's analysis, intentionally or not, implies a tendency towards univocality in Thomas's work that is hard to hear over the din of his echoing catcalls.

The nonsensical wealth of Thomas's work deserves sustained attention, but a look at sonnet VI of the *Altarwise* sequence will at least give an indication of the richness of sound, image, and connotation to be found in the poem as a whole, and in Thomas's corpus. The sixth is perhaps the most indeterminate of all the sonnets in the *Altarwise* sequence. While the words engender numerous possibilities for meaning, and are densely allusive to (among other things) Christian and classical mythology, they never settle down into any definite, definitive sense. Several of the images – for instance, Adam, the cock, the sirens, the cards – connect with the rest of the sonnets in the sequence; others, like the sea, connect with different poems. Words are repeated within the stanza: 'love,' 'lop,' 'pluck,' 'eye,' 'tallow,' 'wax'; so their meanings accumulate. These interrelationships don't help pin meaning down; instead they offer more ways for various lines to mean, more contexts for generating that meaning.

What reverberations lie between 'his' (or the water's) tallow-eyes (l.2) and the 'tallow' the narrator blows from the 'wax's tower' (l.9)? And what resonances lie between the 'manwax' (l.14; the semen from sex with sea-women?) and 'the wax's tower' (candle? phallus?) and the 'old cock' (l.8)? Such 'intratextual' webbing only accents language's manyness.

But to speak of language's manyness seems almost too understated a way of designating what happens in this poem. Words not only relate to one another through deft twists of image and association, but also give the illusion of containing or bearing other words as a result of those associations. The most dramatic example is probably 'the stinging siren' (l.7), which almost asks to be read as 'the singing siren' also. As in Hopkins's poetry, language functions as a palimpsest; one reads through the printed word to the other possible words, or combinations of words, which continually write other senses into the poem.

Thomas's language at once combines a raw physicality with his metaphorical and metonymic tendencies towards linguistic substitution; he uses language at a remove, substituting one term for another like an intensely sensuous dictionary with metre ('What is the metre of the dictionary?' asks the first line of sonnet IV). The comparison is not intended to damn him as prosaic (who could?) or dull (who would want to?); rather the comparison is meant to link him into that Nonsense world of linguistic equivalency and play, of language taken to literal and literary extreme – for he successfully balances both in the multiplicity of his writing.

To augment this variousness of meaning, Thomas uses adjectives that seem to have no immediately obvious relation to the words they modify. These rival Lear for sheer nonsense and fun – for instance, 'oyster vowels' (l.3), those diphthongal vowels that close up on themselves. If proof of the nonsensical orientation of metaphor is needed, this image will surely serve. Yet the image can be read as a delineation of the selecting of meaningful phonemes out of the vast pool of prelinguistic sound. These 'oyster vowels' are 'split through' by the 'tallow-eyed' 'He' of the previous line, as he '[burns] sea silence on a wick of words' (l.4). The sibilance of 'sea silence' is already awash, an amorphous noise to be cut through, sorted out, into meaningful sound, to be sacrificed to the 'wick' (of a candle, of liveliness) of words. The splitting open of the oyster vowels is analogous to the fall into language, the coming into the phonemes of the symbolic and staid reason. Such slicing open of noise, to make it more easily categorized, more univocal, anticipates the lopping of the minstrel tongue later in this same sonnet.

As well, Thomas displaces and juxtaposes words so that they modify in various directions. Because of its placement, 'tallow-eyed' in the sonnet's second line could be referring not only to 'he' but also to 'water,' though how water can be tallow-eyed is a puzzle. And to what does the first line of the stanza refer? Is 'He' a 'cartoon' – a comic, or a sketch for a painting – or is the cartoon the action that occupies the remaining lines of the sonnet? If this latter suggestion is the case, what colouring does this give to the 'characters' – to Adam and the medusa, to the 'old cock' and the sirens, all figures of grave mythical import? Such relational disparity breaks the hold of the symbolic realm of representation, for it makes impossible a definitive reading of the poem. By granting words like 'Adam, time's joker' (l.11) a measure of independence, Thomas insinuates the potentiality for all words to slip away from representation.

There are pressures on morphology here too. The division between words is threatened; rather than using portmanteau words or running words together, Thomas joins words by hyphenating them, works against the '[lopping of] the minstrel's tongue' (l.8) by forcing out words faster, in closer succession. 'Tide-traced' (l.1), 'tallow-eyed' (l.2), 'pin-hilled' (l.6), 'bagpipe-breasted' (l.13): each of these relatively unconventional juxtapositions moves towards the weakening of what syntax designates as a single word. That some of the pairs are alliterative only brings the two words closer together.

Slips in syntax and morphology are not Thomas's sole means of pulling away from singular representation. One need only mention the elusiveness of his allusions and his use of a grab-bag of myths, of possible origins and explanations that all vie for a favourable presentation. Thomas's mythic landscape is chaotic at best – certainly an ironic comment on myths intended to order perceptions of the world; many of these mythic symbols are also intended (in the beliefs out of which they grow) to direct perception away from the order of the world proposed by some of the very mythologies with which they are juxtaposed in this sequence. Thus, Thomas again nods in the direction of manyness.

Like his mythology, Thomas's soundscape is hardly clear-cut; musically Thomas is almost at the height of his powers in this sonnet. The stanza's alliteration and sibilance are but one aspect of this:

'sea silence on a wick of words' (l.4); 'stinging siren's eye' (l.7); 'The bagpipe-breasted ladies in the deadweed / Blew out the blood gauze through the wound of manwax' (ll.13, 14). The onomatopoeic sound of 'Pluck' is followed by a succession of equally brusque monosyllables: 'cock, my sea eye' (l.5). Even the rhyme pattern of this sonnet ($abca1a2b1bcadefe1f$) is hard to stabilize. But many of these rhymes are achieved through a violent wrenching as sound refracts throughout the sonnet, as violent a wrenching, perhaps, as the opening of the first phonic oyster. Half-rhymes and near-rhymes predominate over true rhymes – 'manwax'/'index'; 'till'/'tallow'; 'pluck'/'cock'; 'lop'/'love.' Like Hopkins, Thomas engages in heightened sound play. But the thrust of his play is far from homogeneous; rather it constantly pulls away from any attempt to knit together.

Another nonsensical feature of the poem is its self-consciousness. The denseness of the lines, the unnaturalness of image and juxtaposition constantly remind the reader that this is a construction, an artefact, something outside the natural flow of the world, of language, and of sound. How could a line like 'By lava's light split through the oyster vowels' (l.3) not set itself off? Moreover, if one accepts the interpretation given above, the line not only calls attention to itself because of its arcane imagery, but also reflects upon the very basic issue of the relationship between meaning and language. The awkwardness of the images frames the work with an implicit self-referentiality, and highlights the poet's difficult and skewed relations with language. He is behind all of these images, saying, 'Here I am, back here, orchestrating all these oyster vowels, and it's not easy, given the rifts in the wholeness of sound.'

It would be pointless to say that in the *Altarwise* sequence Thomas contradicts his sense; it would be pointless as well to suggest that Thomas establishes a solid and reliable, albeit hidden, framework of sense. That is why understanding nonsense language is so useful in reading this and other Thomas poems. All these factors taken together don't make Thomas a poet who undercuts the sense of his own poems, but rather one who engages sense viscerally, who gestures towards meaning in an 'un-meaningful' or perhaps 'overly-meaningful' way. For all the abstraction that Jones notes in Thomas's poetic (Thomas 1971, 263), he writes muscle onto the sinew of sense.

What one takes away from this brief glimpse of Nonsense through Kristevan eyes and of poetry through *Bandar*-logical eyes is an awareness that nonsensical language and poetic language function in very similar ways. One of the things the reader of Nonsense looks for is ways in which nonsense language works against meaning and attempts to unstructure sense within a sensical context, or to infuse meaning with meaninglessness. And Kristeva's theory implies that one productive way to read twentieth-century literature – especially avant-garde poetry – is to seek out ways in which it, too, unstructures and *restructures* meaning (see Leon Roudiez's preface to *Desire in Language*; Kristeva 1980, x).

Of course, whenever poetry is analysed one considers how formal systems of expression are shifted and distorted; one looks for ambiguities and multiple possibilities in reference. Although contemporary theoretical readings are urging criticism away from single-mindedness, traditional and practical criticism generally fold perceived ambiguities back into a larger, thematic framework. For instance, Hopkins uses alliteration to reify a theme, to consolidate the inscape of a poem; he wrenches words to demonstrate the inadequacy of language to express the infinite, and on and on and on. Admittedly, Christ is the transcendental signified for Hopkins, but his linguistic play activates other ways of meaning too. Kristevan and nonsense theory both question the possibility of meaning univocally – not just in the hope of serving a higher meaning, or in an effort to negate meaning entirely. These theories explore how a poem can hold meaning and meaninglessness in symbiotic relation, how it can work against its own, almost always undefeatable, inclination towards meaning.

There are dramatic differences between nonsense and Kristeva's theory of poetic language, but the similarities and the potential usefulness of Kristeva's system in analysing Nonsense and poetry certainly justify adopting some of Kristeva's terminology and adapting some of her ideas. Such borrowing is in the spirit of Nonsense: stealing in order to alter, breaking apart what is borrowed.

'Hunting Song of the Bandar-Logician'

———◆◆◆———

The Jungle Book isn't unlike this study, at least structurally. Between its prose chapters or stories are poems – tight poems, quite formal in rhyme, rhythm, and stanza, augmenting some aspect of the story they're 'attached' to. Poetic eruptions in the midst of a prose miscellany, their presence creates a tension, a linear disruption in line with the temporal and geographic nonconformity of the volume. While Kipling is hardly an iconoclastic or experimental poet, when he surrounds one of his poems with less materially-structured language he calls attention to the discrepancy between styles of language; the material or poetic elements of the poems' language are tougher to ignore because of their prose neighbours. Road-Song of the Bandar-log (Kipling [1894] 1987, 78), the companion poem to 'Kaa's Hunting,' demonstrates not only Kipling's strong adherence to poetic form, and so the foregrounding of material elements of language, but also the dissolution of that form when those elements get seriously 'out of hand,' and one order attempts to supplant another.

Sure signs of a formally poetic order are the presence of repetition and of a dominant rhyme scheme; the Road-Song, not surprisingly, has both. Its first two stanzas, of eight lines each, are strongly ordered by rhyme, are, in fact, clusters of rhyming couplets. And the final couplet of the first stanza – 'Now you're angry, but – never mind, / Brother, thy tail hangs down behind!' (ll.7, 8) – appears with slight variations in the final couplet of the second stanza. The change, minor as it is, establishes repetition as a force of flux (since it always occasions change) in the poem, instead of using it, as one might otherwise, as a stabilizing device; the twist in technique is important since the Bandar-log, we're told in 'Kaa's Hunting,' communicate almost wholly through the repetition of other animals' speech, through inhabiting and distorting other creatures' language. Repetition animates the parasitic nature of the *Bandar-log*'s speech, animates as well the subversiveness and anarchy inherent in it.

The third stanza continues the pattern of clustering couplets, and the generative change encouraged by repetition. Rather than ending with a small change to the closing couplet used in the earlier two stanzas, however, it concludes with a triplet that alters that earlier couplet, and then extends it:

> Let's pretend we are ... never mind,
> *Brother, thy tail hangs down behind!*
> This is the way of the Monkey-kind.
> (ll.23–5)

Reworking the form, Kipling uses this final triplet not only to lend insistence to the most important rhyming sound in the whole poem, but also to herald an even greater break from the established form: the introduction of a new stanzaic form, a new rhythm, and a new rhyme pattern.

The last stanza changes entirely; a quatrain with considerably longer lines, it has no couplets. Rather it follows an *abcb* rhyme pattern.

> *Then join our leaping lines that scumfish through the pines,*
> *That rocket by where, light and high, the wild-grape swings.*
> *By the rubbish in our wake, and the noble noise we make,*
> *Be sure, be sure, we're going to do some splendid things!*
> (ll.26–9)

This loosening of the poem's previously rigid rhyme scheme allows other rhyming possibilities to creep in; the phonic movement calls attention to itself by sliding (slantwise) out of one pattern and into another. The stanza's first line ends with a slant rhyme connecting it, tenuously, to all the final lines of the previous stanzas: 'pines' – 'mind,' 'behind,' 'kind.' And the third line of this final stanza has no rhyming coordinate – except internally. In fact, the only lines in the poem without true end rhymes are also the only lines with internal rhyme.

Much of this poem concerns noise, 'the noble noise' (l.28) that the *Bandar-log* make, stealing and jabbering the discourse of the world around them. It's significant, then, that the most noticeable, most jarring, break in the poem's rhyme comes at the point when the *Bandar-log's* jabber is named 'noise.' The noise of the poem, thematic and sonal, is doubly emphasized by this breaking open of the rhyming pattern. 'Pines,' though it has no true end rhyme, can still engage in some phonic patterning without relying upon the rhyme within its line. But if 'make' is to rhyme, it can do so *only* by playing its sound back over its own line, *only* by rerouting the forward flow of the poem's movement.

Such turning back to the line renews attention to the changes in rhythmic structure within it, and the other lines of this stanza, as well. The lines of the first three stanzas each have four feet and balance iambs against trochees. For instance, the first stanza is made up, with very little variation, of lines composed of two iambs and two trochees. A slight tension is created between these feet since the verse never lets one rhythm predominate. The fourth stanza, comprised of four lines of iambic hexameter, throws itself almost wholly over to iambs. The stretching out of lines, and the privileging of one rhythmic foot, allows sound, in a sense, to take over; the temporalizing of sound becomes at once more regular (so more noticeable) and more sustained.

Like the word at the end of its third line, this stanza jars with the rest of the poem's movement, disrupts the patterns already established while instituting another type of regularity; a rigidity of rhyme and a doubleness of rhythm are replaced by a doubleness of rhyme and a rhythm of increased rigidity. Each 'opposition' is orderly and alternative, but the final stanza provides greater room for sound to resonate and a less hesitant – more sweeping – rhythmic movement. Rhyme, rhythm, and sound play are used to emphasize their own abilities to generate meaning, their versatility in exploring alternative orders. Kipling may have styled this a poetic working through of the *Bandar-log's* inability to sustain any sort of order, to follow through on their intentions (a theme of both his poem and his previous chapter), but this spiralling of sound could also be read as indicative of nonsense's explosive unruliness. The formal structure that contains and promotes phonic play is potentially vulnerable to it.

Another equally overt indication of the assault on communicative meaning is Kipling's typographical use of italics. Italics emphasize the one line truly shared by the first three stanzas – '*Brother, thy tail hangs down behind!*' – and the final disjunctive stanza. Each of these uses emphasizes one aspect of semiotic incursion already discussed here: the first, repetition, the other, the dramatic change in sound value occasioned by an undermining of the rhythmic and rhyming patterns of the earlier stanzas.

The other use of italics in *Road-Song* is more intriguing; ' – *so* – ' which ends the fifth line of the poem is italicized. It serves a double function, acting as a parenthetical, demonstrative adjective, a gesture that points at once outside of the poem to an imagined concrete object and inside the poem to the description in the next line, the very description which, by interrupting the flow of the language, it delays. ' – *so* – ' gives the description through gestural language and prevents, momentarily, the relaying of such a description verbally. The technique, itself a gesture, is both futile and full, potent. The word simultaneously resonates with the rhyming pattern it supports to the detriment of uninhibited (or inhabited) communication, and underlines the communicative and referential aspects of language. Similarly it offers both caesura and a partial stop for the end of a line that would, otherwise, continue on into enjambement; the pause is inflicted, not natural. ' – *so* – ' in this context is a highly nonsensical word, an interface between semiotic and symbolic, or a conflation of musical, gestural, and communicative language, serving the needs of each at the same time.

One aspect of the poem remains to be considered; its tendency to deflect speech, to leave things unstated, to ... 'never mind.' The technique, repeated by Kipling in the first three stanzas, does more than add to the characterization of the *Bandar-log*, though by emphasizing their shiftlessness and lack of staying power it does do that. It raises the problem of nonsensical speaking, of things being said and unsaid simultaneously. Given the strength of the rhyme pattern, one is tempted either to view this 'coyness' as being arbitrarily conceived in order to suit the musical structure of the poem, or to substitute other rhyming and rhythmic possibilities, to seek out the words that may lie behind the deflections. If the former is true and Kipling chooses to squash the communicative function of language merely to play to the more material qualities of language, then the poem is surely an example of the privileging of sound as another sort of sense.

Kipling's poem animates in several ways its own nonsense; not only in its use of rhyme, rhythm, and sound play, in its use of italics and deflected speech, but also in its establishing and overturning of orders, the poem's language demonstrates the *Bandar*-logic it describes.

THREE

'There was an Old Man with a nose':

Nonsense and the Body

Add – ... the work of poets who see with their ears, hear with their eyes, move with their noses and speak and breathe with their feet.
  – Louis Zukofsky, 'An Objective'

you infringe upon me in my skin. I must speak then, squeezed like an enigmatic orange.
  – Nicole Brossard, *The Aerial Letter*

Nonsense's relation to the body goes much deeper than the obvious thematic one. True, much classical Nonsense uses the body, the grotesque body, as a springboard for its humour. Lear's work is peopled with bodies seemingly out of control; and *Alice's Adventures in Wonderland* still thrills strict Freudians precisely because Alice's body *is*, at least until her metabolism adjusts to the rhythms of Wonderland, uncontrollable: hysteria working from the outside in. An intensely psychological reading would argue that Lear and Carroll both use Nonsense as a means of working out their own 'socially unacceptable' sexuality and physicality, as frustrated assaults on the sexual strictures of their day. Then their linguistic upheaval would be a more or less conscious result of their physical desires. Such readings abound, but, not surprisingly, tend to exaggerate or simplify each man's sexual orientation.

  Yet Nonsense and the body have a more intimate and structural relation than that argued in purely thematic or 'voyeuristic' approaches. Nonsense is one result of the body's *dwelling* in language, of the rhythms and 'orders' of the psychological body's disturbing sense-making structures. For many writers, the body is a point from which to defy the limitations of logic or patriarchal sense, and so gesture towards nonsense through a sensual intimacy and eroticism. Part of this intimacy is directly located in the senses, in how they make 'sense' of the world around them, in how they make language. For language, like perception, is based on the severing and reconstructing of what is, on the reorganizing and crystallizing of the fluid dynamic between the body and its surroundings. Such language, sensual, physiological, is a common ground on which nonsense and poetic language meet.

'Shoots and Branches':
Nonsense's Grotesque Body

The Old Man's bird-housing beard; the famous curlicue nose; the pin-pointed, harp-plucking chin; that Young Lady's w-i-d-e-eyed stare: Lear's limericks and his illustrations for them are rife with physical deformity. Such bizarre representations of human physiology can't be put down just to dissatisfaction with his own ungainly appearance, though one can argue it is related to Lear's epilepsy and to the distortions of seizure. And it is not merely a case of 'them against me,' a way of singling out the eccentric or the marginal for social abuse – though clearly physical deformity often is the butt of such abuse.

Looking to another of Lear's forays into physical science, his 'Nonsense Botanies' (see, for example, Figure 2, or figures 5 and 6 in this chapter), proves helpful. The ridiculous deformations that result from his parodic Latinisms and literalisms aren't quite so far off the 'real' world as might be assumed; 'Tigerlillia Terribilis' (see Figure 5) does look familiarly like a tigerlily, albeit a terrible one with its petals – plush and purring carnivores. And 'Bluebottlia Buzztilentia' (see Figure 6) is just a few steps for the imagination beyond a bluebell. These are living flowers that exceed even the inhabitants of Carroll's Looking-Glass garden, but their elements are part of Lear's world and our own.

These excesses are the source of perhaps the least painful laughter Lear offers. But they are also indicators of the world of shifting boundaries that characterizes many of his limericks. The worlds of animal and plant, insect and plant, object and plant, mingle. In Part One these botanies helped illustrate the nonsensical result of literal-

Tigerlillia Terribilis

Figure 5 From Edward Lear *Nonsense Botany*

ism, of taking things at their word, by pushing aside the curtain separating words and things. Now a different curtain is pushed aside to reveal not the lively though limited prospect of literalism but rather a different orientation to, and within, the world.

For that is really the 'crime' of the Old Man with the nose (Figure 7): not just having a big nose, but having a nose so big it demands of its viewers a slightly different understanding of the world, and of the place the body makes for itself in the world. No matter what the Old Man may say, his nose is extremely large. So large, in fact, that by ignoring it, one risks tripping over it. This is a fine example of the nonsensical body, which metaphorically challenges the spatial limitations of the body in the world, and literally questions the relationship between the physical 'self' and the world, in much the same way as nonsensical language challenges the location of the

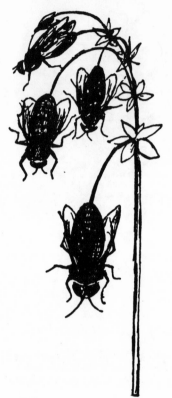

Bluebottlia Buzztilentia

Figure 6 From Edward Lear *Nonsense Botany*

'self' in language. The nonsensical body stretches out into the world beyond and, by doing so, enters into a relationship with the world reminiscent of that found in Mikhail Bakhtin's theorization of Rabelaisian carnival.

Katerina Clark and Michael Holquist credit Bakhtin with articulating a 'semantics of the body' (1984, 299) in *Rabelais and His World*. His is a playful and scatological semantics that relies heavily on the ambiguous nature of excrement and genitals, and seems quite unlike the writing found in Lear's work. But Bakhtin's semantics are not *merely* bawdy, and they can take a reader to Lear:

There was an Old Man with a nose,
Who said, 'If you choose to suppose,
That my nose is too long, you are certainly wrong!'
That remarkable Man with a nose.

Figure 7 From Edward Lear *A Book of Nonsense*

The grotesque ... is looking for *that which protrudes* from the body, all that
seeks to go out beyond the body's confines. Special attention is given to the
shoots and branches, to all that prolongs the body and links it to bodies or
the world outside ... The grotesque body ... is a body in the act of becoming
... This is why the essential role belongs to those parts of the grotesque body
in which it outgrows its own self, transgressing its own body, in which it
conceives a new, second body: the bowels and the phallus. (1965, 316–17;
emphasis added)

'That which protrudes.' Step back from the new body spawned by
Rabelais's out-sized bowels and phallus,[1] and one gets the Old Man's
overgrown nose, a phallus in its own metaphorical right. Yet, even
if one doesn't read into this appendage popular sexual innuendo, it
is a somewhat domesticated version of Bakhtin's 'unfinished and
open body' (1965, 26). What Bakhtin says of the belfry with an im-
pregnating shadow in Rabelais might be said as well of Lear's Old
Man's nose, and of the nonsensical body generally: 'The object trans-
gresses its own confines, ceases to be itself. The limits between the
body and the world are erased, leading to the fusion of the one with

There was an Old Man who said, 'Hush!
I perceive a young bird in this bush!'
When they said—'Is it small?' He replied—'Not at all!
It is four times as big as the bush!'

Figure 8 From Edward Lear *A Book of Nonsense*

the other and with surrounding objects' (1965, 310). Such fusion is also seen in Lear's many illustrations that show a person taking on the appearance of, merging with, the world around him or her (see figures 8, 9, 10).

As those limits are transgressed, so language is transgressed. The body that exceeds itself, visually, thematically, in Lear's limericks, is the same body that exerts itself phonically, rhythmically, playfully, in the linguistic subversion of his Nonsense. It's the genotext overstepping the bounds of the thetic, taking hold of the symbolic's nose and tugging it out of shape.

The language of *Alice's Adventures in Wonderland* seems less phonically, bodily playful, but it is, as Gilles Deleuze points out in *The Logic of Sense*, no less a language related to the body in a state of becoming:

When I say 'Alice becomes larger,' I mean that she becomes larger than she was. By the same token, however, she becomes smaller than she is now. Certainly, she is not bigger and smaller at the same time. She is larger now; she was smaller before. But it is at the same moment that one becomes larger than one was and smaller than one becomes. This is the simultaneity of a

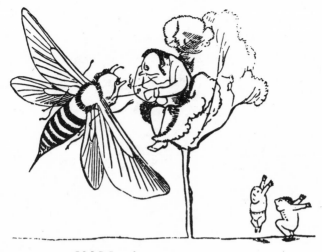

There was an Old Man in a tree,
Who was horribly bored by a Bee;
When they said, 'Does it buzz?' he replied, 'Yes, it does!'
'It's a regular brute of a Bee!'

Figure 9 From Edward Lear *A Book of Nonsense*

becoming whose characteristic is to elude the present ... It pertains to the essence of becoming to move and to pull in both directions at once: Alice does not grow without shrinking, and vice versa. (1969, 1)

The 'paradox of this pure becoming' (Deleuze 1969, 2) carries over into the language of reversal, of pull in two directions, which marks all of Alice's adventures (1969, 3): 'Why, you might just as well say that "I see what I eat" is the same thing as "I eat what I see"!' (Carroll [1865] 1971, 76); 'jam tomorrow and jam yesterday – but never jam *to-day*' (Carroll [1872] 1971, 150).

Even before she encounters the linguistic upheaval that plagues her, Alice must confront her uncontrollable body; this 'becoming' body (becoming larger, becoming smaller), not language, is the initial interface between herself and Wonderland. Physical fluctuations mediate between her own limited assumptions and a seemingly incomprehensible environment. Her elongated neck, her faraway feet: these require of Alice, as much as of the inhabitants of

**There was an Old Man with an owl,
Who continued to bother and howl;
He sate on a rail, and imbibed bitter ale,
Which refreshed that Old Man and his owl.**

Figure 10 From Edward Lear *A Book of Nonsense*

Wonderland, a shift in vision to accommodate her 'renewing' self. And it is this aspect of Alice's body that best serves my purposes now.

There is something comic and carnivalesque about Alice's contracting and expanding body; it blends with Wonderland, and it is most Bakhtinian in its role as conduit, as a point of intersection (Bakhtin 1965, 322). Such intersection is genital and excremental, related to the lower stratum of the body whose symbolism Bakhtin tries to exonerate from what he considers a simplistic and prudish rejection of good 'clean' debasement. But the genital regions are not the only regions that interact with, and affect, the world. The senses (perception) and skin (the surface that mediates between insides and outside) may also be construed as points of intersection. For it is through and at them that the body meets the world, transmits the world around it, or is altered by that world.

Replacing the Senses:
The Possibility of a Perceptually-based Language

In one way or another poetry has always played with the senses. Its roots in music attest to its intimacy with hearing, and imagery has always appealed to the eyes of both mind and body. When, however, poetic language seeks to be what Daphne Marlatt calls a 'direct transmission' (Bowering 1979, 66), rather than a translation, of the senses' perception, it risks nonsense. An odd twist since, as Rieke notes, ' "Sense" begins with physiology, with the body as it takes in data through the five senses. These sensations translate into mental phenomena, perceptions as understanding. Our spoken and written languages then transmit the meaning or sense supposedly in our heads' (1992, 5). Why then should an attempt at an 'unmediated' linguistic experience of the senses result in nonsense?

Because, one might say in Kristevan terms, by ducking mediation, the senses breach a version of the thetic, join the semiotic's revolt against the symbolic imposition of order. The thetic, as mediator between the semiotic and the symbolic, may be seen as a similar point of purported impasse between the actual physical experience of the body and the world, on the one hand, and the verbal embodiment of that experience, on the other. The key term in Rieke's explanation is 'translate.' Communicative language deems sensual perception foreign, garbled, so an attempt to split the body from its dynamic communion with the world, to tidy up perception a bit before articulating it, must be made. Transmitting, as opposed to translating, the senses means allowing their peculiar orders to resonate within the equally important orders of communication.

It is not merely, as André Breton believed, that the senses could, if allowed, *'lead'* to 'a wider horizon [than is] available even to the conscious mind' (Sheringham 1977, 73), though clearly the way that Breton engaged the senses in his poetry produced some very nonsensical work. While Surrealists try to 'dépayser la sensation,' to 'delocalize' the senses, as Sheringham translates it (1977, 74), in order to leap right over rationality and into the unconscious, nonsensical writers (rather than removing rationality from the senses) approach language by retrieving the senses from rationality. That is: rationality, by winnowing out the perceptions of the senses, by translating their effects into organizable phenomena, actually dislocates, delocalizes them. Theoretically at least, Surrealism, like rationality, takes the senses to a further remove from their source in the world, although these removes are quite remote from each other.

The problem is not so much how to *dis*place the senses as how to *re*place them, how to keep them, as Charles Olson says in 'Human Universe,' at the edge, 'the cutting edge' of humanity and the world in language (1966, 62). And how to do so in an actual perceptually-based language, rather than a mimetic version of such a language. Not all of the writers considered in this chapter succeed in their attempts to create this language, as not all are successful in their efforts to 'manufacture' (to hand-make) another type of physical writing, a 'writing of the body.' Both types of physical writing, how-ever, are connected to nonsense. It might be wise to point out briefly how the two differ from each other, before turning to the relationship each has with nonsensical language.

Like much of the terminology of French feminism, the phrase 'write the body' is most useful when read figuratively; a completely physical language is gestural, not verbal – even the most nonsensical of writings remains, ultimately, based in verbal language.[2] However, the phrase has social and political ramifications that need to be kept in view, especially in the latter portion of this chapter. Trinh T. Minh-ha takes exception to those 'male or genderless writers' who 'read "writing the body" as "the (biological) body writing itself."' 'For them writing the body,' she insists, 'means writing *closer* to the body' (1989, 41). She contends that writing the body is both abstract and concrete, personal and political; its physical qualities (vocalic, tactile) '[exceed] the rationalized "clarity" of communicative structures' and so makes 'theory a politics of everyday life' (1989, 44). Minh-ha's distinction between 'writing *closer* to the body' and 'writing the body' is a crucial one. A perceptually-based language does not attempt to write the body, but rather to allow the least possible amount of interference (ideally no interference, though such is literally impos-sible) in the transmission of the senses to words. This would require an attunedness not to the body and its rhythms, though they may influence the shape of the language, but rather to the actual experi-ence of perception. Often the point at which the theory and practice of writing from the senses differ is this point of attention; when there is another 'agenda,' one to privilege or explore the body for instance, the status of perception is lessened and perceptual language may be replaced by an alternatively 'physical' writing.

Listening to the Listenings of the Body:
Olson's Physical Nonsense

Charles Olson was intensely interested in creating a language of
unimpeded senses, and had a measure of success in doing so. In
'Human Universe' he writes,

What makes most acts – of living and of writing – unsatisfactory, is that the
person and/or the writer satisfy themselves that they can only make a form
(what they say or do, or a story, a poem, whatever) by selecting from the full
content some face of it, or plane, some part. And at just this point, by just
this act, they fall back on the dodges of discourse, and immediately, they lose
me, I am no longer engaged, this is not what I know is the going-on (and of
which going-on I, as well as they, want some illumination, and so, some
pleasure). It comes out a demonstration, a separating out, an act of classification, and so, a stopping, and all that I know is, it is not there, it has turned
false. (1966, 55)

Olson's answer to the problem of writing a perceptually- and physi-
cally-based language is the poem of body and breath.
    With the other Black Mountain poets, he sought an 'open' form or
'projective verse' that constituted an opening up of the poet to the
surrounding world, a less active engagement of the selective process
that weeds through, or shapes, the world and exalts the human over
the nonhuman. The distinction, as Olson makes it, is 'between language as the act of the instant and language as the act of thought
about the instant' (1966, 54). His prose manifesto 'Projective Verse'
(first published in 1950) hollers that 'always one perception must
must must MOVE, INSTANTER, ON ANOTHER!' (1966, 17); he '[puts] it
baldly' down to the physiology of the poet – 'the HEAD, by way of
the EAR, to the SYLLABLE / the HEART, by way of the BREATH, to the
LINE' (1966, 19). The best, most kinetic or energetic poetry, he suggests, comes out of a listening to the workings, the listenings, of the
body, out of a transliteration of those listenings.
    In *Proprioception* (1965), Olson modifies his views that the senses
are central to poetic energy, however. And this newer, fragmented,
chart-like essay seems to turn as well from the skin he had cited in
'Human Universe' as an essential location for the poetic act: 'the skin
itself, the meeting edge of man and external reality, is where all that
matters does happen' (1966, 60). Olson now locates two surfaces: the

physiological surface, '(senses – the "skin": of "Human Universe")
the body itself – proper – one's own "corpus" '; and the psychological surface, 'the surface: consciousness as ego and thus no flow
because the "senses" of same are all that sd contact area is valuable
for, to report in to central' (1965, 1). It comes as no surprise that he
writes so condescendingly of the psychological surface, of the conscious ego since he urgently demands, in 'Projective Verse,' that
poetry get 'rid of the lyrical interference of the ego' (1966, 24), yet
with this new notion, 'proprioception,' Olson also seems to dismiss
physical surfaces.

'Proprioception' is 'the cavity of the body,' home to the viscera,
location of 'the old "psychology" of feeling, the heart; of desire, the
liver; of sympathy, the "bowels"; of courage – kidney etc – gall'
(1965, 1). And it is to this place, this viscera, that Olson wants experience brought: 'The advantage is to "place" the thing, instead of it
wallowing around sort of outside, in the universe, like, when the
experience of it is interoceptive: it is inside us/ & at the same time
does not feel literally identical with our own physical or mortal self'
(1965, 1).

Proprioception is the knowledge of the body's depth; 'the "body"
itself as, by movement of its own tissues, giving the data of, depth'
(1965, 2). And if this depth of the body, this inner movement, is the
place of poetry, of poetic energy, it seems that skin no longer is
where what matters happens.

What, I think, Olson desires in *Proprioception* is not the flaying
of the skin, but a swallowing of it, a meeting of inner and outer.
Skin is still where what matters happens, where the world and the
individual meet; but the body's cavity is where the 'skin' needs to
be 'processed.' The skin, as a surface, must not be a barrier between
the world and the body, but rather a conduit for their interchange.
It must be folded into the gut of the poet, into an absolutely physical vision, in a motion the reverse of that advocated in his earlier
poetic manifesto. Now it is the ear, by way of the head, to the syllable; the breath, by way of the heart, to the line. Here is another
incarnation of Bakhtin's grotesque body in which the 'outward and
inward features are often merged into one' (1965, 318). More important, here Olson gives his poetic a slightly different angle, a more
radically nonsensical one. Language inhabits the body, the body
language.

'who looks / some way more':
Zukofsky's Syn-aesthetics

Louis Zukofsky's solution to the problem of writing the senses into language is different from Olson's; his language (Alison Rieke calls it a 'dance of the senses' [1992, 182]) results from synaesthesia, the joining of senses to produce a palpable, tangible language. Poets, he writes in 'An Objective,' should 'see with their ears, hear with their eyes, move with their noses and speak and breathe with their feet' (1981, 17); they cross senses and so cross Sense. Synaesthesia could result from conflating any two senses, though (as Zukofsky says in '[Sincerity and Objectification]'), 'I like to keep the noises as close to the body as possible, so that (I don't know how you'd express it mathematically) the eye is a function of the ear and the ear of the eye; maybe with that you might feel a sense of smell, of taste even. So much of the word is a physiological thing ... that its articulation, as against that of other words, will make an "object"' (1979, 267).

Like that sought through Olson's poetics, this language resists translation, but does so in a very specific manner. Rather than opening up lines of communication and feeling between mental and physical realms as Olson seeks to do ('the HEAD, by way of the EAR'), Zukofsky conflates sensical experience. He 'attempts,' according to Rieke, 'to recover and represent a unified activity of the ear, the eye' (1992, 181). What 'translation' does occur, does so within a wider range of physical response. The strangeness of perception is rendered in his language more faithfully than is usually the case, because it is rendered in terms of another sense; rather than refining sight into sensical words, Zukofsky replaces it, repositions it within its sensual orders, and so calls attention to the orders of perception within and among the orders of verbal langauge.

Peter Quartermain says Zukofsky's 'text is a movement of languages, of *a number of* frames of reference, held in the language of the poem simultaneously, *at once*. And it is a *felt* world' (1992, 88). The felt, the perceived, the sensed – these underlie sense and may be, in Zukofsky's view, 'the part of the whole definition of the word [*sense*] most crucial to his work' (Rieke 1992, 176). But the 'felt world' of his poems is not a linearly sensical one. Rieke suggests that 'Zukofsky's most obscure verses do not make nonsense, but rather make sense in an unfamiliar language' (1992, 161); she is correct if one defines 'nonsense' as 'not sense' – a definition she undermines early in her own study by calling 'the experimental nonsense of Modernism' a 'privileged, enigmatic speech' (1992, 19). But go back to Quartermain's 'movement of languages,' his *a number of* frames of reference.' Or consider Rieke's claim for a palimpsestic writing in *A-23*, where 'liveforever, memory, tradition and history' rub shoulders, altering but never erasing each other (1992, 225), and one comes much closer to the possibilities of nonsense as I construe it.

Both Quartermain and Rieke, Quartermain more so, describe what I name secondary nonsense – the interpenetration of linguistic codes, styles, or types of speech, to create a more meaning*ful* speech. Zukofsky's work is rife with such secondary nonsense: for instance, the transliterations of Hebrew, Greek, and Latin often underlying his odder work, or more openly operating in the 'translations' of Catullus done with his wife, Celia. I want to extend observations about languages that inhabit Zukofsky's work to embrace a broader definition of language, however, to embrace not only Hebrew and Greek, scientific and literary jargon, but also music as language, perception as physical language, mathematics as language. That such fields are in Zukofsky's work could hardly be debated, so obvious is their incorporation. But I suggest they are *not re*presented; this implies too much mimesis. They are present as languages, at the level of language, as much themselves as they can be in a 'foreign' medium, and it is this *presence*, as distinct from representation, which results in nonsense. Thus, Zukofsky attempts to write in mathematical or musical or physical languages as well as in verbal language; he attempts to write into verbal language some of the principles of these others – counterpoint, for instance, or the Pythagorean workings of the number four,[3] or synaesthesia.

I's (pronounced eyes) is one of Zukofsky's more accessible poems and an example of the seen world transmitted by the ear, the joyful music of the eye, where synaesthesia waylays concrete sense. In the poem's title, Zukofsky has already anticipated the movement of its language; revolving around the 'I' of the poet, the title initiates the auditory pun that energizes the entire poem. For 'I' can be read/ heard as 'eye'; sight is the most precious sense for the poet, to Zukofsky's mind (1979, 267). From the outset of the poem, the auditory 'pronounced' has permitted a metamorphosis between 'I's' and 'eyes,' has established the poem as a place where sight has a direct link to the ear, and where sensual play interferes with the norms of verbal language: 'I is'?, 'I's' rather than 'my'? Senses are mixed, languages mussed up some.

As the poem begins, Zukofsky names, renames, his form; haiku, the delicate poem of the eye, born of the visual intensity of an image glistening in the moment of perception, is lent to the ear: 'Hi, Kuh' (l.1). If Zukofsky's poem stretches the limits of its form quite radically, so too does his 'auditory translation,' his homonymic play, undo the literary and critical respect usually given the haiku and animate the subversive potential of his poetic; 'Hi, Kuh' is also, as Rieke notes, a greeting to a cow – ' "Kuh" is German for cow' (1992, 164).

The route between eye and ear is kept open throughout the poem as each sight is shaped by sound, as the entire landscape of the poem and the act of seeing are musicalized. Eyes are already homonymically present in I's, physically present (the cow's golden eyes) and figuratively present (Rieke notes as bees – 'those / gold'n bees / are I's' [ll.2–4], and play off of 'to be,' and as skyscrapers, which like bees touch the sky [1992, 164]). And if eyes inhabit the poem as puns and phonic play, so does seeing itself. 'See / I work' says Angelo, the super's helper (ll.28–9); this first instance of the verb 'see' in the poem stands as both gestural or demonstrative and explanatory; the reader and listener should see and understand. An encouragement that may be from Angelo but is certainly not far from Zukofsky, who writes in Bottom, 'sight is a function of (numerically) irrational biological power of the human animal, which begins as a body, [and] finds a voice that involves or generates intellect' (1963, 67). See and understand; but much of the understanding of any work by Zukofsky is aural, and no less is the understanding of sight aural here. When 'see' reappears several lines later, its sound is showcased: 'TREE-SEE? / – I see / by / your tree' ' – What / do you / see / A SEA ... ABC' (ll.49–56, 62). The echoes and puns are central; words are made objects by exploiting their sound.

Zukofsky uses metalepsis to draw an auditory picture of the sea, its foam shifting phonically as well as visually as it 'claws' and 'cloys' (ll.59–60) its way up the sand. The ah of the first vowel closes over as the water becomes 'close,' closer to the seer. Close sounds for the seeing ear; each push of water just fractionally, phonemically, nearer the hearing eye. And the flashing instant of 'AZURE' (l.71), the colour of 'A SEA,' falls into a linguistic lapping, a sounding of ebb and flow – 'as ever / adz aver' (ll.73–4) – as ever, always, the water and the senses do: the rushing and receding of perception, the tidal pull of a becoming body.

'See' is an important verb in this poem, given its literary and mythic relations with insight and knowledge, but it's not just a verb; it's also a musical note, a letter and his wife's first initial. All this seeing works back to collective beginnings – to see, the perceptual beginnings of intellect; sea, the source of life; ABC, the beginning of the alphabet from which western European languages are constructed; and middle *c*, one centre for sound itself.[4] This sensual, musical engagement with language puts pressure on sense, orchestrates it, so that sense becomes a roving and twisting dancer, no longer stable and stolid.

'IN OMBOLOM BULLORGA':
Nonsense and Other Bodies

Bodies meet with their environments and the objects surrounding them in many ways; senses and skin may organize the world around them, or may be organized by elements of that world. In Lear, the latter is often the case. It is not at all uncommon to find, in the illustrations of his limericks, that the people who are the subjects of the poems are also subject to some startling physical change directly related to the things populating their poems and their 'lives.' Take for instance the *Old Man who said, 'Hush'* (Figure 8), the *Old Man in a tree* (Figure 9), or the *Old Man with an owl* (Figure 10). Each character takes on the characteristics of the animal or insect he is depicted with. Such confusion or submersion of identities confirms the shifting of boundaries in Lear's world. The *Old Man and his owl* is perhaps the best example found in Lear; even the verse, with its pronouns that slide between the two possible antecedents (man or owl), never clearly establishes a division between the two. A simple trick of punctuation and grammar on Lear's part has man and owl bothering, howling, sitting and drinking in linguistic union.

Many other styles of poetry work, often in a more serious vein, towards a similar spirit of nonsensical sympathy between humanity and the environment. In an attempt to dehumanize the universe, to challenge the status accorded to people and to their sense, just such mergers occur. The reasoning for this may lie in the correlation Stephen-Paul Martin makes, in *Open Form and Feminine Imagination*, between the 'open form' of verse and the 'open systems' of life. He remarks upon the similarities between open poetic form and the ideas of chemist Ilya Prigogine that 'everything is "alive" but ... some things sustain themselves through dynamic interplay with the environment (*open systems*) and others are more or less independent of ongoing interplay with it (*closed systems*)' (Martin 1988, 53). It is in responding to this animated world, be it closed or open, that poetry again articulates nonsensically. Responding to? Responding with. For, as Zukofsky says, poetry of 'direct contact' is a 'thinking with the things as they exist,' beginning 'in a physiological response' (1981, 12). It requires tapping a 'primal' energy, one that is the experience of the semiotic in an other form of life. It requires the implementation of the prelinguistic.

In an unpublished paper on Ted Hughes's language, Jamie Bush discusses Hughes's attempt to put the natural into words:

For Hughes ... the term 'pre-linguistic meaning' has a special significance. His effort to make vocal the inner essence of things, and so to connect with the elemental energies in the natural world, is ... evident in the usually tightly restricted, synchronic rather than diachronic temporal line of the poems, and in the tendency to bore in on one thing – a pebble, an animal, or a fern's frond – and then either to describe it in a proliferation of metaphors, or to adopt its perspective, or to personify it. (1987, 3)

But as Bush notes, and as Hughes's invention of a language for *Orghast* (Peter Brook's experimental dramatic 'work-in-progress') attests, conventional language, one that is all, or almost all, communicative, doesn't serve the needs of someone 'so concerned with expressing what lies between and beneath and inside the interstices arbitrarily fixed in the conceptual continuum' (1987, 3).

What Bush has described as Hughes's method, this boring in, is a secular version of what Tim Lilburn calls '*Haecceitas* ... the insight of Christified sensibility, a knowing-in-love; ... the source of what is strong and strange in verse' (1987, 35), an outgrowth of Duns Scotus's *haecceitas*, 'the ultimate reality of the being' (1987, 35), and a close friend of Hopkins's inscape. It is the 'thisness' of a pebble, an animal, a fern's frond, of a stone, a pumpkin, a tree, 'as it exists in relation with its loving observer, the tree-known-in-love' (1987, 35). Such 'thisness,' caught up in language, stretches it considerably.

Following part of Lilburn's definition can lead to a more plausible union between nonsense and inscape than might initially seem likely.

Inscape, *haecceitas*: it requires a presence, usually in both objects and language, found in systems of thought that recognize the existence of an Absolute, a 'transcendental signifier' at which the sense stops for good: the hub of the wheel that stabilizes. And inscape requires an Idealist turn of mind in its positing of the existence of an 'essence' – the essential tree, the essential stone, articulation through the essential word. Such Idealism, generally considered to be quite far removed from the materialist forum of nonsense, does not necessarily assume an essential link between word and thing, but it does seek to infuse the word momentarily with the essence of a thing, even if such infusion requires the wrenching of the word.

If 'surface' nonsense provides stability,[5] in an admittedly parodic version of a transcendental signified, if it offers the temporary hiatus in which the word and the sign 'mean' together (Deleuze argues that the nonsense word means itself), then it offers as well the means to express a faith in presence that language, as a materialist system, does not allow. This is one of the most paradoxical and slippery functions of nonsense yet; it undermines univocal Sense, but simultaneously incarnates linguistically just what and how that Sense would be, if it could be. By being its own sense, nonsense is essentially the naming of its own essence as well.

It seems only natural for Martin to insist that the process of locating those elemental or 'essential' energies, the writing out of the fullness of being of the 'object,' lies in employing 'unconditioned physical senses,' the listening to the listenings of the body so important to Olson and Zukofsky. Unfettered perception facilitates an organic materialism that allows in-dwelling and is best articulated in the very rhythms within which it falls. Such perception, he suggests, allows one to become ignorant again, as Wallace Stevens requires in 'Notes Toward a Supreme Fiction.' For, 'no longer seeing only what we have been taught to see ... [we] find ourselves in a vivid non-rational world where the interplay of elemental energies re-assumes the prime significance it had in ancient matriarchal societies' (Martin 1988, 142).[6]

Because Hughes finds conventional, 'civilized' language lacking when he seeks to infuse it with the life of thisness, Bush claims he seeks his 'ignorance' in a 'primitive language,' one related, for him, to the originary condition of integration with nature and the elemental power of the universe, rather than one of metaphysical deferral. For Hughes, 'primitive language corresponded to this existential fullness, for men communicated intuitively, through a language of sound, a non-conceptual language of essential presence' (Bush 1987, 9). Within this language of sound, the voicing of phonic articulation, Hughes locates human primal energies, and their kinship, blood-relation, he locates within the world around them.

Hughes's convictions about language come closest to being realized in the *Orghast* experiment. In creating *Orghast*, he purposely attempted to leave behind the arbitrariness of language (Smith 1972, 42), 'to offer the actors sounds from a physiological basis, which would, in the most literal sense, embody the mythic narrative he was composing' (1972, 43). Sometimes he used onomatopeia; other times he would 'concentrate on what was to be expressed, and intuitively seek the sound for it' (1972, 44). Here's a sample of *Orghast* with the translation Hughes provided for the actors:

BULLORGA OMBOLOM FROR   SHARSAYA NULBULDA BRARG
darkness opens its womb   I hear chaos roar

IN OMBOLOM BULLORGA
in the womb of darkness

FREEASTAV OMBOLOM   NILD US GLITTALUGH
freeze her womb   rivets like stars
(Smith 1972, 50)

Because of its heavy reliance upon sound and the physiological production of language, *Orghast* was meant to speak 'directly through the body,' to be a language in which 'all conceptual thought was a metaphor of what the body, first, had perceived' (1972, 51). Yet Hughes's statement seems naive; the consistent use of 'OMBOLOM' for the word 'womb,' for instance, implies a good deal of conscious determination. And, while one can certainly understand the need for a translation like the one above, especially during the workshopping of *Orghast*, its existence does curb the spirit of Hughes's probings. A sensical language seems an unavoidable foundation.

Orghast was, however, at the very least, an *attempt* to devise 'a language that reveal[ed] the body as a map of human experience' (1972, 78). So it's not surprising that, while creating it, Hughes pondered the relationship that the body has with language generally. 'The deeper into language one goes,' he explained to Smith, the chronicler of Brook's theatrical experiment, the less visual/conceptual its imagery, and the more audial/visceral/muscular its system of tensions. This accords with the biological fact that the visual nerves connect with the modern human brain, while the audial nerves connect with the cerebellum, the primal animal brain and nervous system, direct. In other words, the deeper into language one goes, the more dominated it becomes by purely musical modes, and the more dramatic it becomes – the more unified with total states of being and with the expressiveness of physical action. (Smith 1972, 45)

While Hughes's intensely physical and prelingual language is unrealizable and rarely glimmers beneath the surface of his work, the implications of his ideas are exciting: buried beneath the sense and abstraction of language are ways of articulation that oppose or undermine linear, linguistic sense. The body, music, sound – these elements are borrowed from other ways of meaning, other (*Hughes* might say 'earlier') ways of being, to build up the verbal system. These are the same elements that, when resurrected in excess, can break open the system whose foundation they contributed to.

It's a very little leap from this Hughes to the *Bandar-log* running riot in the Cold Lairs or the *chora* huffing and puffing at a straw-house-thetic. For Hughes's claims of the originary status of sound, the sound that he appeals to for a prelogical and nonsensical language, is an Idealistic echo of the importance sound plays in the dishevelling of communicative language, in articulating a subtextual, contradictory 'sense.'

'the soft letting-go':
Feminism and Nonsense

One need only look at the writing coming out of the feminist movement to question those critics who suggest that 'women don't favour nonsense' (Haughton 1988, 31). Such statements suggest not only an over-narrow definition of Nonsense, or nonsensical writing, but also a failure to recognize shared methods of disturbing sense. Like nonsense, much feminist writing dwells on and in bodies, specifically women's bodies. Sexually and erotically energized, *écriture féminine* (feminist writing at its most nonsensical) makes demands: 'Woman must write her body, must make up the unimpeded tongue that bursts partitions, classes, and rhetorics, orders and codes, must inundate, run through, go beyond the discourse with its last reserves'

(Cixous 1975, 94–5). Feminine writing must be disruptive, circular, blurring; it must be steeped in the blood and rhythms of physical, periodic experience and so outside of male-dominated culture (Clément 1975, 8). It must 'steal into language to make it fly ... , pleasuring in ... routing the sense police' (Cixous 1975, 96). Cixous calls on women to write in the 'white ink' (1975, 94) of their breast milk, to write out of, along with, their bodily rhythms, their unique fluidity. The evocations of this body language may be highly metaphorical, or (as we'll see shortly) metonymic, but its implications are no less important for that.

The concerns that motivate this physical writing may be extremely different from those which underscoring the perceptually-based writing discussed earlier, but the results are equally disruptive of the sensical standards of communicative language. Central to both this writing and the movement[7] that encourages it is the belief that women have been oppressed in all socio-historical respects, especially in the matter of discourse, since the world is determined by language and language is made by men.

'so many terms for dominance in English are tied up with male experiencing, masculine hierarchies and differences (exclusion), patriarchal holdings with their legalities. where are the poems that celebrate the soft letting-go the flow of menstrual blood as it leaves her body' (Marlatt 1984, 47). So Daphne Marlatt wonders in 'musing with mothertongue,' the essay that concludes her book *Touch to My Tongue*. This essay and the poems to which it's attached work in both form and content to subvert such hierarchies, to infuse language with women's visceral experience.

Admittedly, purely communicative language doesn't accommodate any aspect of the body with ease. The God/Law/Definition, which Kristeva associates with the symbolic, is often construed as the seat of an 'androcentric' power (one I'm not inclined to distribute simply according to gender, though throughout history men have certainly been seduced by it), which actively curbs the semiotic. It is endemic in language, however, that the 'social' should attempt to prevent the 'individual,' the sexual, from disturbing language. A sexual and sensual decorum excludes certain physical experiences from language, and limits one's abilities to express other seemingly inoffensive (usually nonhuman) experiences.[8]

The evocation of sexuality or desire, be it male or female, arises only in a disrupted, nonsensical language that allows other orders to be asserted within, between, beneath the conventional orders of verbal language. For instance, Marlatt abandons punctuation, lets association, rhyme, and rhythm guide her through this prose love poem:

eating

a kiwi at four a.m. among the sheets green slice of cool going down easy on the tongue extended with desire for you and you in me it isn't us we suck those other lips tongue flesh wet wall that gives and gives whole fountains inner mountains moving out resistances you said ladders at the canyon leap desire is its way through walls swerve fingers instinct in you insist further persist in me too wave on wave to that deep pool we find ourselves/it dawning on us we have reached the same place 'timeless' you recognize as 'yes' giving yourself up not in we come suddenly round the bend to it descending with the yellow canyon flow the mouth everything drops away from time its sheets two spoons two caved-in shells of kiwi fruit. (1984, 24)

The words Marlatt uses are not 'different' or difficult, nor is her syntax irremediably disturbed; by exploiting the rush of words, the associative blend of ideas – articulated by pulling the punctuation, the stops, out of language – she attempts to bring her poem, sensuously, to an edge of sense. The poem at once imitates the flow of desire and captures the dissolution inherent in such desire. Verbal language's tendency towards compartmentalization, division, and linear structure is partially defeated by Marlatt's eclipsing of sentence divisions, while her use of stream of consciousness technique imitates the unconscious's associative ordering principles.[9]

There is reason, then, to see a connection between nonsensical and feminist writing; in feminist theory, too, connections can be found. 'Women have served all these centuries,' writes Virginia Woolf, 'as looking-glasses possessing the magic and delicious power of reflecting the figure of man at twice its natural size' ([1929] 1977, 35). In *Speculum of the Other Woman*, Luce Irigaray extends this metaphor, claiming that women must either reflect a narrow, grown-up, masculine world view, and so corroborate it (which creates, philosophically, artistically, psychologically, Pygmalions who can do just that), or be silent; preferably both. She concludes that a woman becomes 'another specularization. Whose twisted character is her inability to say what she represents' (1974, 134). The twisted character of a reflected woman reveals her inability to speak herself. To speak she must twist in another direction, bringing her into contact with the *Bandar*-logical poet, whose twists reveal the mirror itself to be twisted, and who also shows up and parodies the dominating sense system. Irigaray argues for a tactile 'womanspeech'; her erotics of a woman's language concentrates on touch: 'For in what she says, too, at least when she dares, woman is constantly touching herself' (1977, 29). Such touching circles back not only to Bakhtin's carnival of genitals, in an admittedly more enlightened way,[10] but also to Alice's shifting body. But no matter how close they stand to each other, Irigaray's womanspeech and nonsense are looking different ways: feminism infuses language with a socio-political body in order to reclaim both, and thereby to acquire women's self-determination. Not self-determining but self-referential, nonsense language ingests the drives of the body for the exposure of sense – a potentially political act with no programmatic intention or purpose. Nonsense is, at best, a(ll)political, outside of any *one* political system, but insidiously tangential to all.[11]

Women must twist language because they are excluded from it by the nature of words themselves, argues Irigaray. She quotes Jacques Lacan to show that this perception is held not only by women, and that the perspectives about such exclusion may be quite different: 'There is no woman who is not excluded by the nature of things, which is the nature of words, and it must be said that, if there is something they complain a lot about at the moment, that is what it is – except that they don't know what they are saying, that's the whole difference between them and me' (quoted in Irigaray 1977, 87).

Lacan's attempt at what one hopes is humour is more than a different take, albeit a confirming one, on women's exclusion from language. He is, after all, the one who holds that language and the unconscious are organized along the same lines, and his theories represent a major point of access for those who link sexuality and writing. His remark can be made to argue for the need to articulate women's sexuality, to help women know what they are talking about, and how they are saying it – precisely what Irigaray, Cixous, and the other proponents of *écriture féminine* are after.

They envision a discourse relating, in several ways, to a highly-sexualized female body, to the entertainment of the Other. Cixous talks of writing as the experience of an Other, of a multiple 'oneing' within the individual:

Writing is the passageway, the entrance, the exit, the dwelling place of the other in me – the other that I am and am not, that I don't know how to be, but that I feel passing, that makes me live – that tears me apart, disturbs me, changes me, who? – a feminine one, a masculine one, some? – several, some unknown, which is indeed what gives me the desire to know and from which all life soars. (1975, 85–6)

She attributes the ability to write in this way to a bisexuality that is not a matter of sexual orientation, but rather of the existence of both sexes within one person and the consequent 'multiplication of the effects of desire's inscription on every part of the body and the other body' (1975, 85). For her, the most natural model of this entertainment of the Other is maternity (1975, 90).

Kristeva, in an interview quoted in Leon Roudiez's introduction to *Desire in Language*, makes a connection along similar lines, with an admittedly different emphasis. 'The arrival of a child is,' she says, ' ... the first and the often only opportunity a woman has to experience the Other in its radical separation from herself, that is, as an object of love' (Kristeva 1980, 10). Indeed, Kristeva suggests in 'Stabat Mater,' an essay presenting Christianity's idealization of the Virgin as an attempt to contain and constrain femininity within the symbolic mode, that maternal love and death, its antithesis, are outside of language: 'Man overcomes the unthinkable of death by postulating maternal love in its place ... Such a love is in fact, logically speaking, a surge of anguish at the very moment when the identity of thought and living body collapses. The possibilities of communication having been swept away, only the subtle gamut of sound, touch, and visual traces, older than language and newly worked out, are preserved as an ultimate shield against death' (1983, 252–3).

The symbols of maternal joy and pain – breastmilk and tears – 'are the metaphors of new speech, of a "semiotics" that linguistic communication does not account for' (1983, 249). Kristeva's use of 'semiotics' here has a double, a flexible, status; it entertains simultaneously the traditional sense of the word and her own redefinition. Breast milk and tears are related to the semiosis of the *chora* and the death drive (which the maternal replaces or covers over) and also to a system of 'signs' and signals outside of our own linguistic or verbal sign system. A highly nonsensical conflation with its introduction of other, nonlingual orders of meaning into language.

If language is born of the continual, and constantly unsuccessful, search for union with the Other, and if that sense of lack (articulated by the symbolic but expressive of the semiotic) can be even momentarily assuaged by the experience of pregnancy and childbirth, then it would seem that women (especially during pregnancy with its paradoxical union of mother and child) are closer somehow to the semiotic than are men, that the desire to return to the womb can almost be realized by carrying a child in the womb. And pregnancy and childbirth can temporarily *erase* the thetic, ease the divisive separation of orders of sense.

Such implications could be counted as an unhealthy biologism; an ungenerous reading might well locate French feminism within Freud's 'dark continent.' Yet neither Kristeva nor Cixous limits her ideas about the entertainment of the Other to women. Pregnancy may well be one way of experiencing the Other, of momentarily filling the lack that motivates language, but different methods of erasing, of easing, are conceivable: the madness dealt with in Kristeva's dissertation is another method, and another reason for connecting this writing with nonsense. Kristeva doesn't exclude men who are excluded from the physiological experience of pregnancy from the production of semiotically sated literature; in fact her doctoral thesis, part of which has been published as *Revolution in Poetic Language*, deals exclusively with male writers.

Nor does Cixous limit 'woman's' writing to women. Her example of a man capable of bisexual stretch is Jean Genet (1975, 84). It's not so much Genet's sexual orientation that makes this stretch possible as his ability to infuse his texts with the presence of an Other, and another 'order.' Cixous cites the tendency of Genet's texts to 'divide,' 'dismember,' and 'regroup' as indicative of a 'proliferating, maternal femininity' (1975, 84). This tendency to derange is indicative of femininity because women are outside the structure of order as defined by the current discourse of sense; they are by nature 'derangers' (1975, 85).

This language, these metaphors of 'white ink' and maternity, cause problems for many only marginally acquainted with French feminism. However, both Cixous's and Irigaray's works need to be read with the understanding that metaphor and metonymy are their structuring literary tropes. Diana Fuss, in *Essentially Speaking: Feminism, Nature and Difference*, takes exception to the proliferation of literalistic, and consequently negative, readings of French feminist writers. She points out that many critics 'demand that metaphors of the body be read literally, and they then reject these metaphors as essentialistic' (1989, 62). Fuss continues, 'for Irigaray, the relation between language and the body is neither literal nor metaphoric but *metonymic*' (1989, 62). And Katherine Binhammer, in a volume of *Tessera* devoted to the issue of essentialism, makes a related claim for Cixous: 'Feminine does not mean female but that is not to say there is no relation at all – it is a metaphor and also not a metaphor, a metonymy ... Feminine is not identical, but contiguous with female' (1991, 75).

The slide between literal and tropic, between sex and gender, is too often and too easily made. Metonymy allows a space for difference, room for movement. 'The metonymic field,' Binhammer explains, 'is based on contiguity and combination rather than on identity and similarity. This difference allows us to escape the either/or established by traditional articulations of the essentialist problem – i.e., either one reads the relation of feminine to female literally, therefore, biologistically and anatomically, or one reads it metaphorically and thus having no relation to women' (1991, 74–5). Reading these works metonymically requires acceptance of displacement and replacement, of continually renewed contexts; here is an ironic language of usurpation that cannot speak itself within the symbolic mode of discourse – these works, according to Fuss and Binhammer, speak beside themselves.

Irigaray's metonymy provides a link other than maternity between proliferation, division, disorder and femininity. Women's sexual 'organs' and erogenous zones are prolific and scattered: '*woman has sex organs more or less everywhere*. She finds pleasure almost anywhere ... the geography of her pleasure is far more diversified, more multiple in its differences, more complex, more subtle, than is commonly imagined' (1977, 28). Sexual geography is a key to syntax. Male sexuality is limited to the penis, she says (with what seems to be disturbing insensitivity if read literally), hence the univocal, 'one-way thinking' (Brossard 1985, 111) attributed to systems, even language systems, arranged around a masculine economy.[12] Because women have a multidirectional sexuality, Irigaray contends, they require a multifoliate language; by extension, 'feminine' discourse is also multifoliate: a fluid, '[wholly] fluent' (1977, 216) syntax, released from the 'shadow shaped something like the letter ''I'' ' (Woolf [1929] 1977, 95). Such a purely fluid syntax is unachievable because of the interdependence of forms of sense (communicative, physical, musical, for instance); even Irigaray admits this syntax is hard to define, but, she speculates, 'there would no longer be either subject or object, "oneness" would no longer be privileged, there would no longer be proper meanings, proper names, "proper" attributes ... instead, that "syntax" would involve nearness, proximity' (1977, 134). It is a syntax, thus, of metonymy. Irigaray's discussion of sexuality and syntax, of language as multifoliate once it entertains the rhythms of the body, is a startlingly exact description of what a purely semiotic language, were one possible, would be.

The writing envisioned by Cixous and Irigaray could be construed as a nonsensical writing if it acknowledges the need for many orders of sense. By definition subversive, and in many ways a 'feminine' writing, it does move closer to imitating the rhythms of women's bodies, and the rhythms of any body in the world, through its engagement with the *drives* of the body. But the term 'feminine writing' in their context is too easily and uncomfortably misread as an indication of literary biologism.

Drawing a distinction between feminist texts and feminist writing, Nicole Brossard (herself at times seemingly guilty of biological oversimplification) argues that the body is not a specifically feminist domain:

Though we may speak of feminist texts, it seems to me that we cannot speak of feminist writing. Insofar as I conceive of writing as a way of using the body, that is, how the body physically asserts itself to gain its formal status in linguistic terrain, I can speak only of feminine and/or lesbian writing. Certainly, the body has ideas and feminist thoughts but the body itself is not feminist ... Feminism can make a place for a 'body politic' but it cannot offer us a writing of the body or of the skin. (1985, 91)

Brossard's definition of writing, the body exerting itself linguistically, is a Barthesian one. The influence is clear; she alludes to him in 'The Aerial Letter' (1985, 68). But her notion of writing as it applies to women steps past his idea of 'language lined with flesh' (Barthes 1973, 66), an idea that many feminists pick up and elaborate upon. Brossard's feminine text results when the body meets the world from a feminist point of view, when selection of sensory perception is governed by an informed feminist consciousness. For her, feminine writing goes beyond the recording of the body and its unconscious rhythms; in order to be feminist, it must use that physical/musical energy within a clearly formed, politicized sensory framework.

Nonsense might be able to offer *écriture féminine* a new, and perhaps 'clearer' terminology, but I suspect that the confusion elicited by the gender-related terminology of *écriture féminine* is also part of the political message. To read it effectively is to enter its discursive community, to enter into a metonymic language, to be beside oneself.

'Becoming Visceral'

———◆◆———

'Our whole life a translation / the permissible fibs,' begins Adrienne Rich's *Our Whole Life*, a poem of vivid social and political commitment, one in which words *mean* intensely according to their 'accepted' definitions, despite Rich's cry against the limitations of language, the curbing of political minorities' speech by official (oppressive) language. In this poem two apparent paradoxes resonate: the first, that Rich writes such a powerful poem in a language that (so the poem itself suggests) oppresses her – language may not be true to her experience, but it allows her to voice her objections; the second, that a poem so bent on communicating a specific meaning entertains nonsense's subversiveness. But that's what one finds upon reading this poem closely. Beyond, beneath the rhetoric of Rich's poem are movements straining against the poem's perceived order. These nonsensical incursions may well be examples of a voice jarring with the language it uses; whatever reasoning one applies to them, there is no denying the tensions that they animate throughout the poem.

Our Whole Life transforms its speaker into word; she becomes word by association, because of the inadequacies of language to express her experience. Her life 'is' a translation. I put that 'is' in quotation marks because in a very real sense the speaker 'is not.' There is a noticeable absence of the verb 'to be' in this poem; the only appearance it makes is negated – 'there are no words for this' (l.14). If Marilyn Farwell is right, and Rich's tendency is to emphasize experience, to see a poem 'as a verb instead of a noun' (1977, 196), then this lack is a substantial one. It is still substantial if one reads Rich's poetry not as verb-oriented (or polarized diachronic) but as adjectival poetry. A poetry that frees attributes from a substantivizing or stable centre, and whose movement away from a noun/verb opposition is emphasized by the shifting images created by her use of adjectives.

The poem concerns a life of absent or negated existence, of missing words and 'dead letters' (1.8). It is essentially a series of dislocations or fragments, a form that challenges at least one possible interpretation of the title: *Our Whole Life* – 'whole' as 'unified,' as 'complete.' In many sections of the poem, and often between the sections (or stanzas) themselves, there are no firmly articulated connections; words are suppressed. The poem establishes a hesitant balance between speech and silence, between saying something and saying nothing (or perhaps more to the point here – being *unable* to say something), which is highly reminiscent of Nonsense. Words and meanings that are never raised in the poem are entertained in it nonetheless, because of the power of Rich's use of silence, metaphor, and fragment; these devices become palimpsests covering possible other ways of saying and meaning, allowing associative meaning where more direct 'truths' cannot be stated.

Lines and sections resonate with potential meaning, build towards the final three sections that stand as one disjointed unit. Indeed, the sectioning of the poem itself is unstable; associations that lurk in the silence between the sections suggest various ways of realigning lines. And since the poem has no complete sentences, the logic of grammar and punctuation don't contest these realignments. Capital letters are structural rather than syntactical, and so lump the lines of the poem into groups of four, then three, then two, and finally six. They are indicators of a possible order other than that presented by the section breaks themselves, an order spanning the silence of the breaks.

The most obvious order that the poem seems to establish, the order of the section breaks (two stanzas composed of two lines and then one composed of one line) is quickly, nonsensically, undercut. By joining what should be the next single-line stanza and so should, structurally speaking, stand alone, to the following stanza of two lines, Rich is destabilizing the poem's expected stanzaic structure. The number of lines in the poem is sufficient to continue the stanza composition, mentioned above, three times; the poem quickly undermines that order, however, with stanzas composed of three, two, and finally one line. So the line count of stanzas reads 2, 2, 1, 2, 2, 3, 2, 1; the last three stanzas set up a pattern of diminishment, which will be discussed later.

This slide away from the earliest stanza patterning is facilitated by the poem's only simile, its only outright statement of 'this is like that': 'meanings burnt-off like paint/under the blowtorch' (ll. 5–6). Throughout the poem, Rich speaks covertly, relying upon metaphor to insinuate her meaning. While her use of a simile here is still a deflection of direct speech, a reliance on a figure of speech to relay a point that cannot be stated outright, this simile is the most overt of all her images, the closest she comes to a declarative statement in *Our Whole Life*. It is a near breakthrough and affects the poem's structure. Always the poem has been spoken at a remove, with the words that forge connection between ideas and images remaining unspoken. This one 'like,' connected to its horrifying image, requires that the poem be reordered. The poem's tendency to be associative, to restructure itself in order to speak its message more openly, urges a noncentrist and asyntactical reading, one that is simultaneously diachronic and synchronic, which moves towards the grasping of a 'whole life' at once.

'Our whole life a translation / the permissible fibs' (ll.1–2) – there is a leap in logic here as two seemingly disparate things, 'translation' and 'fibs,' are associated, reminding the reader that there is a problem with the validity, the veracity of translation, positing the unreliability, instability, of language. This suggestion of failure is heightened when the 'fibs' are followed by 'and now a knot of lies' (l.3), a correlation that at least tentatively implies a causal connection and which, despite the shift in intensity, provides a bridge between the first two sections, and almost threatens to pull the second line away from the first, tying it up to the third line.

The first line, as well, links up with the third last, by virtue of a parallel structure: 'Our whole life a translation'; 'his whole body a cloud of pain' (l.13) – the structure supports the analogies of our life / his body, translation / pain, joining the speaker and the unnamed Algerian as they experience inarticulable oppression. While the second and second last lines do not continue the paralleling, the association of fibs with a lack of words furthers the idea of language lying, or feigning a reality that it is incapable of presenting.

The knotting of the lies in the third line is not only an entangling in, and so a trapping, but also a phonic negation: knot, not. Such sound and word play is central to both feminist and nonsensical writing because it reveals the 'lie' that the symbolic makes of language in trying to exclude the body from articulation. The lies here are a translation into a language in which adequate words are not allowed to exist; such lies, by their very existence, negate experience and 'silence' the speaker.

The fourth line, 'eating at itself to get undone,' continues the idea of the destructiveness of entrapment, and speaks of a movement not unlike that of the semiotic as it works against the symbolic's restraint, distorting and disfiguring the very language that it must rely upon to express it. While this fourth line has some alliance with the third (with which it's paired), there is a strong pull at the line to join the fifth line, which stands alone, turning in upon itself in the act of devouring – 'Words bitten thru words.' This shortened, commercial-ese, form of 'thru' looks partially eaten already, and exhibits the sort of short-hand collapse that results from a heightening of the sound value of a word. The difficulty of envisioning this line's reference (just how *do* words bite through words?) also challenges the way language works.

There is no metaphorical carry over, no drawing together of the fifth and sixth lines. Rather than expanding further the images of devouring, Rich turns to quite another image, equally aggressive: 'meanings burnt-off like paint / under the blowtorch.' Using an image of paint stripping, in the process of which a paint surface blisters with heat and then is removed, Rich questions the relationship between meaning and a word; a word, the more physical, concrete thing that is merely covered over, adorned by a removable meaning. Momentarily, this section floats by itself, dislocated, surrounded on both sides by quite unrelated sections. But the idea of 'burning' connects with the twelfth line, where that participle describing the Algerian floats by itself, isolated from the poem and from the 'village' by the only punctuation mark in the poem. Meanings, like the Algerian, are burnt; the Algerian, burning, becomes a word himself, the only word for himself; his pain, meanings destroyed and devoured, present themselves as the only means of truly speaking within the 'oppressor's language.'

The fifth stanza, too, stands alone – 'All those dead letters / rendered into the oppressor's language' (ll.8–9). The 'dead letters' can be both lifeless bits of alphabet, or undelivered mail, messages written but never received. Whether the letters were dead when written, or are dead because unread, whether the silence is caused by complete lack of articulation or the suppression of what meagre attempts at articulation occur, is unclear. A subtle thematic link turns upon the verb 'rendered,' for it can mean 'surrendered,' 'depicted,' 'given over,' and, quite significantly, 'translated' or 'reduced by heat.' The reading of the verb supports either reading of the silence, supports either form of imposition. As well, the resonance of translation means that a link between the first line and the ninth does, in fact, exist, but is more or less obscured by language.

The poem seems to reach a natural division between the fifth and sixth sections; the sections, after the fifth, are much more clearly connected than the earlier ones, and, through Rich's use of simile, the poem is located in a more concrete political reality than it previously was. These sections progress in a pattern of diminishment – three lines, two lines, one line – underscoring the breaking down of language to its gut meaning, the rendering of language to a more visceral speech. This diminishment is also styled in the first half of the poem through Rich's use of capitals.

Thus the poem can be read nonsensically, despite the relative scarcity of more 'traditional' Nonsense strategies – morphemic collapse, rhythm, and rhyme. Its sensical movements and arrangements work against each other; lines move away from their partners, seem drawn through metaphor to other lines, sections seem only loosely united within and, sometimes, without themselves; capitals and themes urge a unity, which the gaps and spaces between lines and between metaphors 'silence' at one level. Spaces between sections, however, are highly active, saying as much as the words of the poem do. *Our Whole Life*, formally, turns in upon itself, like the words that bite themselves. As the lines elide, as the form fluctuates against itself, the nature of the poem becomes the critical speaking that cannot be articulated in the words of the 'oppressor's language.' In a sense, the poem too is on fire, burning like the Algerian, becoming visceral.

FOUR

'as birds as well as words':

Nonsense and Sound

That makes a sound that gently sings that gently sounds but sounds as sounds It sounds as sounds of course as words but it sounds as sounds. It sounds as sounds that is to say as birds as well as words.
– Gertrude Stein, 'What is English Literature'

The fish is indeed the most oral of animals; it poses the problem of muteness, of consumability, and of the consonant in the wet/palatalized element – in short, the problem of language.
– Gilles Deleuze, *The Logic of Sense*

The Duchess was wrong, or partly wrong. 'Take care of the sense, and the sounds will take care of themselves,' she advises Alice (Carroll [1865] 1971, 97); but in Carroll's Wonderland, and in Nonsense generally, sounds not only take care of themselves, they 'take care' of sense too. Even her moral is proof. While she moralizes, taking care with the sense, a slight phonemic shift grants a traditional axiom ('Take care of the pence and the pounds will take care of themselves') a liberation of sound; the very liberation, independence, which her moral implies.

Of course, such phonic liberation reverberates of the heart of nonsense. The language of nonsense sounds, as Stein puts it, 'as birds as well as words' (1935c, 30). Almost every theory of Nonsense includes a consideration of how manipulations of sound, like the frequently cited pun, can fracture the sense of ordinary language. Locating nonsensical sound in the body, however, is not common. Deleuze, for instance, categorically denies the location of classical Nonsense *in* the body.

His distinction between classical (or surface) Nonsense and schizoid nonsense precludes Nonsense's separation from the body. Sense, as he sees it, is part of the 'skin' of things, 'not *localized* at the surface, but ... rather bound to its formation and reformation' (1969, 104). It is the result of a process of infinite regress because of 'my impotence to state the sense of what I say, to say at the same time something and its meaning' (1969, 29). In other words, one can't say 'I'd like to fry that cat' and simultaneously explain just what 'to fry' is, and what a 'cat' is, and which cat 'that' cat is, and how a cat could be fried. So the sense of that sentence exists at a remove, in the sentence or phrase that explains it. His is a type of relational sense that grows, perhaps obliquely, out of Saussurean linguistics, in which sense (the sense of each word) is paradigmatically and syntagmatically relational.

But nonsense, the nonsense word and what Deleuze names the 'esoteric' word ('it,' 'that,' etc.), 'says its own sense'; '[it] is a word that denotes exactly what it expresses and expresses what it denotes' (1969, 67). Deleuze's nonsense adds a dash of entropy to the regress of sense because it doesn't accommodate explanation; how, Deleuze wonders, does one explain what a 'Snark' is (1969, 67). Well, to adapt Gertrude Stein, a snark is a snark is a snark. In the word lies the thing. Its definition is contingent upon its paradigmatic relations, unless Carroll's 'answer' to the whole mysterious Hunting is used as a way to get out of this mess: 'For the Snark was a Boojum, you see.' But, as Deleuze implies (1969, 66), 'Boojum' is as problematic as 'Snark.' For a Boojum is a Boojum is a Boojum, you see.

And it is this momentary pause in regress, this point of temporary stasis where the word is the thing, which 'donates' to sense some signification (1969, 69), which grounds sense. Deleuze argues that, within any given series of signification, a term 'has sense only by virtue of its position relative to every other term' (1969, 70). Such a position involves both its placement and function in a sentence, and its systemic relationships with these other terms. However, 'this relative position itself depends on the absolute position of each term relative to the instance=x,' the nonsense or 'self-defining' word. Sense, he continues, 'is always an *effect*' (1969, 70); never a cause. Nonsense at one and the same time breaks and strengthens the chain of sense; its challenge to sensical deferral merely provides, for Deleuze, the pivot upon which that deferral may more successfully, more meaningfully, turn.[1]

Deleuze is right in his assertion of the copresence of sense and nonsense, and in his attribution to nonsense of an active role in the manufacture and deferral of sense and meaning. But the 'effect' he claims for nonsense, that of offering a moment's stability to sense, isn't any more important than other 'effects' of nonsense, such as its exposure of how meaning is created. He speaks often of the paradox of sense and nonsense, and it is indeed paradoxical that the nonsense word which grounds sense also reveals, as Stewart argues so deftly, the whole process of sense-making. However, by revealing it, the nonsense word opens this process up to a critical probing, which Deleuze does not acknowledge.

Nonsense helps expose the very process that it supports; and that fact surely suggests that nonsense is much more than a meaning-preserving activity. Nonsense simultaneously 'stabilizes' (in Deleuze's rendering of it) and encourages a questioning of meaning, perhaps stabilizes meaning precisely *to* move a reader to question it. This is not exactly a 'preservation.' In fact, I wonder to what degree, to what level of intensity, nonsense may stop the flow of sense, may 'mean' itself, and still preserve meaning. For providing its own sense isn't merely the provision of its own syntactical and signifying relationship; there are other ways that nonsense can mean, that it can be a self-defining object. Nonsense can mean visually (as do Lear's limericks, whose sense is significantly altered by the accompanying illustrations), physically, musically, or mathematically. By meaning in such varied ways, nonsense actively cuts open, cuts through, the illusion it creates of a Stable and Meaningful Language.

But if nonsense makes linguistic sense possible, according to Deleuze, what makes language itself possible is its distinction from other bodily noises (grunting, yawning, farting) (1969, 166), even as musical sounds are distinct from noise. 'What renders language possible,' he writes, 'is that which separates sounds from bodies and organizes them into propositions, freeing them for the expressive function. It is always a mouth which speaks; but the sound is no longer the noise of a body which eats – a pure orality – in order to become the manifestation of a subject expressing itself' (1969, 181).

Such a distinction lies in Deleuze's notion of the 'event.' Foucault, in his 1970 essay about Deleuze's early works, 'Theatrum Philosophicum,' summarizes Deleuze's position:

We should not restrict meaning to the cognitive core that lies at the heart of a knowable object; rather, we should allow it to reestablish its flux at the limit of words and things. (1977, 174)

To summarize: at the limit of dense bodies, an event is incorporeal (a metaphysical surface); on the surface of words and things, an incorporeal event is the *meaning* of a proposition (its logical dimension); in the thread of discourse, an incorporeal meaning-event is fastened to the verb (the infinitive point of the present). (1977, 175)

Deleuze's event, as it relates to language, is sense, the same sense that is so intimately dependent upon what he describes as surface nonsense. The event mediates between the cause and effect of his radically reconstrued causality in much the same way that nonsense joins sense and senselessness, by validating the former through the latter. The event 'desubstantializes' or dematerializes the physical core of cause and effect, extracts their component being as articulable but ultimately kinetic, incorporeal; the event is the abstract and constantly repetitive occasion that links the bodies of cause and effect.

But nonsense is another sort of mediator. Poised between language and the body, it is one of the many frontiers of language where distinctions begin to break down, just the sort of distinctions that are rendered feasible by Deleuzes's theory of the event. If the event occasions language by making sound incorporeal, then nonsense as I understand it reverses the event. For nonsense is an attempt to resubstantialize language, and to do so in its own kinetic fashion. Nonsense explores the kinesis, the instability of the body by rematerializing language.[2] With the help of a 'vocalic,' polyphonic 'maternal' body ('throat, voice, and breasts: music, rhythm, prosody, paragrams, and the matrix of the prophetic parabola' [Kristeva 1974b, 153]), nonsense both establishes and undermines sense.

Curse of the Mummy's Tomb:
Nonsense, Poetry, and the Possibilities of Sound

When asked if there would be a dictionary of *Orghast*, Ted Hughes replied 'Where is the dictionary of music?' 'There is one – in your body' (Smith 1972, 209). Hughes's rhetorical question and his unexpected response recall his statement quoted earlier: 'The deeper into language one goes, the less visual/conceptual its imagery, and the more audial/visceral/muscular its system of tensions ... the more dominated it becomes by purely musical modes' (Smith 1972, 45). Hughes ties the body and language together at a primal level; and it is, as has already been suggested, a metonymically, metaphorically primeval position that Cixous points to when she locates in women's bodies 'the first, nameless love [which] is singing' (1975, 93).

Yet, even if one removes this originary or metaphorical notion, this primeval myth, from the body and music, an undeniable connection with verbal language remains. The body produces the sound that informs language, or at least spoken language, so the two must interact. In *Lyric's Larynx*, Steve McCaffery writes: 'It is sound more so than meaning binds / the body to language' (1986, 178). A writing intimate with sound (as is nonsense) is bound to the body.

An obvious counterargument: poetry and nonsense are usually written forms, meant to be read silently. Avant-garde composer R. Murray Schafer takes just such a stance when comparing music and language. Despite the numerous similarities between the two, he concludes that 'in language words are symbols standing metonymically for something else. The sound of a word is a means to another end, an acoustic accident that can be dispensed with entirely if the word is written, for then the writing conveys the word's essence, and its sound is totally absent or unimportant. Printed language is silent information' (1988, 202). Print is a 'sarcophagus' (1988, 171) for sound, he contends.

There is a limited logic here. Superficially, at least, one has to admit that the printed word is silent, voiceless. But to what extent does the *printed* word constitute language, or, going to the opposite extreme, to what extent is it a notational form, a scoring for language? What one must ask oneself is not does language, unlike music, exist to communicate (that will be dwelt upon later), but rather what is the relationship of the printed word to language. Surely the written alphabet, the visual medium of language, is not verbal language per se, not the entirety of that language. To suggest that the printed word is the ultimate or only incarnation of language is to sell short our communicative system. If writing is considered in part a notation for language's intimacy with sound, or considered only one facet of language (whether or not, as is usually the case, that language is directed at a meaningful end), then one can begin to open up language to its phonic possibilities. Print may be silent, but the reader of print, and so the process of reading, is not – even as I write and reread these lines my mind's ear hears each word, syllable, letter. The same is true of most silent readings.

Such questions about sound and writing cannot be asked, and such tentative conclusions can't be reached, without confronting Derrida's grammatological deconstruction of the privileging of speech. He argues in his early works, *Speech and Phenomena*, *Of Grammatology*, and *Writing and Difference* (1967), that the opposing of speech and writing and the subsequent privileging of speech over writing are the result of Western civilization's historical worship of the logos, a transcendental absolute that is an unprovable figment of its own philosophy. Such a hierarchy presupposes a presence, a fullness of being, associated with speech that is not, or cannot be, found in writing. Such an opposition implicitly defines writing as 'a parasitic and imperfect representation' of speech (Culler 1982, 100).

Derrida, however, claims that writing, or what is meant by his redefinition of writing, precedes speech. Christopher Norris explains it this way: 'Writing, for Derrida, is the "free play" or element of undecidability within every system of communication ... Writing is the endless displacement of meaning which both governs language and places it for ever beyond the reach of a stable, self-authenticating knowledge' (1982, 28-9).

It is the 'arche-trace' that is present in, and so comes before, all origins. Speech is not indicative of a fullness, of a link to the primal origin; all origins are already displaced from the arche-trace, defined by their difference (or differance) from that trace. Here is Derrida on this trace:

The (pure) trace is differance. It does not depend on any sensible plentitude, audible or visible, phonic or graphic. It is, on the contrary, the condition of such plenitude. Although it *does not exist*, although it is never a *being-present* outside of all plenitude, its possibility is by rights anterior to all that one calls sign (signified/signifier, content/expression, etc.), concept or operation, motor or sensory. This differance is therefore not more sensible than intelligible and it permits the articulation of signs among themselves within the same abstract order – a phonic or graphic text for example – or between two orders of expression. It permits the articulation of speech and writing – in the colloquial sense – as it founds the metaphysical opposition between the sensible and the intelligible, then between signifier and signified, expression and content, etc. If language were not already, in that sense, a writing, no derived 'notation' would be possible. (1967a, 62–3)

All language is 'written,' then, even that which is spoken, for all language bespeaks a state of lack.

As soon as nonsense admits a participation simultaneously within language and within pre- or nonlingual modes, admits its incorporation of a Derridean arche-trace, it reconstrues one of the premises of deconstruction. By wilfully incorporating the nonsensical equivalent to Kristeva's semiotic within its articulation in a very definite and disruptive way, by comparing that 'free play' with a musicalized 'maternal' body, nonsense is *responding to* lack and difference. The interdependence of the semiotic and symbolic may preclude this lack ever being singularly satisfied, and nonsense may require Deleuze's version of sense – the continual, relational deferral of stable meaning – to give it purpose, but nonsense goes a considerable distance towards responding to this lack and towards blurring the boundaries that separate lingual and prelingual modes. It entertains and exploits this lack self-consciously.

Rendering an account of 'human delusion,' voicing, that is, his version of the Rousseauistic premises central to phonocentric civilization, Derrida writes: 'Man *calls himself* man only by drawing limits excluding his other from the play of supplementarity: the purity of nature, of animality, primitivism, childhood, madness, divinity. The approach to these limits is at once feared as a threat of death, and desired as access to a life without differance. The history of man *calling himself* man is the articulation of *all* of these limits among themselves' (1967a, 244–5).

What Derrida sets up as the factors oppositional to Rousseauean lingual humanity in order to expose humanism's binary basis, are some of the many elements related to nonsense. Nonsense is not childhood, madness, divinity, nature, animality, or primitivism; yet, as the taxonomy in Part One argued, it participates in almost all of them, through its engagement with play, the irrational, and materiality. It spans or blurs the sorts of opposition that deconstruction seeks to undermine.

Such blurring of boundaries is integral to nonsense's difference from deconstruction. The deconstructive principle is, according to Vincent Leitch, one that emphasizes the gap between traditional oppositions in order to encourage a questioning of the premises upon which these binaries are constructed (1983, 180). Nonsense inverts and highlights such oppositions as well, but does so not to open up a gap between them but to close one down. Rather than replacing meaning with the meaninglessness of a constantly receding meaning, nonsense requires that the two, meaning and meaninglessness, coexist.

And if nonsense is that place where meaning shades into meaninglessness, where sense shades into senselessness, it is no less the place where other oppositions blend while still maintaining their oppositional force. Each pole is demonstrably a function, an integral and parasitic resident of its opposite. Nonsense implies, to apply Charles Bernstein's words on a different (albeit marginally related) topic, a 'deeper reality of the interpenetrability and interdependence of all oppositions as appositions' (1986, 287). Meaning is as parasitically related to meaninglessness as meaninglessness is to meaning. And speech is as parasitic to writing (in the common sense of the word, not Derrida's) as writing is to speech.[3] Yet integral as these oppositions may be to each other, they retain their own integrity. Unlike the traditional dialectic process, in which thesis and antithesis merge to make a higher, more valuable synthesis, nonsensical blending, as is the case with negative dialectics, never devalues its 'thesis' or 'antithesis,' never privileges its 'synthesis' over its component parts.

Many of the writers I have been and will be discussing might be termed phonocentric, whether or not one conceives of it as a pejorative term. That does not mean, however, that nonsense is phonocentric. Phonocentrism would find a *grounding* in sound, which nonsense does not have. I'm inclined to borrow Foucault's description of Deleuze's theory as 'phonodecentring'[4] (1977, 180) to describe nonsense. Nonsense is an intimate and tenuous meeting of sound and print; as such, it is at once both, and neither, phonocentric and graphocentric; the same movement that centralizes sound, decentralizes it. Lear's limericks delicately poise the visual and the lingual with and against each other; the illustrations illustrate, extend, or undermine the verses. The same is true of the interrelationship between sound and print in nonsense. Because nonsense is at heart a balancing act, neither sound nor print can ever tip the scales.

To return to Schafer's metaphor: if print is a 'sarcophagus' for sound, then nonsense is a Saturday-afternoon-at-the-movies-grade-B-quasi-Freudian-flick – *Curse of the Mummy's Tomb*. Sound may be buried, but it's not dead yet; it's undead, won't *stay* dead. Elements of sound stalk through printed language raising the reader's spirits, spirits of a wholly other sort. Schafer might even give qualified assent to this suggestion; in *The Thinking Ear*, he quotes a small boy he once taught who defined poetry as 'when words sing' (1988, 235), a definition that hardly suggests the printed language of poetry has both feet in the grave.

Nonsense relies on the hesitant fusion of speech and writing, of sound and print. But sounding out words in the mind, weighing their sound against their printed version, also facilitates poetry. The organic life of the object is best reflected in the organic, melodic life of the word, in what Martin calls the 're-affirmation of its *physical* properties, its visual shape and aural resonance' (1988, 38). Zukofsky's definition of writing is more than the 'thinking with things as they exist' related in chapter three to a perceptually-based language; it is also, as he continues his statement, 'directing them along a line of melody' (1981, 12). Zukofsky's poetics come startlingly, but not surprisingly, close to music. He presents them succinctly in *A-12*:

$$\int \frac{\text{music}}{\text{speech}}$$

> An integral
> Lower limit speech
> Upper limit music.
> (1978a, 138)

His poetry is an integer composed of both speech and music, a mediator between them. Writing and print, one notes, isn't mentioned; Zukofsky stands firmly on the side of sound. An even clearer articulation of his passion for sound is found in 'A Statement for Poetry'; he posits the imagining of a speech wholly separated from writing, one that is purely 'a movement of sounds' – this is his 'musical horizon of poetry' (1981, 20). But it's arguable that nonsense is also a musical horizon of poetry. If that's the case, one might recast Zukofsky's famous poetic equation quoted above along lines suggested to me by Charles Bernstein:

$$\int \begin{array}{l} \text{poetry} \\ \\ \text{nonsense} \end{array}$$

An integral
Lower limit nonsense
Upper limit poetry.

Rubbing against the Grain:
Language and the Semiotics of Music

This discussion risks imprecision. When, if ever, does the use of the term 'musical' cease to be metaphorical? Kristeva points out that 'the best metaphor' for the rhythmic assertion of the *chora* is 'a piece of music or a work of architecture' (1974b, 126), but her paradigm allows for a nonmetaphorical use of the term as well. Before looking more closely at how nonsense and poetry can mean musically, it will be helpful to determine what is meant by 'music' and how it differs from verbal language.

In *Silence*, John Cage asks, 'If words are sounds, are they musical or are they just noise?' (1961, 42). The question is part of 'Composition as Process,' a lecture comprised entirely of questions. It is also part of his larger attempt to question the limits of music and language, to promote a phonic continuum in which sound is never silent, and music incorporates all sorts of sounds – even unplanned noises. His ideas are important to this discussion because they provide an alternative to Deleuze's theory that language is made possible through its distinctness from sounds.

For Deleuze, words are not sounds, or at least are sounds severely qualified by their dissociation from the body. Cage acknowledges such distinctions by highlighting their arbitrariness. 'Yes,' he might say, 'but what's the nature of those distinctions: why are they made?' He purposely incorporates bodily noises into some of his lectures, pencils in when to cough or blow his nose (see '45' for a Speaker' in *Silence*), so that the idea of such distinctness can be questioned. These bodily noises become part of the 'meaning-event' (Foucault 1977, 174),[5] which is his presentation, the process of inquisition which evokes sense. By virtue of their inclusion within the lecture's structure, these bodily noises resonate with meanings. But they resonate with imprecise meanings that cannot be individually defined apart from the sounds' broadly gestural flaunting of the conventions of language and lectures. No one cough means separately from the other coughs, sneezes, or snorts; yet each means beyond the realm of basic bodily signification. Cage's sounds challenge Deleuze's theory by presenting incorporeal meaning corporeally, and thereby questioning the rigidity of his divisions between sound and language. Cage's experiment also confronts the distinction between sound and music; if, as has been suggested, music is an arrangement of sounds meant to be listened to (see Schafer 1988, 18), then Cage's words as well as his snores, grunts, hisses, and gargles are also music, for they have been arranged to be heard.

Cage's probing of the border between language and sound, and between music and sound, may put a crimp in Deleuze's argument, but it doesn't supply a ready answer to his own question – 'If words are sounds, are they musical or are they just noise?' This question raises another problem that Eduard Hanslick had already anticipated – a 'fundamental difference' exists between language and music: 'while sound in speech is but a sign, that is, a means for the purpose of expressing something which is quite distinct from its medium, sound in music is the end, that is, the ultimate and absolute object in view' ([1922] 1957, 67). Language, unlike music, has a field of reference outside of sound (Springer 1956, 506), so it is, on at least one level, 'sound as sense' (Schafer 1988, 202).

'Pig,' for instance, is more than a group of sounds strung together. It denotes that porcine animal that all too often ends up on the breakfast table, or that, in *Alice's Adventures in Wonderland*, is just 'a phonemic breath away' from a fig (Miller 1987, 70). That seems to be the case, at least, when Alice tells the Cheshire-Cat about her experience with the Duchess and her baby, who has turned into a pig. The cat interrupts Alice to ask: 'Did you say "pig" or "fig"?' (Carroll [1865] 1971, 74). Edmund Miller, commenting on this passage in 'The *Sylvie and Bruno* Books as Victorian Novel,' contends that the 'sound image floats free to attach itself to any other sound with which it has the slightest association' (1987, 70). His point is that, in this Nonsensical world, the baby is only a hair's-breadth away from being a 'fig,' or a 'wig,' or a 'twig,' or any other 'ig' word one can think of. The content, 'what' the baby becomes, matters far less than the actual sounds of its name.[6] But there is no avoiding the fact that whether or not sounds govern the sense, as the Cheshire-Cat's question implies, the sound also relates to a sense. The baby did become a pig, the physical referent of the sound word. Nonsense nods towards the referential function of language; it may show such references to be arbitrary, but it exploits reference as well as controls it through sound.

Music points to nothing outside of itself, however. And because this is the case, music is itself concrete; it 'stands for the concrete experience of the unique, sensed reality of sound in process' (Orlov 1981, 133). Like a Deleuzian nonsense word, which means itself, music has no 'recognizable identity' beyond itself (Orlov 1981, 135). Since each note refers to nothing, it is indefinable; no other meaningful note lends it substance. The same is true of musical compositions as a whole: each piece of music, Winn suggests, 'must establish *within itself* the "conditions for understanding it"' (1981, 293). Even variations on a preestablished musical theme can do no more than perpetuate a regressive referral back to music, and so to itself. If a Snark is a Snark is a Snark, then a note is a note is a note.

Walter Ong comments upon the phonocentric paradox: sound's evanescence contributes to its concreteness, to its presence in the present because it must 'emanate from a source here and now discernibly active' (1967, 112). This is precisely the tradition that Derrida responds to, but in the field of music this tradition is less susceptible to his scepticism. Even its notational system doesn't ground music since the notes point only to their phonic counterparts and to nothing else. Whatever music may evoke (and the responses it elicits, like those elicited by humour, drama, and colour, are culturally determined [Orlov 1981, 136]) is entirely separate from what it 'means.'

If music conveys any meaning at all, that meaning is its form. As John Blacking claims, 'In music, code and message are inseparable: the code is the message' (1981, 185). Contemporary literature's tendency to unite form and content finds a perfected counterpart here, and so does nonsense's inclination to mean itself. Blacking goes on to argue that any attempt to make music symbolize something outside of itself nullifies it; when 'music is treated as an arbitrary symbol in essentially social, political, economic, or religious interaction, ... it ceases to have meaning as *music*' (1981, 185). This does not mean music is senseless – it is too rooted in the physical senses for that to be the case; both Hanslick ([1922] 1957, 49) and Zukofsky (1963, 423) urge this understanding of music. But it does mean that music is more useful than verbal language 'for revealing the purely structural requirements for a symbol *system*' (Blacking 1981, 186). There's no meaningful baggage to trip up a person wending her way through musical structure, no abstractions tempting her to detour from the immediacy of the sound.

Kristeva takes Blacking's contention one step further by calling music the furthest limit of a sign system. Actually it is not, she argues, a system of signs at all because it has no signified; the signifier, signified, and referent of music have all melted into one (1981, 309). Perhaps this blending of disparates is one reason why nonsense is equated with music by some critics; Cammaerts considers classical Nonsense to be 'by its very nature, pure music' (1925, 52). Both reach across the gap of signifier, signified, and referent. But music, according to Kristeva, fuses the three; nonsense joins them while retaining their individuality.[7]

Music, like language, is a differential system. But it has, for Kristeva, no semantic meaning (1981, 310) and so can be regarded as exclusively semiotic (in her redefinition of the term) (1974b, 24). Language is musicalized when it is 'drawn out of its symbolic function (sign-syntax) and is opened out within a semiotic articulation; with a material support such as the voice' (1974b, 63). Her argument seems pulled towards paradox since music is so rigidly structured; even jazz with its improvisational form is dependent upon a series of accepted structures and quite dependable rhythms. But as will be seen later, rhythm, despite its highly structured nature, is integral to the semiotic; structure per se is *not* found solely in the realm of communication and syntax.

Henry Orlov sees language and music as 'autonomous and mutually complementary domains,' each having 'its own sets of patterns and values, field of competence, and view of reality' (1981, 132). Though such a view is not wrong-headed, its prevalence has led inadvertently to an almost habitual pairing off of music against language in criticism. They are made to fall into binary oppositions: expressive/communicative; nothing/something; emotion/intellect; concrete/abstract – such dualities can be found in a range of critics. These oppositions are often useful because they provide a clear, simple, and dramatic view of one particular perspective, but they almost all reduce or misrepresent either language or music. For instance in response to claims that music is expressive and emotive (a myth that Winn claims rose with German Romanticism [1981, 259–70]), Pierre Boulez offers Stravinsky's insistence that music doesn't express anything, it merely orders (1966, 4). And language, because it involves a sensical referent, extracts a meaning from sound, but that does not eliminate its sound component.[8] Language can't be qualified as merely abstract, only as more abstract than music; Gerald Bruns, in *Modern Poetry and the Idea of Language*, contends that 'language, being sound, appears as a malleable substance capable of being shaped into an infinity of forms' (1974, 18).

Cage writes: 'Nothing more than nothing can be said' (1961, 111) – a statement that might, given that the context is a lecture on nothing, be taken as a pun; when one is talking about nothing nothing can be *said*. Such reemphasizing is reminiscent of the many claims that poetry says nothing. Cage's logical paradox (he's clearly saying *something*, even if it's nothing) can be taken as a qualified 'nothing,' however. It is obliquely related to his appeal for an ideal language rooted in a musicalized landscape. An ultimately ineffective, empty something is, in Cage's book, a nothing: 'Since words, when they communicate, have no effect, it dawns on us that we need a society in which communication is not practiced, in which words become nonsense as they do between lovers, in which words become what they originally were: trees and stars and the rest of primeval environment' (1979, 184). Which brings one back to an insistent relationship between words, things, and beings similar to that found explicitly in Hughes and implicitly in Lilburn.

The idea of words being germinated in the surrounding world is appealing on many levels; it's an idea that Nonsense embraces and rejects simultaneously. But it is also an idea that moves full circle to a theoretical position that has already been left behind. Such circling is an acceptable Nonsense strategy, a sort of active stasis, but it doesn't work in a theoretical argument. And neither, ultimately, does Cage's contention about a metaphorical, almost mystical, tie between language and music. Language needs to be broken down into its component parts, to be encountered from an ignorant position, in order to confront its similarities with music. This may be arguing the obvious, but it is essential for the understanding of how language can work musically.

Facing language out of ignorance or unfamiliarity is, in effect, facing it musically. Deleuze suggests, 'If the child comes to a preexisting language which she cannot yet understand, perhaps conversely, she grasps that which we no longer know how to grasp in our own language, namely, the phonemic relations, the differential relations of phonemes' (1969, 230). Language is at its most musical (or is appreciated with a most musical frame of mind) when it is not comprehensible, when its phenotextual aspects are short-circuited. That's why people may appreciate the sheer 'music' of poetry read in a foreign language. And why the 'pig'/'fig' example, discussed above, so strongly demonstrates the musical rebelliousness of Nonsense; it isolates the phonemic instant in language, makes that instant of ignorance and new recognition count as much as meaning does.

Deleuze's suggestion about an ignorant grasping of phonemes unwittingly supports Springer's contention that the phonemes, the smallest units of language, offer 'the most significant parallels' between linguistic and musical theory. Phonemic systems relate, Springer suggests, to scales (1956, 509). A partial proof for this suggestion can be found in ancient Egyptian vowel music. Egyptian priests, while singing hymns, would utter vowels in succession; 'the sound of these letters,' according to Demetrius in *On Style*, '[was] so euphonious that men listen[ed] to it in preference to flute and lyre' (quoted in Winn 1981, 2). The sounds were appreciated sensuously (1981, 3) and behaved very much like the 'neume,' of which Derrida writes in *Of Grammatology* – it is 'pure vocalization, form of an inarticulate song without speech, whose name means breath,' 'a song and an inarticulate language, [a] speech without spacing' (1967a, 249). Here, at the level of the phoneme, or of breath, music and language coincide.

In *The Music of Poetry*, T.S. Eliot describes the music of a word as a product resulting from the intersection of both the relationships the word has with the other words in its immediate context and the range of its lexical meanings (intended or not) (1942, 19). While some of a word's contextual relationships may well be phonic, Eliot's version of music is, for the most part, cerebral and metaphorical, as sensically compromised as language itself; that compromising of sound is the whole problem of music in language. Following Springer, I would argue that a word can come closest to a 'literal' music via the phonemes that combine to create it.

Since music is material, one way language can move towards musicality is by downplaying its phenotextual or abstract aspects in order to emphasize its phonic and phonemic interrelations. 'The anteriorities / of language' are carried by sound, writes McCaffery in *Lyric's Larynx* (1986, 179). But his is not another Cagean plea for a return to primeval language. One doesn't need to return nostalgically to the anteriorities he speaks of because they exist in and with language: 'the body at all times houses the / linguistic and pre-linguistic' (1986, 178). One wonders, then, if the anteriorities of language are carried by music as well. The suggestion may be that music and language are different growths from a similar source. Such an extrapolation is hardly Derridean, but it is Kristevan. McCaffery is well versed in Kristeva's theory of poetic language, as is evident from his work. If those anteriorities constitute the semiotic, or part of it, then it seems likely that they are also found in music and so form one possible interface between it and language. Nonsense explores and exploits this interface when playing with language's most minimal and musical elements, phonemes.[9]

Barthes turns to Kristeva to offer another interface, or to put that interface into different words. In an essay entitled 'The Grain of the Voice' he names the interface 'the *grain*, the grain of the voice when the latter is in a dual posture, a dual production – of language and of music' (1977, 181). Of course, he is concerned for the most part with the singing of lyrical music, but his argument can be applied to a poetry intended to be read, to the 'written' poem and poetic language. He speaks of the 'geno-song,' 'that apex (or that depth) of production where the melody really works at the language – not at what it says, but the voluptuousness of its sounds-signifiers, of its letters – where melody explores how the language works and identifies with that work' (1977, 182). This 'voluptuousness,' this sound-body of letters, is embodied in the grain of the voice. But that grain works against another grain – the grain of a phenotextual language, the grain of musical and literary criticism, which wants to keep language and music distinct.

'Akin jabber':
Nonsense, Poetry, Rhythm, and the Zukofskys' A

'Above everything else,' writes Wallace Stevens in 'The Noble Rider and the Sound of Words,' 'poetry is words; and ... words, above everything else, are, in poetry, sounds' (1951, 32). Nonsense, poetry and poetic language have everything to do with sound. Ede finds some parts of Lear, especially 'The Story of the Four Little Children Who Went Round the World,' to be language functioning 'purely' as sound (1975, 58), while Cammaerts, as was noted above, equates Nonsense and music (1925, 52). Certainly the pronouncedly rhythmic disposition of Nonsense verse to which Cammaerts appeals lends a measure of credibility to his claim. Dennis Lee's *Quintin and Griffin*, for instance, whether one classifies it as Nonsense or a slightly tamer form of children's verse, patterns sounds with tongue-twisting revelry:

> Quintin's sittin' hittin' Griffin,
> Griffin's hittin' Quintin too.
> If Quintin's quittin' hittin' Griffin,
> What will Griffin sit'n'do?
>   (1977, 11)

Lee's verse is not pure music, nor, despite Cammaerts's claims, Nonsense; but Cammaerts's observations lead in the right direction for an exploration of the musical elements in Nonsense and poetry.

Rhythm is sound considered in its temporal dimension, and is inextricable from Kristeva's *chora*. Toril Moi highlights the relationship between the two: 'The *chora* is a rhythmic pulsion' (1985, 162). Because the *chora* is the 'source' of the semiotic, its rhythms are integral to nonsense. Robert Haas perhaps intuited as much when he argued: 'Rhythm is always revolutionary ground. It is always the place where the organic arises to abolish the mechanical and where energy announces the abolition of tradition' (1978, 98). He contends that 'new rhythms are new perceptions' (1978, 98), but even old rhythms offer alternative perspectives. Strongly articulated rhythms can shift emphasis from sense to sound, from meaning to material, and in the process can foreground how sense is made. That in itself is revolutionary.

Communicative language is rich in structure, but it doesn't exhaust the possibilities of structure. Criticism of Nonsense's tendency to use rigid structures misses the point because structure is not antithetical to a writing of the body. Lear's limericks are no less nonsensical for their tight form. Some of the most nonsensical works of modern and contemporary literature, for instance *Finnegans Wake*, embrace intricate, albeit unusual, structural rigours. In fact it seems appropriate to conflate Kristeva's terming of music as pure semiosis with the seemingly opposite, and frequently given, definition of music as pure structure to argue that 'pure' semiosis *is* pure structure. Pure structure as (opposed to) pure meaning; form as opposed to content, and form that points to itself *as* content.

All disorders are orders of another ilk. An infusion of 'disorder,' of another language's structure into grammatical language can pervert its structure without doing away with grammar, can bring two or more opposing ways of meaning together. Boulez writes that structure is the point of contact between poetry and music and 'that poets [among them Joyce] who worked on language itself are the ones who left the most visible imprint upon the musician' (1966, 53). Such a crossover implies that musicians and experimental writers are, as this chapter is, most concerned with the structure of sound.

Robert Bringhurst (1986, 116) and James Winn (1981, 297) each characterize Joyce's work as *chordal*. An especially helpful term when read in light of Winn's description of chords as 'intersections of contrapuntal lines' (1981, 334).[10] This definition points towards a facet of intertextuality, or what Kristeva (to avoid confusion with its popular and imprecise use) calls 'transposition,' that 'passage from one signifying system to another' (1974b, 60), which emphasizes the manyness, the polyvalence of each enunciated object. Her term, taken from the musical term for rewriting a musical composition into another key, succinctly denotes not only the passing from one signifying system to another, but also the character of the relationship between nonsense and music. Nonsense is a converging, intermingling, transliterating that moves in and out of various sign systems and, in doing so, takes with it the residues of those systems.

When the rhythmic structures of music move into language, two sign systems are walking in step. Sometimes, when she was small, my daughter (a confluence of ancestors) would plop herself onto my foot, wrap her arms around my leg and ask me to walk her into the next room. Something similar happens when a confluence of sign systems (musical, visual, and verbal have been mentioned, though several others, including mathematical and philosophical as Carroll's work proves, are also possible) situates itself in a language, transposes itself into a medium that, laden with all these elements, must radically alter its movement. Nonsense is a silly walk. Of course because the nonsense considered here is oriented to words, it always toes in towards verbal language. But a nonsense that toes towards music, or mathematics, or any other component is conceivable too.

Cage, for instance, creates a form of nonsense in his poem sequence *Empty Words*, which is arguably more musical than linguistic. Following Norman O. Brown, he calls syntax the 'arrangement of the army' (1979, 11), and insists upon the 'demilitarization of lan-

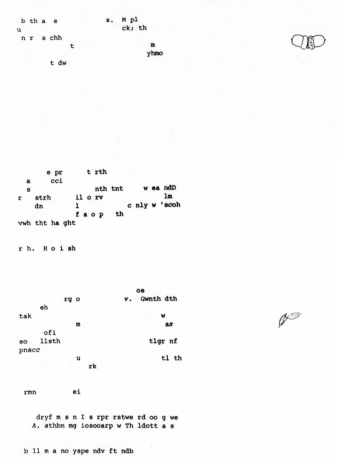

Figure 11 From John Cage *Empty Words*

guage: a serious musical concern' (1979, 184). He attempts to demili-
tarize it by moving through its five component materials (sentences,
phrases, words, syllables, letters [1979, 11]) until his poem's final
section offers only an arrangement of letters on the page (see Figure
11), verbal language gone AWOL. It's a matter of perspective whether
Empty Words is nonsense or gibberish, but the sequence does juggle
a meaning, and quite a polemical one, encoded by some seemingly
random and supposedly meaningless letters that actually *refer* back
to earlier sentences and phrases.

Cage has not escaped Springer's contention that even nonsense words have 'rudimentary morphemic associations' (1956, 508) – though there are few morphemes here. However, he has in part reduced verbal language to a tonal construct, has made it 'multidimensional,' multifoliate; it has been given a manyness of meaning (Orlov 1981, 134). But is he left with words or with a visual representation of their anteriorities? Is this a musical 'score' or a concrete poem? It is possible that he has pushed verbal language over the edge that separates it from music, as he suggests (Cage 1979, 65). However, if he has done this, he has pushed it into a nonsensical music. His use of letters in *Empty Words* allows a symbolization that threatens the piece's ability to mean musically, or so Blacking would contend. Rather than transposing music onto language, he may have transposed language onto music. Moreover, this nonsense only exists musically if one accepts the premise that disorder is a form of order, and so accepts the existence of a structure, which is not readily identifiable, within the work. As literature, Cage's work is closest at this point to sound poetry, a category of literature that bends notions of poetry almost to breaking.

A different example of language being articulated as music is found in bp Nichol's *Book 5* of *The Martyrology*. This is no surprise coming from Nichol, a renowned sound poet and experimenter with the tonal and visual aspects of verbal language. In *Book 5*, Nichol tries to establish 'a system for using text to generate melody' (Dutton 1989, 9) by writing part of the text on a musical staff. Paul Dutton explains that 'when a letter in the text was the name of a note, the text moved to the line or space corresponding to that note, remaining on that line or space until the next note-name letter occurred' (1989, 9). (See figures 12[a] and 12[b] for a sample.) The text is chanted; the duration of each pitch depends on the amount of text on the given line. The resulting music sounds, according to Dutton, 'somewhat reminiscent of Gregorian chant – or should I say, given its aleatoric basis, Gregorian chance?' (1989, 10). Though Nichol's experiment, in this instance, doesn't quite match Cage's for sheer flaunting of the musical residue in language, his playful exploitation of the alphabetical intersection of musical and linguistic notation points to the possibilities inherent in viewing written language as a notational system for its more concrete aspects. Jonathan Albert, in his essay 'A Language of Spoken Movement,' suggests that the alphabet can be viewed as a 'series of directions' rather than as a 'naming system'

dour yo umeett
hemor talit
ypl aininon year home
as w as t
he ot
her opens[6]

Figure 12(a) From bp Nichol *The Martyrology Book 5*

(1982, 14–15). As such it is a symbolic representation that shares similarities with musical notation. By forcing certain letters of the alphabet to incorporate their musical functions within a lingual context, Nichol implies the musical possibilities for *all* letters.

A somewhat tamer, but much extended experiment with presenting verbal language musically is Zukofsky's '*A*'-24, originally titled *L.Z. Masque*.[11] A work for five voices arranged by Celia Zukofsky, '*A*'-24 counterpoints the classical order and control of Handel's Harpsichord Pieces with the chaos of four other competing voices, each reciting

Figure 12(b) From bp Nichol *The Martyrology Book 5*

excerpts from Louis's stories, poetry, drama, and thought (or criticism). And it raises several questions about language and form that critics of Zukofsky have not yet dealt with sufficiently. Very few have written exclusively on it: most refer to it simply as the consummation of Zukofsky's poem. Guy Davenport describes the movement with the wonderful analogy of 'a family reunion of [Zukofsky's] work, inside and outside the poem, a grand Jewish family affair, with everybody cheerfully talking at once' (1974, 22). He adds that in performance it sounds like indecipherable noise, being intensely polyphonous (1974, 22). This emphasis on performance is important, for *L.Z. Masque* is meant more for the ear than the eye; Celia refers to the text as a score, and it does indeed read like one.

'A'-24 jettisons the overt spectacle and dance of a traditional masque, but keeps its fusion of music and drama; one might look to the dramatic line for help shifting through the medley or muddle of voices. Celia's prefatory remarks support such a reading strategy, and in the score itself the dramatic line is centrally located as the third of the five voices. But looking again one finds that, rather than repeating the drama as Louis wrote it, Celia has drastically reorganized it – making each scene of the masque a monologue for one character and patterning it after a distinct musical form: for instance, Act One, Scene One is named 'Cousin: Lesson' and so includes all of and only the lines spoken by Zukofsky's character 'the cousin.'[12] Dramatic tension and dramatic coherence are set aside; drama is rearranged into song, into character, and becomes the counterpoint for thematic variations in the genres of music, thought, story, and poem.

The tranditional English masque was plagued with 'the problem of how much the burden of meaning and the presentation of character may be allowed to challenge the primarily choreographical and musical movement,' writes John Arthos (1974, 475). Celia Zukofsky's masque also turns on that problem, for it challenges conventional meaning; dislodges the development of dramatic character, since each character now acts and speaks in isolation; and through its musical arrangement of the verbal supplements the partial overturning of meaningful structure (both linguistic and poetic) in the earlier parts of *'A'*.

Each scene can be read as reverberations of character: music, thought, story, and poem harmonizing with drama's melody. But as in so much of Louis's work, language is itself a character. And although reading *L.Z. Masque* as a play upon character is true to the genre, reading it as a play with languages, or with verbal language as music, is equally true to Zukofsky. Always his work has leaned this way, towards making words as musical, as music-laden, as possible. Randolph Chilton points out that 'Zukofsky used sounds as a musical composer might use them – to produce aesthetic effects by manipulating relations between sounds' (1981, 238), and Davenport suggests that the whole of *'A'* is 'a series of metamorphoses in which thought turns into music' (1974, 21); *'A'-24* is the most literal (or *musical*) realization of that metamorphosis. For the tangle of voices both interferes with and supplements the sense-making process; it moves words towards music.

Louis says in his closing dedication of '*A*'-24 to Celia that she 'hears / the work / in its recurrence' (1978, 806). And it is Celia the listener, the hearer, who begins *L.Z. Masque* with three voices speaking of and as this movement towards music – four if one counts the Handel:

Thought: And it is possible in imagination to divorce speech of all graphic elements, to let it become a movement of sounds.
Story: This story was a story of our time. And a writer's attempts not to fathom his time amount but to sounding his mind in it.
Poem: Blest/ Infinite things/ So many/ Which confuse imagination/ Thru its weakness, To the ear/ Noises. (1978, 566–7)

Even in the drama, with the cousin asking distractedly 'How do you catch such a bird?' (1978, 568), one can hazard connections. Catch a bird? a song? music? But also words – as early as '*A*'-7 Louis writes 'each bird a word' (1978, 39), playing no doubt upon the rhyme and upon the fact that 'bird' *is* first and foremost a word.

Such thematic recurrences are not always so obvious, nor need they be for '*A*'-24 to cohere musically or verbally. Celia has, of course, caught such a bird, or 'diverse birds chirping harmonious discord' (1978, 789), has caught it as both verbal and musical language, where both languages intersect in a strange version of negative dialectics. If context is a determinant of meaning, then here music exists on a par with words, thematically reiterating, underscoring, the 'sense' of the words. But more important, words exist musically – even if their semantic meaning is able to rise above musical overscoring, above simultaneous cacophony, they are most evidently a movement of sounds in performance.

Writing about the difficulties of performing '*A*'-24, Bob Perelman observes that while the analogy of 'language approaching music should allow for an approachable "verbal harmony"' it is actually misleading (1984a, 292). For verbal language and music occupy time differently, and unlike music whose 'unities are instantly "transparent," so to speak,' a word's 'phonemes, the units of "verbal music," aren't transparent, can't be superimposed without ambiguity'; 'a phoneme doesn't sound like a word' (1984a, 292–3). The two can't blend inextricably. Words don't *become* music, nor music words; the one doesn't cancel the other out. Rather the ear comes to negotiate a delicate balance between music and language, becomes alive to the fact of words' daily inhibitions about their own musicality, of music's inhabitation of Zukofsky's words. Each word – orchestrated: drawn out, spoken quickly, staccato, shouted, whispered,[13] and almost inevitably recontextualized by concurrent voices – becomes the site of the meaningful confluence generated by its own nature but illuminated by its companions.

All this concerns how th *hear 'A'-24*, not how to read it. Yet when approaching the whole of '*A*', no matter how finely ears are engaged, eyes serve as conduit to those ears. How do these newly musicalized words, this thicker nonsensical language, appear on the page? If, as I suggest, nonsense is an intimate and tenuous meeting of alternate sign systems, and if that intimacy is carried over into print, then nonsense is at once both, and neither, graphocentric and phonocentric; in *L.Z. Masque*, the movement that centralizes sound also decentralizes it by seeming to obfuscate it. Writing and sound are both priviledged and upset. Such, then, is the experience of reading '*A*'-24.

On first turning to this movement of '*A*', one might feel a surge of panic and not without cause, for *L.Z. Masque* presents itself multiply to the eye. Such panic might be considered in the character of the movement itself: musical, sensual, riotuous, and tricky – this is a wise and a goaty peom, despite what Guy Davenport recognizes as Zukofsky's Apollonian affinities (1974, 18), and it is best approached with such in mind. Reading it, the eye strays, dances in, out, up, down, backward, forward; a sustained linear reading is impossible. The eye seeks out echoes and equivalencies, verbal cousins, mothers, fathers, sons (the relations of *Arise, Arise* and '*A*' embodied in words, as words). Such relations are at times thematic, but mentally holding together five concurrent texts in order to sift through for larger connections is a tall order. Rather, the eye rests on visual resemblances; the mind's ear pauses over pockets of sound, rhyme; fingers reconsider rhythms' and the pages of *L.Z. Masque* are read and reread in ever-shifting configurations of line and voice. The very act of reading becomes fractured, splits into vectors or tangents of possible association, and language (this time written, verbal language) becomes another series of movements. Of pages, of phrases. Larger movements than those of the phonemes that threaten to overwhelm during the hearing of this piece, but movements nonetheless once more collected around sound, rhythm, and graphic representation as a means of facilitating meaning.   .

The masque's most disorienting quality is its simultaneity of competing texts, so it could be argued that, whatever the masque's effects upon language, Celia Zukofsky is actually writing nonsense at a larger, structural level, at the level of genre (though she doesn't write generic Nonsense per se). But this is precisely what makes 'A'-24 so fascinating from a nonsensical point of view – Celia attempts at the level of genre what Louis has striven for at the level of the word, and as such, makes more emphatic the very nature of verbal language, generally, and of Louis's writing specifically. Celia has both synthesized and extended his work – extended it in the direction he was heading but to a distance that Louis, lacking Celia's musical training, perhaps could not have gone.

On a more accessible and, one might argue, more insidious level, rhythm,[14] the temporalization of sound, is working in grammatical language when it remains on this side of the border between language and music. Ezra Pound gives his now famous definition of *melopoeia*, in 'How to Read': 'words are charged, over and above their plain meaning, with some musical property, which directs the bearing or trend of that meaning ... [and have] a contrary current, a force tending often to lull, or to distract the reader from the exact sense of the language. It is poetry on the borders of music' (1937, 170–2)

Melopoeia is 'a function of language in which the rhythmical organization is developed internally' (Welsh 1978, 234). It matches Valéry's story about the primacy of rhythm in writing, and how that rhythm is related to the body. Valéry relates in 'Poetry and Abstract Thought' being '*gripped* by a rhythm' one day while walking in Paris, and then by another rhythm, so 'certain strange *transverse* relations were set up between these two principles' (1958, VII:61). These rhythms were, he concludes, the result of the confluence of the external world, the body and the mind (1958, VII:62). And they were the physical experience of the rhythmic body spawning ideas. While he says these particular rhythms were too complicated to be worked into poetry, he uses the story to acknowledge that poetry often finds its impetus *first* in a rhythm, not an idea.

Much of Andrew Welsh's *Roots of Lyric* deals precisely with this melopoeic poetry, which he links with 'primitive' charms and chants, whose sole motivations, he suggests, are sound and rhythm respectively (1978, 145, 162). Just how estranging such melopoeic poetry can be, and how connected it can be to 'primitive' art forms, is dramatized in *A-23*, where, as Quartermain notes (1992, 63), Zukofsky transliterates an Ojibway chant:

> we see knee (windsong bis)
> we knee we see hay
> io we hay we see
> hay io wé see knee
> hay io we hów we
> see hay io we see,
> no wee knee no wa –
> (1978a, 539)

A translator might have tried to make sense of the chant, with certainly more success than Zukofsky's reader will have making sense of this transliteration; Zukofsky's insistence upon remaining true to the rhythm and sound of the original governs this portion of his poem's sense entirely, as it earlier governed his *Catullus*. For him the sound of words is 95 per cent of their poetic presence (Corman 1979, 315); rhythm, not metaphor, is a poem's most important element (Dembo 1979, 287). What is left may be 'akin [to] jabber' (*A-23* 1978a, 539), but it is also a poetry which, to use Cage's phrase, '[allows] musical elements (time, sound) to be introduced into the world of words' (1961, x).

Not for Wallflowers:
Sitwell's Rhythmic Disposition

Edith Sitwell calls the preface to her *Collected Poems* 'Some Notes on My Own Poetry' ([1957] 1982), though she might well have entitled it 'Notes for Wallflowers' because in it she defends her experimental writing style from the criticisms of those unwilling to enter into her poetic dances.[15] In order to stretch itself beyond the overworked stylistic clichés found in poems influenced by the high Victorians, she claims her writing investigates 'the effect on rhythm and on speed of the use of rhymes, assonances, and dissonances, placed at the beginning and in the middle of lines, as well as at the end, and in most elaborate patterns ([1957] 1982, xvi).

'Rhythm,' she holds, 'might be described as, to the world of sound, what light is to the world of sight. It shapes and gives new meaning' ([1957] 1982, xv). Following this metaphor, Sitwell choreographs her poems, gives them the aural shape of nursery rhyme and of dances like the waltz, the polka, the mazurka, and the hornpipe; she chooses over and over again to let sound and movement dictate her use of language. The result: wonderfully flowing poems that augment their distinctive rhythms with strangely catachrestic images. A nonsensically timid, wallflower-ish reader is left quite out of any intelligible dance, tapping her foot.

Sitwell's 'dances' are intelligible, though in a somewhat irregular way. 'When sounds become signs,' writes Charles F. Altman in 'Intratextual Rewriting,' 'their sound value is all but discarded, for to play it up would "becloud the intelligibility" of language' (1981, 49). But this is precisely what Sitwell does: play up the concrete aspect of her language, not to becloud sense but to revitalize it. And though the resulting language is hardly staid, it still maintains a discernible, albeit subordinated, meaning. Or rather, it maintains a meaning in part constituted by rhythm. Often the poems in her best known volume, *Façade*, are named after particular dances, a clear gesture that the rhythmic movement of the poem, which attempts to imitate the movement of dance, is a particular node around which meanings collect. Such is the case with *Fox Trot* ([1957] 1982, 137–8).

Fox Trot is given essentially from a child's perspective. In it, Sitwell conflates innocent perceptions of the nursery with the nursery rhyme and with the basic one-two-three-pause rhythm of the fox trot. The poem meets Zukofsky's poetic requirements – 'a context associated with "musical" shape' (1981, 16) – explicitly, letting its shape and order grow out of its musical patterns. It does so most appropriately, because the poem deals in part with order growing out of the rhythms of life, and with the way human activity (symbolized by hunting, farming, reigning, and the eating of the egg [a mythic allusion to the creation of the world] at afternoon tea – itself a civilizing ritual) enhances, controls, directs, and protects the fertility of nature.

But that merger of form and content, that decidedly musical intent, results in an obscuring or estranging of sense, a shifting quasi-surreal movement resulting from Sitwell's belief that 'rhythm is one of the principal translators between dream and reality' ([1957] 1982, xv). Her work is neither nonsense nor not-sense; words don't collapse in upon themselves, portions of the poem aren't indecipherable, but the reader is caught in the struggle between meaning and movement, the struggle of meaning *as* movement. She must decide whether to sift through the thickly rhyming sentences and order their mythic and commonplace allusions into some sort of message, or to forsake all that and let her tongue do some 'pantomimic dancing' (Paget [1930] 1963, 202).

'Will you, wo'n't you, will you, wo'n't you, will you join the dance?' (Carroll [1865] 1971, 108) run the lyrics of 'The Lobster-Quadrille'; the Mock Turtle and Gryphon's 'invitation' to join the dance is an opportunity to accept a set of rules that defy the narrow perspective of Alice, who neither understands the quadrille nor wishes to join it, indeed is happy to see it end. Sitwell's poem, though its language is less permeable than that of 'The Lobster-Quadrille,' offers the same opportunity: to join this dancing poem, but at the cost of the reader's preexisting notions about how words mingle and poems mean.

The first three slow and firmly pronounced lines, or steps ('Old / Sir/ Faulk'), are followed by longer, brisker lines made up of several stressed and unstressed syllables – the unstressed syllables, quick steps before a pause. The strongly articulated rhythm, though decidedly more intricate than those of nursery rhymes, still maintains part of that flavour. But its changes in speed distinguish it from the more regular movement of the nursery rhyme. Those first three downbeats are repeated throughout the poem in various configurations – 'Tall as a stork' (l.4); 'Sit / And / Sleep' (ll.11–13); 'Meadows / Where' (ll.21–22); 'Water / Hissed' (ll.39–40).

More akin to nursery rhymes are *Fox Trot*'s quite regular end rhymes: 'gun'/'sun'; 'sheep'/'sleep'/'weep'; 'cry'/'sigh'; 'Meg' /'peg'/'egg'; 'he'/'tree'/'the'; 'crane'/'strain'/'again'. Sometimes these true rhymes are placed right next to each other ('why cry?'; 'I sigh' [ll.15, 16]), giving, as Sitwell supposes, the effect, that they 'leap into the air' as if 'they have light and bodiless endings' ([1957] 1982, xxiii). It is ironic, considering the sense of the words themselves, that Sitwell would give them these added lilts, lilts that are unignorable in their placement at the ends of succeeding lines. They're twice as springy because that first little leap ('why cry?') is so soon repeated ('I sigh').

Sitwell adds complexity through her tightly woven internal rhymes. Such sound play folds lines back in upon themselves, or over other lines: 'Oh, the nursery-maid Meg / With a leg like a peg' (ll.17–18); 'Picked it up as spoil to boil for nursery tea, said the mourners in the' (l.26). These true rhymes underscore the rhythm of light and lightness that she aims for, and are representative perhaps of patches of light in among the moving.shadows of country land-scape, as Sitwell suggests ([1957] 1982, xxvii), or rare glimpses of the fox (itself associated with light in the image 'reynard-coloured sun') darting (trotting) through the early morning cornfields. Reading the true rhymes in this latter fashion suggests that the poem's title is a punning with the reader and a playful inquiry into the metaphorical nature of the dance's name.

The fact that the fox is never *literally* named gives it the tenuous, slinking presence it must have for Sir Faulk, the huntsman who is, one assumes, chasing it away from the hen-house. The fox here is both a presence and an absence, dramatizing the slipperiness of stabilized meaning. His pseudonym ('sun') finds a true rhyme in 'gun' – a loaded gesture ultimately revealing an innocence of vision; in this poem lion and lamb, or rather hunter and fox, share lullabies.

But the poem is, according to Sitwell, not merely an attempt at incorporating the kinetic rhythms of dance in language; it is also an experiment with assonance and dissonance, those sound patterns that make up the various shades of darkness in her rhythmic landscape. She thus pairs off words like 'Faulk'/'tall'/'stork'/'stalk'/'walk' /'smock' – 'dissonances, so subtle they might almost be assonances' ([1957] 1982, xxvii). These function in much the same way as the internal true rhymes, overlapping lines and sentences, but they never quite let the edges meet, a faint lisp to counterpoint the more inno-cent true rhymes. At times they give a hesitant unity to contraries, not unlike that found in nursery lore; the slant rhyme of 'huntsman' and 'reynard-coloured sun,' especially in line 15, 'The huntsman and the reynard-coloured sun and I sigh,' strengthens the nonsensical tie between hunter and hunted.

Sitwell lets assonance 'smooth' out her lines. A line like 'Among the pheasant-feathered corn the unicorn has torn, forlorn the' (l.8), she claims, 'might consist of one word only were it not for the change from sunniness to darkness' ([1957] 1982, xxvii). Such a view may be hard to swallow, but it indicates an important underlying assumption – these words exist for their sound far more than for their sense. That sound runs them into one another with a washing flow similar to dance music and to the dark rhythms of Hopkins's *Spelt from Sibyl's Leaves*, though with decidedly different results. Sitwell's poem may leave the reader with the upside of civilization

– staving off the Flood – but she is nevertheless inundated by an ocean of sounds, a rising and falling tide of rhyme that leaves her wondering if the best reader of Sitwell might not have gills, perhaps, or sport a shell.

Dancing is in many ways a nonsensical pursuit – a series of motions that have meaning only within their own context, that define themselves. It falls into many of Huizinga's categories of play – especially his contention that play involves a set of arbitrarily established rules that set the governed action apart from the outside world. Valéry, comparing dance to poetry, calls it 'a system of acts, but acts whose end is in themselves. It goes nowhere' (1958, VII: 207). While Valéry's concern is poetry's refusal to communicate on a merely businesslike or prosaic level, his analogy holds for Sitwell's work twice over. Set against the 'progression' of this dance (a movement through a series of prescribed steps only to return to the first step and begin again) is the regression of the rhyme, a continual turning back in upon itself, joining hands with the words that have gone before and resisting each line's attempt to go 'somewhere' – that is, on to the next line. Not only, then, does the actual incorporation of so dominant a rhythm introduce a nonsensicality to the poem, but also the tightly woven, almost incestuous play of these rhymes echoes and forestalls the action of the dance precisely because they turn in upon themselves.

'on edge primmed private *privet*':
The Sense of Zukofsky's Sound

'But I would remind you, first,' writes Eliot in The Music of Poetry, 'that the music of poetry is not something which exists apart from the meaning. Otherwise, we could have poetry of great musical beauty which made no sense, and I have never come across such poetry' (1942, 13). His position may be open to a criticism of rigidity and unfairness, even though it does allow for a musical poetry that parodies, as opposed to makes, sense. His example, the work of Edward Lear; 'his nonsense is not vacuity of sense: it is a parody of sense, and that is the sense of it' (1942, 14). Since Lear's poetry has a sense, Eliot feels justified in praising its musicality, which at times, he contends, is related to the 'blues' (1942, 14). Eliot can stretch his notion of the sense and sensibility of music in poetry enough to accommodate Lear, but his brief comments on Lear's nonsense miss its complex and radical response to traditional sense, and one wonders if he could stretch much further. Could he stretch it far enough, for instance, to embrace the later works of Zukofsky? If the works of anyone challenge Eliot's notion that there cannot be a musical poetry without sense, Zukofsky's do. Some of his poetry relies so heavily on the orchestration of linguistic tones that its lexical meanings may elude the reader almost entirely. Such poems rest on the edge of sense – private, musical, linguistic puzzles. Take, for instance, *Privet* from *80 Flowers*:

> League gust strum ovally folium
> looped leaf nodes winter icejewel
> platinum stoneseed true ebony berries
> gray-jointed persistent thru green hedge
> ash-or-olive order white panicles heavy
> with daffodil doxy red blood pale
> reign paired leaves without tooth
> on edge primmed private *privet*
> (1991, 328)

The title gives a starting clue, and, having wended her way all the way through the poem, the reader is rewarded with the title reiterated as an italicized, emphatic summary. This circling motion implies a totally enclosed world of sound and words, a hermetic universe akin to that of Nonsense.

Despite the disconcerting and unrelenting juxtapositions between its title and its final word, this poem has an alternative order relating back to the visual/aural synaesthesia that Zukofsky is so fond of. The 'syntax' of this poem, gesturally maintained despite its lack of punctuation, is the line of the poet's sight as he explores a privet hedge, taking in leaves, branches, berries, seeds. An important part of this exploration concerns the words themselves, the components of this lingual hedge. The visual order is equally rooted in a thick series of sounds not unlike the density of the privet Zukofsky contemplates.

Each word, juxtaposed with other, seemingly incongruous words, resonates, sends out sonal shoots. Sometimes those shoots anticipate words that aren't there. Cid Corman, by picking up on the equation of ashes and death, finds in 'ash-or-olive' the phrase 'dead or alive.' Other times, the sounds hide words that are actually there, nesting within a weave of syllables. The first line, for instance, is a homophonic translation of the Latin name for privet – *Ligustrum ovalifolium* (Corman 1979, 308); it hides the Latin original underneath its English phonic equivalents. The line begins the intertwining so typical of the poem: the *gu* of 'League' branches out into 'gust,' whose final two letters edge into 'strum'; the *um* in 'strum' slips around to the end of 'folium' while the first and last syllable of 'ovally' meet in the middle of 'folium.' Other sound patterns work throughout the piece too: alliteration ('looped leaf'; 'ash-or-olive order'; 'daffodil doxy'; 'primmed private *privet*'), a sort of hind-end alliteration or the sharing of final phonemes ('red blood'), internal rhyme ('strum'/'folium'/ 'platinum') and slant rhyme ('pale'/'paired') all make appearances.

As Corman argues 'the ear finds its way to sense – if attentive' (1979, 308); Zukofsky's 'thrust [is] towards getting us to SOUND the words and discover the sense – to bring us into play – to participate' (1979, 306). His language is not reduced to empty sound, as Tigges writes is the case with Nonsense (1988, 155),[16] but rather aptly fits Orlov's characterization of tone as 'multidimensional' (1981, 134). The reader is 'left off-balance' (Quartermain 1992, 71), and language is overburdened with meaning that resides in the intimate associations of words. Zukofsky's poem publicizes the private struggle of the semiotic to move meaning towards sound. In response to this struggle, in the face of its overwhelming affront to stable and stolid sense, the reader reads *Privet* from a position of ignorance, as one coming to a new language and hearing its particles musically. Each word in the poem, by meaning phonically as well as sensically, opens the horizons of the poem; once a reader pierces the privacy of Zukofsky's meaning, she's inveigled into leaping the hedge, residing in a field that is circumscribed (as is the poem) by *privet*. The sounds of the poem generate associations ad infinitum; they crescendo and fade away. And in doing so they tie together separate words, break other words down into syllables, morphemes, phonemes as the language shifts, grows, a living plant.

Zukofsky and his wife Celia use a similar sound sense in their 'translations' of Catullus (1969). The translations were widely maligned within the community of Latin scholars, who failed to understand the Zukofskys' intention and the rigorous method that governed their work. One critic, in fact, was so confused and outraged by their *Catullus* that he questioned their sanity (Hatlen 1979, 351).

The translating principle that so offended the critics was a homophonic one. Each word of the original becomes for the Zukofskys a nugget of sound to be partially trans*literated* into English; each translation contains the same number of lines and syllables as the original and 'as far as possible the length and the sound of the English syllables echo Catullus's Latin syllables' (Hatlen 1979, 349). In their introduction to the translations, the Zukofskys explain that they have '[followed] the sound, rhythm, and syntax of his Latin – [tried], as is said, to breathe the 'literal' meaning into him' (1969, n.p.). 'The Zukofskys remind us,' writes Burton Hatlen, 'that the "*littera*," the letter, is an aural and visual shape, not a "meaning" ' (1979, 348). They privilege the sound of the poetry, treat each word as a series of sound units and try to translate the aural shape, the kinesis they find in Catullus's poems over and above his meaning. This return to the *littera* of literal is the essence of musicalized poetry. By breaking language down to its most basic element, they 'reduce' it to its most scalar level, its clearest point of intersection with music.

The Zukofskys come closest to writing pure nonsense here, where their words mean first musically. They refuse, Hatlen insists, to '[assume] that words are mere husks, to be stripped away so that we can get at the "meaning" ' (1979, 347). Lines like these from the translation of Catullus's poem 32 show just how closely the Zukofskys followed the sound of the poem:

> nequis liminis obseret tabellam (line 5)
> no case, limb, menace, obscure your tableland;
> pertundo tunicamque palliumque (line 11)
> pert under the tunic, pulling up the quilt.

Pulled out of context, of course, these lines make even less cerebral sense than they do in the translations. They do, however, make the sense of sound, hearing, the operative link between poet and reader. And they demonstrate how important the relationship between the Latin original and the English 'version' is, as sound is *echoed* in the translation, never reduced to an easily shed accoutrement to sense. The substance of Catullus is as much sound as sense; rhythm, cadence, and sound are at least as important as the meaning. The Zukofskys move towards language as 'pure sound value' (Hatlen 1979, 351), though of course such is ultimately unrealizable.

As Hatlen argues, the Zukofskys actually maintain the essence of Catullus's sense as 'a half-heard melody' that 'hovers behind the words' (1979, 349), and they extend that sense to incorporate its implicit ramifications. To recognize this sense requires a long hard look at and listen to the words, but attentive ears reward a reader; the Zukofskys succeed in fusing Poundian melopoeia and logopoeia (1979, 352).

A brief glance at just one element in Hatlen's reading of poem 32 demonstrates this roving and expanding meaning admirably. For instance, he argues that the sonal/metaphorical translation of the first word 'amabo,' into 'I'm a bow' was 'latent' in the Latin version, just 'waiting to be freed' (1979, 351). Though the association of the bow with Cupid and so with love couldn't have been lost on the Zukofskys, the bow, to Hatlen's mind, is not a literal bow but an erect penis, which is 'a "bow"' in at least three senses: it curves like a bow, it is aimed at an object of desire, and it is ready to shoot' (1979, 351). Hatlen's metaphor underlines the sexual, often bawdy nature of Catullus's poetry. But the transliteration may go further, offering a homonymic reading of bow as 'beau' – murmuring underneath the metaphorical sensuousness of the English, which Hatlen so astutely identifies, is a quaint, countrified, innocent sexuality as well, a witty and incongruous conflation made possible only by the sonal quality of the writing.

There are lines in these translations where, as Guy Davenport puts it, 'Catullus has come alive, as alive as if he were breathing garlic in your face' (1979, 369). Davenport's light-hearted description implies that the Zukofskys have done what they set out to: 'breathe the "literal" meaning with him' (Catullus, 'Preface' 1969, n.p.). Their breathing together with Catullus, their 'conspiracy,' holds the grain of his verse. By letting the letters, the sounds, of Catullus mean equally with the sense, these translations exploit and explore that nonsensical interface between language and sound.

The Zukofskys are not alone in their use of homophonic translation, of course. Numerous examples of this technique exist, some less serious in intent than theirs. For instance, Mots d'Heures: Gousses, Rames The d'Antin Manuscript (van Rooten [1967] 1980) uses the homophonic translation of forty Mother Goose rhymes into French as the basis for a wonderfully witty parody of scholarly pretension.[17] The 'discoverer, editor and annotator' of these poems, Luis d'Antin van Rooten, claims the 'curious verses were part of the meagre possessions of one François Charles Fernand d'Antin, retired school teacher, who died at the age of ninety-three in January of the Year of our Lord, 1950, while marking papers' ('Foreword' [1967] 1980, n.p.).

And, while he himself could do little more than annotate parts of the poems, he '[hopes] some more perceptive scholar, with the help of [his] notes, will bring greater clarification to these esoteric fragments' ('Foreword' [1967] 1980, n.p.).

Van Rooten then goes on to present the poems. The first, a homophonic translation of *Humpty Dumpty*, and a few of its annotations, will suffice to illustrate the flavour of the work and how the book challenges meaning not only through its emphasizing of sound but also through its literal misdirections:

> Un petit d'un petit
> S'étonne aux Halles
> Un petit d'un petit
> Ah! degrés te fallent
> Indolent qui ne sort cesse
> Indolent qui ne se mène
> Qu'importe un petit d'un petit
> Tout Gai de Reguennes
> ([1967] 1980, n.p.)

The footnote explaining the first line claims that 'Un petit d'un petit' is 'the inevitable result of a child marriage.' A much longer one, glossing 'Ah! degrés te fallent,' suggests that 'the poet writes of one of those unfortunate idiot-children that in olden days existed as a living skeleton in their family's closet.' More obliquely, the poet may be referring to 'some famous political prisoner, or the illegitimate offspring of some noble house. The Man in the Iron Mask, perhaps?' ([1967] 1980, n.p.)

The footnotes supplied by van Rooten do more than send up scholarly pretensions that overlook the obvious for the obscure; they exemplify the nonsensical pull that marks the book. Susan Stewart comments that footnotes are one way of splitting the direction of a text, because they fracture the unity of direction and view that may be offered (1978, 74). Such is certainly the case in *Mots d'Heure: Gousses, Rames*; the movement of the homophonic translation to let sound mean as sound, or as sonal likeness, is continually interrupted by van Rooten's sham explanations. Even that initial movement, however, is hardly unified since the words that van Rooten uses to translate Mother Goose do not, as is the case with the Zukofskys' *Catullus*, relay any of the sense of the original nursery rhymes. The poems, then, mean on at least four levels all the time: they mean as sound, and they mean according to the original meanings of their English equivalents, according to their literal French translations, and according to their annotations. It is this confluence, conflict, of meanings that urges these playful phonic puzzles towards nonsense.

'Uthlofan, lauflings!':
Velimir Khlebnikov's Beyonsense

From translation with a chuckle, tongue-in-cheek, to the translation of a laugh, full-bodied and belly-breaking. Russian Cubo-Futurist poet Velimir Khlebnikov's most famous poem is undoubtedly *Zaklyatie smekhom* (translated from Russian as *Incantation by Laughter*), an eleven-line guff-iggle of prefixes and suffixes and riotous play on 'smekh,' the Russian root for 'laugh.' A few lines will suffice to show how flexible Khlebnikov's language is, how much stretch it demands of a reader and, especially, of a translator:

> Hlahla! Uthlofan, lauflings!
> Hlahla! Ufhlofan, lauflings!
> Who lawghen with lafe, who hlaehen lewchly,
> Hlahla! Ufhlofan hlouly!
> Hlahla! Hloufish lauflings lafe uf beloght lauchalorum.
> (1985, 22)

Those are the first five lines of Paul Schmidt's English language *translation*. In his version, Schmidt has clearly moved into an area of English equivalent to the realm of Russian, which Khlebnikov opened. Like Khlebnikov, he uses archaic and dialectic forms of words and invents several of his own. For *Zaklyatie smekhom* emphasizes that verbal language, as Khlebnikov knows it, is plastic, or perhaps more appropriately plasticene – to shape, stretch, press, and pull. Khlebnikov models and remodels a variety of lingual units – the sentence, the word, the syllable, the phoneme. And when one turns to translate his work, one must infuse the host language with a similar spirit of malleability; one must turn that language on (and towards) its ear.

In the introduction to *Snake Train*, a collection of Khlebnikov's poetry and prose, Edward J. Brown suggests that this poem is the best example of Khlebnikov's ability to offer a reader 'an experience with the materials of the Russian language' or of the basic units of language generally (1976, 12). Indeed, this was central to Khlebnikov's poetic, this making of words based on the models already provided by language. As Charlotte Douglas explains in her introduction to the Harvard University Press selected of Khlebnikov's work, 'Much of [his] writing ... has to do with the texture of language, with poetry as *made words*. His puns and neologisms are attempts to lay bare the meanings that may be hidden in the wornout language of every day' (1985, 13), to reinfuse language with the power it once had.

But beyond that desire to resuscitate verbal language is Khlebnikov's perhaps even greater desire to discover a university common language that proves sound's governance of the universe, to find an organic relationship between the language which expressed one's experience of the world and the physical laws which shape that world. Khlebnikov's play with language as if, as he says in 'Our Fundamentals,' its 'scraps of sound are used to make dolls and replace all the things in the world' (1987, I:383) is a means of exploring language, of reconnecting with it. And *zaum'* is his finding, was to be his universal language. Along with its coinventor, Alexei Kruchonykh, Khlebnikov believed, as Douglas writes, that 'sounds would convey emotions as well as abstract meanings forcefully and directly, without the mediation of common sense,' that 'stable units of sound material could be uncovered beneath the seemingly disorganized surface variety of language' (Khlebnikov 1985, 3). Sound is, in fact, *so* stable for Khlebnikov that it provides a key both for the spatialization of the world and for the generation of meaning. In 'To the Artists of the World' an essay written in 1919, he contends that 'the simple bodies of a language – the sounds of the alphabet – are the names of various aspects of space, an enumeration of the events of its life. The alphabet common to a multitude of peoples is in fact a short dictionary of the spatial world' (1985, 149). And he goes on to suggest that the consonantal sound with which words begin affects their meaning (1985, 149; see also 'The Warrior of the Kingdom' [1987, I:292–5], in which Khlebnikov discusses not only the influence of initial consonants, but also the role played by internal vowels in determining the meaning of a word). While Khlebnikov's systematization of sound and language is highly suspect, as Raymond Cooke notes it is certainly not 'irrelevant' since 'people *do* associate certain sounds with certain concepts' (1987, 77–8).

A stronger argument for not wholly discounting this system as a crackpot's musings (and Khlebnikov was nothing if not eccentric) is its relation to another tangent of his thought, the interplay, the juggling for power of sound and sense. For what he seems to be getting at is that, whether on an affective or an intellectual level, sound and sense colour each other; a clear separation of the two is both impossible and undesirable. In 'On Contemporary Poetry,' he describes an interrelationship between sound and sense that is unquestionably nonsensical:

The word leads a double life. Sometimes it simply grows like a plant whose fruit is a geode of sonorous stones clustering around it; in this case the sound element lives in a self-sufficient life, while the particle of sense named by the word stands in shadow. At other times the word is subservient to sense, and then sound ceases to be 'all-powerful' and autocratic; sound becomes merely a 'name' and humbly carries out the commands of sense; in this case the latter flowers in another round of this eternal game ...

This struggle between two worlds, between two powers, goes on eternally in every word and gives a double life to language: two possible orbits for two spinning stars. In one form of creativity, sense turns in a circular path about sound; in the other sound turns about sense. (1987, 373)

This unending jockeying for position and prominence, this unending struggle marks almost of all of Khlebnikov's creative work – prose, poetry, and drama. And it gives his language a musical intensity rarely found in even the most experimental work. His 'beyonsense' language is among the twentieth century's extraordinary examples of nonsense.

'A New Way to Blow Out Candles':
The Nonsense of Sound Poetry

Making light of something that he recognizes as an intensely important exploration of language, Steve McCaffery quips in 'Sound Poetry: A Survey' that sound poetry is just 'a new way to blow out candles' (1978a, 18). Sound poetry, of all the poetries and poetics touched on in this study, is, with Khlebnikov's *zaum'*, perhaps most akin to nonsense; its overt musicalization of language makes finding any directly communicable meaning in it almost unheard of. In a more serious mood, McCaffery names it an attempt at 'the deformation of linguistic form at the level of the signifier' (1978b, 72), and the exploration of language at the purely phonic level of the phoneme. These explorations were pioneered by, among others, German Nonsense writer Christian Morgenstern and the Lewis Carroll of *Jabberwocky* (McCaffery 1978a, 6); this heritage ties it with classical Nonsense too. The phonemic exploration of sound poetry has been furthered considerably by the Dadaists and Futurists of the early twentieth century, and by the numerous avant-garde artists influenced by them. Among them were Gils Wolman and Francois Dufrene, who, in the 1950s, according to McCaffery's survey of the history of sound poetry, gave it 'megapneumes,' highly reminiscent of Derrida's ancient neumes, by '[pursuing] language back beyond the threshold of the word and letter to breath, energy and emotion,' thereby '[demonstrating] the full implication of a pneumatic centred communication' (1978a, 15).

McCaffery, who performed in Canada's most important sound poetry ensemble, The Four Horsemen, with Paul Dutton, Rafael Barreto-Rivera, and bp Nichol, relates sound poetry to Kristeva's theory of the subject-in-process (1986, 183n). This attribution, even more than his earlier claims about ancestry, or about the influence of the Nonsense tradition on it, places sound poetry squarely in the range of nonsense theory.

> Saussurean linguistics posited
> a system of language from which
> the agency of
> the subject was
> excluded. The sound poem (or
> a text-sound writing) re-inserts
> the primary agency of the subject
> as an instinctual
> body-as-self
> (1986, 181)

In this very much 'not-sound' poem, *Lyric's Larynx*, McCaffery theorizes and poeticizes about the nature of sound poetry. He asserts that sound poetry is not merely a return to the materialistic basis of language (1986, 181), not merely semiotic: 'it is an agency for desire production, for releasing energy flow, for securing the passage of libido in a multiplicity of flows out of the Logos' (1978b, 72). It is not, he argues, 'any kind of nostalgic return to a pre-sociosymbolic matrix' (1986, 124). McCaffery isn't denying the link between the body and sound, or that the sound of language is related to the prelinguistic (a distillation of Kristeva's ideas). Rather he contends that, like all works of the Kristevan subject-in-process, sound poetry blends the semiotic and the symbolic. It requires the symbolic, if only to have something to break down as it releases libidinal forces. Though it is closer to the absolute disintegration of lingual madness than, say, Lear's limericks, even sound poetry is not without its restraints.

Winn suggests that the centrality of meaning to poetry and the inevitable association of meaningful concepts with phonemes and morphemes make a semblance of sense inescapable in sound poetry (1981, 321). Hugo Ball, the Dadaist sound poet believed as much; his words were meaningful by virtue of 'being *reminiscent* of other words, or rather sounds,' writes John Elderfield in his introduction to the English translation of *Flight Out of Time* (Ball 1927, xxvii). Such is the premise behind my reading of Colleen Thibaudeau's *from Throgmoggle & Engestchin*, which might be considered a very mild and syntactically restrained variant of the contemporary sound poem.[18] After all, even musicalized language, according to Kristeva, 'is not without signification' and so must contend with its own communicative impulses (1974b, 63).

When McCaffery talks about how the 'acoustic' poem works, his words are vaguely reminiscent of Hughes's discussion of the physicality of music quoted at length in chapter three, and recalled earlier in this chapter. What is essential here is the skirting of the cortex, 'that interface of language and matter ... the deciphering department of the mind' (1978b, 72). While Hughes and McCaffery seek distinctly different languages, both want one that acts on a directly physical level. The fact that a theory of nonsense is useful for understanding this newly evolving language of direct contact can be extrapolated from McCaffery's call for 'a whole new critical vocabulary based on a semiotics of drive and flow and patterned over a schema of the neural' (1978b, 73).[19]

Other sound poets, like Britain's Bob Cobbing, play up the 'pre-sociosymbolic' origins of sound poetry more – 'PARTLY it is a recapturing of a more primitive form of language, before communication by expressive sounds became stereotyped into words, when the voice was richer in vibrations, more mightily physical' (1978, 39). But Cobbing emphatically puts qualifications on this relationship with the primeval by writing 'PARTLY' in the upper case. Larry Wendt comes close to the mark when he writes that sound poetry is an amalgam of nature and technology (1978, 70), of the 'primal' and the 'civilized.' Here is another way in which sound poetry is nonsensical; nonsense, as was argued earlier, urges the meeting and mingling of such nature/culture distinctions.

This hesitation to embrace 'primitive' sound as the sole source of sound poetry doesn't completely eradicate the primeval sounding that Cage calls for in Empty Words, and that Hughes and Lilburn articulate in wholly different manners. Nor does it prevent one from attributing to sound poetry a portion of the orality that Deleuze saves for schizophrenic language. Once again a reader is faced with a language, like Cage's noises, so involved with its own material production and with the way the body can modulate sound (and how the machine can then distort and mix that sound), that Deleuze's distinctions are rendered vulnerable. Once again noises – especially when tape recorders are used – become incorporeal, in Deleuze's terms, but retain so much of their corporeality that they seriously challenge abstract meaning. Sound poetry is a nonsense of the body, a 'singing' of the desires over against the demands of communicative expression in which words, sounds, vocables regain their autonomy (Ball 1927, 22).

Paula Claire makes her sound poetry a nonsense not only of her own body, but also of other bodies. And in so doing, she has dramatically changed the notion of what can be considered textual notation. She often '[receives] "song signals" from natural objects: a cross-section of a cabbage, a stone, a piece of rope, the textures surface of bricks, cloth etc.' (McCaffery 1978a, 14);[20] these signals are perhaps analogous to the 'signals' Lilburn received when he imagined how a pumpkin would sing. (See the poetic results of this imagining in Pumpkins, the subject of the next interchapter.) As Claire writes in 'The Notation of My Sound Poetry,' 'I began to realise that all patterns and markings could be considered as primitive codes, dictating to human perception much earlier than alphabets, provoking a response in sound' (1984, 56). And she describes a group sounding at which she and her audience dropped to the floor and 'read' the wood knots in the auditorium's floor (1984, 62).

A more common textual strategy in sound poetry, however, is the use of 'optophonetic' notation ('typographic variations in size to indicate proportionate variations in pitch and volume' [McCaffery 1978a, 8]) developed by Dadaist Raoul Hausmann and still quite prevelant in sound poetry circles. Drawings and collages (often valued as much as works of art as they are as scores) loosely chart

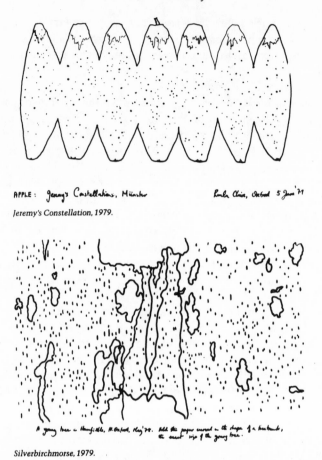

APPLE : Jeremy's Castellations, Münster   Paula Claire, Oxford 5 June '79

Jeremy's Constellation, 1979.

A young tree in Hampstalls, N.Oxford, May '79. Add this paper around in the shape of a headband, the exact rip of the young tree.

Silverbirchmorse, 1979.

Figure 13 *Jeremy's Constellation, 1979* and *Silverbirchmorse, 1979* from Paula Claire's *The Notation of My Sound Poetry'*

vocal renderings. (See, for instance, visual scores by Paula Claire, and by Steve McCaffery and bp Nichol – figures 13 and 14). It is, per-haps, when its notation reaches these extremes that sound poetry most challenges traditional notions of what poetry is. One would be hard pressed to justify calling a cabbage a poem (as opposed to the inspiration for a poem), but if the notational rendering of sound poetry *is* its text, its cues for performance, then that is just what Claire's experiments require.

STEVE MCCAFFERY & bpNICHOL
discarded text for SIX GLASGOW TEXTS

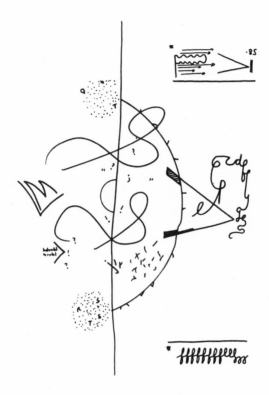

Figure 14 From Steve McCaffery and bp Nichol *Sound Poetry: A Catalogue*

A loose interpretation of Claire's statement, quoted above, might lend itself to Derridean interpretation – patterns and markings being a physical manifestation of the arche-trace that precedes and informs speech and sound. But McCaffery's qualification of the idea of a text upsets such an interpretation, revealing the priority of sound over writing and demonstrating just how far from traditional poetry this 'writing' stands, how much the grain is emphasized: 'Text iself [*sic*] as a dialectic term, not a score (the anchor of repeatability) but the thetical surface from which a performer reacts, projecting out into the unique flowings of the fissure created by that rebellion against the fixed' (1978b, 73). The acoustic text becomes a radical example of 'borderblur' – a term Nichol borrows from Argentinian poet Dom Sylvester Houedard to describe the generic indeterminacy of much postmodernist 'writing' (1987, 19). And it is only in its privileging of sound over writing, despite the inventiveness of its texts, that sound poetry risks exclusion from a nonsense canon.

Writing in the poetic context of the 'L=A=N=G=U=A=G=E' movement, McCaffery views sound poetry as an assault on the capitalistic denigration of language, on its reduction of language to a merely meaningful commodity. 'Against the order,' he writes,

> of
> word, meaning, nomination
> and syntax (i.e. against the
> socio-cultural system of communication)
>
> place the gestural body, attaching
> itself to sound and rhythm
> as autonomous discharges (expenditures)
> outside the utilitarian
> production of meaning
> (1986, 182)

The radical infusion of sound in experimental poetry is an attempt to place this gesturing, polyphonic body into, onto, or next to language. The writing that results is often nonsensical. Some of the most adept practitioners of a musicalized poetic, Gertrude Stein and the poets associated with the journal $L=A=N=G=U=A=G=E$, remain to be considered.

'O jongleurs, O belly laughs'

———◆———

The first thing the eye meets on the page of Tim Lilburn's *Pumpkins* (1986, 42–3) is a huge patch of *o*s; big and little, they proliferate, reckoning the shape of the pumpkins whose praises the poem sings. The page is the garden, thick with vegetable letters, a 'rioting plot' whose long lines tumble about, sinuous vines stringing together those pumpkinesque vowels. The other thing that immediately strikes the looker – Lilburn is a poet whose embrace is as wide as the page, sometimes wider.

But this poem is not just a rush and tangle of verbiage or herbiage. Lilburn takes full advantage of the play of the voice he hears in the pumpkins, the voice with which he imagines a pumpkin would sing if it could sing. His answer to the implicit question of how does a pumpkin sing: clearly from the diaphragm, the seat of phonic fullness. The 'Oompah Oompah Oompah' (l.1) of these pumpkins rolls out of the mouth with the roundness and substance of a pumpkin of mammoth proportions. A brassy, bass 'tuba girthed' pumpkin. A pumpkin with lungs to match.

The *oo* of 'Oompah' is voiced again in the rest of the pumpkin's songs: 'Booompah' (l.3), 'Doo dee doo dee doooo' (l.14), 'Carro-car-roo' (l.23). These are onomatopoeic, words that mean what they sound, as well as Deleuzian nonsense words, which mean themselves. They are a point of intersection between music and word, and also between hoer and hoed. For the sound, the song's musical sense, is woven into the speech of, and picked up by, the speaker, 'I, weeding farmer, I, Caruso,' that

... , dung-booted serf, whose unhoed brain,

the garden's brightest fruit, ones
communion with the cowfaced cauliflowers,
cucumbers twinkling like toes, and you,
clown prince,
sun dauphin of the rioting plot.
(ll.26, 41–6)

The 'identity' of the 'weeding farmer' grows directly out of the song of the pumpkin ('carroo'/'Caruso'[ll.23, 26]); he joins, 'dung-booted,' in the *oo* sound play, when he names the pumpkins 'My Poohs' (l.24).

Creating within the poem an echo of the nonsensical body (with its distorted and blending borders), sound functions as a way of 'merging' pumpkin and farmer, and as an indicator of *haecceitas*. The interdependence of identity that the pumpkins and the farmer share argues for a mimetic copresence, an earthy imitation of the bodily presence that is so fundamental to the Christian (especially the Roman Catholic) principles of the Eucharist and the Incarnation.[1] For the 'geno-song' (to use Barthes's term) establishes a type of communion between the characters of pumpkin and farmer, and articulates a contemplative (as opposed to actual) indwelling on the part of the poet.

There is another unity of sound, an alliterative and assonantal unity, which mirrors the oneness, the communal 'oneing' of poet and plant as well. Lilburn's stretching of this word's use, making it work as a verb, reinforces the all-inclusiveness of that communion. Verb and noun stand joined: 'one' now contains active and static, being and object, open and closed systems of life. And it is this 'joy esperanto, [this] intense Archimedean aha / of yellow' (ll.40–1), the music of praise, which underscores such closeness. 'Communion with cowfaced cauliflowers,' 'cucumbers,' 'clown prince'; 'bruited busied, blessed these being-ward, barn-big, / bibulous on light' (ll.32–3); 'puffing like perorating parliamentarians' (l.2); 'self-hefted on the hill and shot' (l.21) – the wild writing and writhing of sound employs the entire exuberant, 'exaultant' alphabet.

Partial rhymes and internal rhymes that fold lines back in upon themselves or span whole stanzas add to the proliferation of sound: 'Oompah'/'Boompah'; 'suburban'/'burp'/'brumpht'; 'popeyes'/'apoplexies'/'flexed'; 'dolphin'/'dauphin'; 'Carro-carroo. Are you well' (l.23). Such rhymes lace the poem with an attempt (not entirely unlike Hughes's) at 'primal' energy, the energy of growing, blossoming life that spills out in its long lines, and leaps across stanza breaks: 'How do? How do? How do? // Doo dee doo dee dooo' (ll.13-14). The repetition of individual words supplements this 'primal' energy too. Such repetitions in a row, like the one quoted above, do more than multiply the poem's sound games. They help move sensical words into the realm of nonsensical words; 'How do? How do? How do?' begins to define itself as its echoing reiteration pours over into 'Doo dee,' and so closer still to music itself. But this phonic merging doesn't create an onslaught of sound of the sort in *Spelt from Sibyl's Leaves*. The pace of *Pumpkins* keeps the sounds from massing, lends to the poem a serious frivolity. And this pacing is, perhaps surprisingly given the 'lungs' those Oompah boompahs imitate, really quite puffy.

Caesura helps create that puffing effect throughout the poem; it is present more often than not as commas, full stops, or just large gasps between 'Oompah's.' But as caesura accrues and alternates with more fully breathed lines, the puffing becomes a chug, the chugging a rocking momentum verging on dance: ' ... dancing (thud), dancing (thud, / brumpht, thud, brumpht) with the Buddha-bellied sun' (ll.6–7). This movement is found in the very first lines: 'Oompah   Oompah   Oompah, fattening / on the stem, tuba girthed, puffing like perorating parliamentarians' (ll.1–2). The large spaces between the first three words close down to the mere wisp of a pause, the gulping of breath before the line's energy pushes over in enjambement to the second line. Again there is caesura, though brief. But after each caesura the cluster of words grows, gains length and so breath-force till the next caesura-laden line is reached: 'Boompa   Boompah   Booompah.' This line repeats the same process of lengthening and expanding breath and, after a brief end stop, plunges into the first full line without a caesura. Such play with full and partial stops mid-line energizes the whole poem.

A central source of the energy, too, is the epithets that run throughout the poem; they are an outpouring of the reverence, the spirit of this psalm. And, because they never appear in isolation, they continue to generate the puffing-chugging-rocking dance:

... God's jokes. O jongleurs, O belly laughs
quaking the matted patch, O my blimpish Prussian

generals, O garden sausages, golden zeppelins
(ll.11–13)

Popeyes, my dears, muscular fruit
(l.19)

my sweets, pleasure things, my baubles, my Poohs
(l.24)

clown prince,
sun dauphin of the rioting plot
(ll.45–6)

Each string of epithets does more than augment the rollicking rhythm of *Pumpkins*, though. Some measure of alliteration adds fuel to the momentum which accretion is building up. But of equal importance is the zany juxtaposition of 'items' within these strings; Lilburn brings together in these moments, and throughout the poem as a whole, a slew of seemingly disparate bits and pieces of life. This bricolage adds both humour and seriousness to his attempt to cross barriers. If a poem can work as well as this one does and still cross the borders that seemed to exist between Zen Buddhism, German opera, Easter Island, St Francis, the suburbs, and cauliflower, then the stretch between pumpkin and poet is minimal at best.

Such juxtapositions and the images that grow out of them, out of the poem's spiritually and religiously flexible world view ('vegetables on a ball and chain' [l.36]; 'garden elephants ... yahooing a yellow / which whallops air' [ll.5, 9–10]), share the whimsy of the finest of the Nonsense tradition; think of the odd mixing together of 'The Owl and the Pussy-cat [who] went to sea / In a beautiful pea-green boat,' or the many creatures (the Stork, the Duck, the Frog, the Fimble Fowl with a Corkscrew leg, the small Olympian bear, the Blue flute-play-ing Baboon and the Attery Squash, among others) who went to live in the Quangle Wangle's hat on the Crumpety Tree, or the Jumblies who went to sea in a sieve (they did!). Here is Nonsense's noncontra-dictory opposition, a 'copresence.'

Lilburn's poem is a psalm, a particularly, peculiarly serious psalm, whose nonsense reaches past dour-faced religiosity to a harmony achieved through a vegetative gesture towards transubstantiation, the 'bodily' mixing of poet and plant, word and music. This harmony is neither pantheistic nor monistic, 'because the union between poet and stone, poet and tree, poet and history is not a oneness of substance, but a oneness in relation, in election, in solidarity. The bonds are affective not physical, though the recognition of these erotic bonds completes the physical form of things. Streams, persons, hills, the dead – all are fully what they are when they are known as linked, in community with one another' (1987, 36). Such community, such harmony, grows out of Lilburn's unique use of nonsense.

FIVE

'A Silly Corpse'?:

The 'L=A=N=G=U=A=G=E' Poets, Stein, and the Nonsense of Reference

Does not every means desire to become an end as well? Consider the beauty of language set free from its ends. The hedge that forms the hedge-row bears hedgeroses also.
– Velimir Khlebnikov, 'The Burial Mound of Sviatagor'

The move from purely descriptive, outward directive, writing toward writing centered on its wordness, its physicality, its haecceity (thisness) is, in its impulse, an investigation of human self-sameness, of the place of our connection: in the world, in the word, in ourselves.
– Charles Bernstein, 'Three or Four Things I Know About Him'

Writing about a paragraph of experimental prose by Barret Watten, Ron Silliman wittily comments, 'Referentiality is not merely dead, it makes for a silly corpse' (1987a, 78). Silliman's comment isn't only a quip, however; it's indicative of a serious query, about the status of reference and referentiality in language, which is central to much of the work of those writers loosely called 'L=A=N=G=U=A=G=E' poets. Not surprisingly, that query finds many and various answers in the experimental works of this 'group,' but all of these answers involve the relationship between the world and the word, and the ways language helps construct one's perception of reality.

The movement, whose members usually deny it *is* a movement, is named for convenience after *L=A=N=G=U=A=G=E*, an American journal that offered a forum for their poetic investigations during the late seventies and early eighties; Silliman claims that *L=A=N=*

$G=U=A=G=E$ was 'the first American journal of poetics by and for poets' (1986, xvii). In 'Repossessing the Word,' Bruce Andrews and Charles Bernstein, editors of $L=A=N=G=U=A=G=E$ and of *The $L=A=N=G=U=A=G=E$ Book* (an anthology based on the first three volumes of the magazine), claim that the journal's purpose was to '[foreground] compositional issues and styles of reading' (1984a, ix). As a result of such foregrounding, almost all of its participants engage in dramatic questionings of the nature of meaning and its relationship with the political status quo, and with language's materiality. To do so they cite such writers and thinkers as Thoreau, Dickinson, the Russian Futurists, Stein, Zukofsky and Olson, Wittgenstein, Barthes, Derrida and Kristeva, and offer an alternative poetic tradition radically opposed to New Criticism and its formalist and 'modernist' offshoots. The list of names from which this various poetic springs may already suggest an affinity with nonsense as it has been construed throughout this study.

'The Writes of the Reader':
Another View of Audience, Author, and the Self

First, to rethink the name. Many 'L=A=N=G=U=A=G=E' poets object to being collectivized by this term because their inquiries are not specialized or made unique by virtue of their engagement with language. Almost all poetry maintains an intimate, probing relationship with language, and by its nature highlights language's delicate workings. But 'conservative' poetry is less *partial*, goes further towards making its exploration and exploitation of linguistic principles subtle, quiet. It doesn't demand of its casual reader a conspiracy of 'wording.' A 'L=A=N=G=U=A=G=E' poet's questioning of, disruption of, language and linguistic norms cannot be overlooked; it occurs at such a basic level, in such a dramatic manner, that a reader is *required* to participate, to question, to probe, to leap from word to syllable to sound, to disorganize and reorganize the words presented.

A writer of 'L=A=N=G=U=A=G=E' poetry writes most successfully when readers willingly join in the process. Jackson Mac Low, a literary precursor of the movement, suggests calling the work 'perceiver-centred' instead: 'Whatever the degree of guidance given by the authors, all or the larger part of the work of giving or finding meaning devolves upon the perceiver' (1986, 494). Mac Low contends that the reading process is one 'in which perceivers are perceiving their own minds at work' (1986, 495), not, as in more traditionally conceived writing, the minds of the authors.

'L=A=N=G=U=A=G=E' poetry is not inscribed with a readily discernible (some would say 'consumable') meaning. Rather, its meanings are 'inseparable from the language in process' (Messerli 1987, 3). Lyn Hejinian argues in 'The Rejection of Closure' that such 'open' writing 'is generative rather than directive. The writer relinquishes total control and challenges authority as a principle and control as a motive. The "open text" often emphasizes or foregrounds process, either the process of the original composition or of subsequent compositions by readers' (1984b, 134-5).

There is for these writers no one hypothetical mind supplied with the background details necessary to infer an author's intention. Their works are geared to a complex of readers, unique individuals with a common trait, an acceptance of the redefinition of reading that Bruce Andrews gives in 'Text and Context' – 'READING: not the glazed gaze of the consumer, but the careful attention of a producer, or co-producer' (1984b, 36). Such a reader might serve many modernist texts no less well than she would these 'postmodernist' ones. Likely it is a matter of the degree of involvement required that separates Andrews's reader from that of Pound or Eliot.

And such a reader would be quite unlike Alice, that spoilsport in a verbal Wonderland. As Michael Palmer points out in an interview with Lee Bartlett, a reader '[has] to decide what [her] relationship to the poem is. It is a kind of poetry that insists that the reader is an active part of the meaning, that the reader completes the circuit' (1987, 128). Alice may escape Wonderland by sceptically confronting its inhabitants, but the *responsible* reader of 'perceiver-centred' poetry has no such out. She 'cohabit[s]' (Grenier 1986, 533) with the poem, its writer, its language. She chooses to remain in Wonderland for the whole of the text and longer since the lines drawn between text and world are tenuous at best.

Hejinian's *My Life*, as the final interchapter will demonstrate, is in many ways typical of the movement. It offers a fabric of verbal resemblances that seem rooted obliquely in the world as one knows it; 'A pause, a rose, something on paper' (1987, 7) – these are words and grammatical forms that one recognizes, that one might even be able to pin to exterior referents, yet that function within the volume as a whole in ways beyond one's normal expectations of a word, and of poetic convention. These 'refrains' not only accrue meanings through frequent repetition and recontextualization. They also achieve a heightened status as words. Because they continually appear within new frameworks, they begin to matter as *matter*, as arrangements of letters, syllables, sounds that mean in relation to the other arrangements of sound surrounding them. They become reconfigurations of the other letters, syllables, sounds, around them, fluid nodes that crystallize, for the space of a moment, aspects of the verbal weave of Hejinian's work. Hejinian's words are possibly more accurate representations of reality than the staid words that typify a more intentionally communicative, descriptive discourse, like that I'm engaged in here. And she needs a reader like the Mad Hatter, or the Cheshire-Cat, or the Mock Turtle – one who will play her (quite serious) game.

It is this insistence on the participation of the reader in the making of the text's meaning, in the playing of its 'language games' (Wittgenstein's term is frequently adopted by these writers), that supplies an opening for a strategically Nonsensical reading. In *The Raven and the Writing-Desk*, Francis Huxley defines generic Nonsense in this way: 'Nonsense, then, is a logical game played with feeling by at least two people, in a spirit of self-contradiction, in such a way that one thing leads on to the other to the constant surprise and mutual enthusiasm of both parties' (1976, 10). Huxley's definition is more restrictive, more rooted in logic, than the physical and subversive version of nonsense construed in this study. By suggesting that Nonsense resides solely within a logical continuum, he ignores its psychically disruptive effects and implications; he fails to clarify that, as a logical game, Nonsense involves alternative forms of logic, and that often a poet's (or Nonsense writer's) logic is 'illogic' (Palmer 1987, 136).

However, Huxley's Nonsense reader plays, contradicts herself and what she has been taught to be the fundamental indications of self and world. The important relationship between play and reading is borne out in 'perceiver-centred' writings as well, in what Vicki Mistacco calls 'ludism' – although her definition seems to argue for a proliferation of *meanings*, rather than the stretching of meaning or the multiplicity of *ways* to mean that is crucial in nonsense: ' "Ludism" may be simply defined as the open play of signification, as the free and productive interaction of forms, of signifiers and signifieds, without regard for an original or ultimate meaning. In literature, ludism signifies textual play; the text is viewed as a game affording both author and reader the possibility of producing endless meanings and relationships' (quoted in McCaffery 1986, 149).

'L=A=N=G=U=A=G=E' poetry urges play and participation by using many of the materialist strategies that are central to nonsense and Nonsense – puns, juxtaposition, phonemic variation, the privileging of sound and rhythm – and also by using metonomy and parataxis.[1]

Such poetry is also based fundamentally on self-contradiction. This is not the self-contradiction that Huxley intends, for 'language-centred' writing's contradiction undermines the notion of self, a stable and fixed identity. Here is another affinity with a *Bandar*-logical style of nonsense and with Kristeva's notion of the subject-in-process. Kristeva argues for a self continually fluctuating and reconstituting itself, continually being shaped by its intercourse with all forms of language, events, and instinctual drives. This self in flux, continually unmaking and remaking itself, is central to the slipperiness of nonsense and its location within the world of the text. The protean forms of Nonsense, which itself seeks to construe and construct a verbal universe, imply a reality in perpetual metamorphosis. For 'L=A=N=G=U=A=G=E' poets especially, this implication extends to the very being of writer and reader, and can be related to a Heraclitean recognition that all things are in continual flux. Randa Dubnick argues that Stein's use of repetition constructs such a Heraclitean reality (1984, 21). This fluctuating self can easily be related to the slipperiness of 'L=A=N=G=U=A=G=E' writing with its diminuation of the role of poetic voice and its reconceiving of author and audience, as well.

Marjorie Perloff, in 'The Word as Such: L=A=N=G=U=A=G=E poetry in the eighties,' contends that 'the poet's voice functions as no more than a marginal presence, splicing together the given "data"' (1985, 221). Rather than language being the medium through which the poet's voice or personality (or that which she assumes for each poem) is transmitted, the poet's voice sparsely supplements the transmission of a linguistic 'reality,' serves as the almost invisible thread that sews the poem's verbal patchwork together. The 'voice' presented in 'L=A=N=G=U=A=G=E' poetry resonates in the fractures and leaps, the fissures and echoes of the words themselves. It appears often as nothing more than the principle governing 'selection,' as the eye (rather than 'I') that collects and directs data. Since such writing works against a transparency of meaning, it evokes the shifting of a subject engaged in the very process of 'being' which constitutes the act of writing and reading the text. The process by which the reader ferrets out the potential meanings of the text is also the process by which she relates the 'vocal' idiosyncracies of the 'author' to the idiosyncracies of her own perceptual world.

In a telling critique of some extratextual applications of Derridean theory, Bernstein argues:

> The lesson of metaphysical finitude is not that the world is just codes and as a result presence is to be ruled out as anything more than nostalgia, but that we can have presence, insofar as we are able, only *through* a shared grammar. That our losses are not based on the conceptual impossibility of presence in the face of the 'objects' of presence not being 'transcendentally' locked into place, but rather on grounds that each person must take responsibility for – the failure to make ourselves present to each other, to respond or act when the occasion demands. (1986, 182)

This kind of relationship with language or a 'shared grammar' of meaning in use or context (Bernstein admits a strong Wittgensteinian influence) results in a social, albeit fluctuating, self. A self, or presence, constructed out of the physical (as opposed to metaphysical) structures of language whose meanings are communally agreed upon. Such presence, tentative in comparison to the crystalline logocentricity of formalism, is constructed through verbal agreements, interactions, explorations, through the graphic, phonic, and sensical elements of a language that continues to 'be,' in flux.

Bernstein's stand on presence and language provides a useful response to radical deconstructionists; but it may also be borrowed to serve, if slightly stretched, as a cogent defence for nonsense against charges of phonocentrism and metaphysicality. Nonsensical presence, as Lilburn's *Pumpkins* demonstrates, is communal, genotextual; it determines its own axis for the production of meaning and invites a reader to participate in a community-creating reading. By cocreating a shared grammar that articulates a limited presence, nonsense and 'L=A=N=G=U=A=G=E' poetry blend, in admittedly differing ways, the roles of reader and writer. What Bruce Andrews says of 'perceiver-centred' poetry can equally be said of nonsensical poetry; it 'resembles a creation of a community and of a world-view by a once-divided-but-now-fused Reader and Writer. This creation is not instrumental. It is immanent, in plain sight (and plain-song), moving along a surface with all the complications of a charter or a town-meeting' (1984b, 35).

This communal process is self-determining in several ways; not only does it enable reader/writers to determine, temporarily, their 'selves,' it is also established for individuals or a community by themselves and so *not* imposed upon them as are most forms of meaning. Andrews's poetry bears this out too, as the following passage from a poem in *Wobbling* (quoted in Hartley 1989, 40) shows:

gaps

shocks through

absorbing

hover

the subjunctive

we're

less

thoughts

Strange as it may first seem, the poem is a strong argument against culturally imposed constraints on reading, and for seeking out new ways of reading and constructing meaning. Reading as one would normally attempt to – line by line, top to bottom, left to right – little 'sense' can be made.

It's quite likely that much of the poem's impact would be lost if it were performed, since performance would probably limit the range of interpretative strategies available to the reader/listener; the performer would take on much of the burden of reorganization which, in the written version, falls to the reader. What Andrews's poem demonstrates is that alternatives, in the style of reading and expectations of the outcome of that process, do exist and can result in various forms of sense. One can try to follow the traditional manner of reading and end up concentrating on each word individually; one can read from bottom to top, from right to left, or randomly. The most sustained and normative sense seems to result from reading inwards from the left margin – reading the words in an order based on their proximity to that margin; this method at least results in grammatically-acceptable phrases: 'thoughts absorbing less hover we're gaps shocks through the subjunctive.'

This sense culled from the poem also supports, in terms of content, Andrews's claims about form and thought. Thoughts do hover, stand in still-motion, when they aren't absorbing, working with, responding to their surroundings; though one wonders what they absorb 'less' of. And it doesn't seem a theoretical stretch for Andrews to say 'we're gaps' – especially if 'we're' hovering through language in neutral, not actively engaging it or experiencing its process. If one doesn't work with and through language, one is a hole, a fissure in the communal constitution of the world; she is a 'shock' (disruption) 'through the subjunctive' (the conditional/self of existence). I wouldn't want to contend that such a reading of/into Andrews's poem is its ultimate or intended meaning; that would be contrary to the spirit of the poem and the poem itself. However one decides to reconfigure it and to deal with its scattering of words,[2] the poem helps a reader question the process of reading; it requires a new, exploratory relationship between writer, text, and reader. These oddly spaced words are a means of creating community.

The issues of the self, the reader and the writer are tied to a much larger concern for many 'L=A=N=G=U=A=G=E' poets. In 'An Interview with Tom Beckett,' Bernstein points out that 'a poem exists in a matrix of social and historical relations that are more significant to the formation of an individual text than any personal qualities of the life or voice of an author' (1986, 408). He's not discounting the value of the author's 'patterns of language ... and corresponding behavior or relevant quirks' (Hejinian 1984a, 30) scattered throughout a poem in order to be forged into a tenuous communal meaning here; rather he is recognizing that the socio-political context, more so than the author or reader, forms and informs the meanings of a text. 'Language is taken as the representative social form per se,' Jerome Mc-Gann writes, as 'the social form through which society sees and presents itself to itself' (1987, 643).

To Shew or Eschew the Fly?:
Nonsense and the 'L=A=N=G=U=A=G=E' Poet's
Concern about Referentiality

'What is your aim in philosophy? – To shew the fly the way out of the fly-bottle,' muses Wittgenstein in *Philosophical Investigations* ([1953]

1958, I.309). This is his response to the restrictive classifications, grammatical and referential, of Russell and Moore as they argued for a philosophical use of language devoid of flux or socially generated meaning, a use whose hard and fast classifications created rather than resolved paradoxes. For instance, since the word 'mind' is a noun, Moore and Russell contended that in philosophical discourse it should *behave* as a noun does – have location and attributes, some sort of concrete existence. But this, of course, contradicts the 'sense' of 'mind.' Wittgenstein's metaphor implies that the 'fly' is always, would always be, free of the linguistic bottle if philosophers paid attention to the ordinary usage of language. Language's general, social, and material functions prove the nonexistence of the fly-bottle. What Wittgenstein argues for, here and in other places, is a renewed consideration of the social character of language and, in part, a re-materialization of language.

When McCaffery uses the metaphor as a springboard in the opening of *Evoba*, his meditations on the *Investigations*, he leaps in quite a different direction, and urges poetry to leap with him: 'If the aim of philosophy is, as Wittgenstein claims, to show the fly the way out of the fly-bottle,' he writes, 'the aim of poetry is to convince the bottle that there is no fly' (1987, n.p.). No fly? No reference, no contained or containable meaning? McCaffery's metaphorical twist departs from Wittgenstein's original in several ways, not the least of which is his use of fly (or my understanding of that use) to connote some sort of stable meaning.[3] A socially based meaning such as that Wittgenstein promotes is neither stable nor containable in the long run. McCaffery's fly cannot exist in Wittgenstein's philosophy. Whether McCaffery's bottle can be convinced by poetry of the fly's nonexistence, a fly (or *many* flies) do(es) exist. In an attempt to liberate language McCaffery goes far beyond decontextualizing and twisting Wittgenstein's metaphor, however; he posits the impossible.

The notion that reference is culturally determined is widely accepted by almost all of the 'L=A=N=G=U=A=G=E' poets; their position grows out of readings of theorists like Sapir, who promotes the highly controversial theory that people live 'at the mercy of the particular language which has become the medium of expression for their society' (quoted in Silliman 1987a, 7). But McCaffery has extended that notion in some quite radical ways. He argues, like many other 'L=A=N=G=U=A=G=E' poets, that capitalist society and its distinctly classist version of reality are transmitted through language by dematerializing it. However, he goes on to characterize and condemn reference purely in terms of a capitalist market economy. 'The Capitalist rationale is: you can produce and consume everything and everywhere providing it flows and providing it's exchangeable. Reference marks a point of extreme liquidity in the Sign. It is, in fact, the line along which the Signifier liquidates itself, exchanges itself for the Other by means of the flow occurring along the surface of a grammatical meaning' (1984a, 161).

Reference, he suggests, being an exchange-oriented commodity, is merely a 'surplus-value' (McCaffery 1986, 13).[4] In fact, McCaffery goes so far as to suggest that reference is an example of commodity fetishism in language, and 'derived from an earlier theologicoling-uistic confidence trick of "the other life"' (1984b, 189). His point is, as Marjorie Perloff succinctly explains, that '[language] ... is itself always already politically and ideologically motivated. The positioning of the subject as panoptic and controlling "I," for example, is itself a political statement that calls into question whatever professedly "radical" content is expressed in that I's monologue' (1990, 295).

What McCaffery seems to want is a language of use-value, not of surplus-value, a language that emphasizes the signifier and so the production, not the consumption, of language (McCaffery 1986, 14). Such a view is purposefully polemical; like the other writers of this movement, he takes an extreme stance, pushing the issue of materiality as opposed to reference to an illogical, almost Idealist, limit.

In his often insightful study *Textual Politics and the Language Poets,* George Hartley suggests that 'McCaffery imagines a point at which one can transcend meaning and achieve a pure presence of the material signifier, a pure use-value or – to the extent that "use-value" carries with it instrumentalist connotations – a pre-use-value' (1989, 67).[5] What this call for a 'pure presence of the material signifier' suggests is that McCaffery really wants a nonreferential language. Or wanted – he admits in 'Nothing Is Forgotten But the Talk of How to Talk: An Interview by Andrew Payne' that aspects of this approach have 'certain naivetés' (1986, 124); indeed this approach's extremity pushed it into the realm of the unrealizable. A purely material language does not exist, unless perhaps as music or gesture; it has no verbal incarnation. Such a language is also not nonsensical, since, to borrow McCaffery's early terminology, nonsense needs both use-value and surplus-value, both materiality and reference, to be effective.

However, while McCaffery admits there are limitations to his initial emphasis on the purely material, he still contends that even if reference is not entirely fetishistic,[6] and if the invitation to the reader to join in the process of creating/completing the text smacks of 'ideological contamination,' literature should be read 'not as forms and structures, but as operative economies. Here,' he continues, 'the notion of expenditure, loss, the sum total of effects of a general economized nature, would emerge to relativize the more "positive" utilitarian ordered reading' (1986, 124).

McCaffery represents on extreme version of what can be called, roughly speaking, one side of the split over referentiality among 'L=A=N=G=U=A=G=E' writers. His is a radically anticapitalist interpretation of the workings of language, an approach that, finally, is neither easily combined with nonsense nor a successful defence of noncapitalistic linguistic interaction.[7] Nonsense's inability to respond to or alleviate the concerns expressed by this essentially nonreferential position is ironic since some of McCaffery's theoretical work (as chapter 4 has shown) contains ideas that can be contrued as sympathetic to nonsense. However, nonsense is not ever entirely nonreferential, nor for that matter is language. Balancing meaning and non-meaning, sense and not sense, requires not that reference be completely undermined, but that on some level reference be employed against itself within nonsensical writing.

That is what Ron Silliman's approach to reference argues. Silliman, an influential 'L=A=N=G=U=A=G=E' writer, begins from what appears to be the same point as McCaffery. But through some fine discriminations, he develops a much more workable (and, incidentally, nonsensical) understanding of the relationship between language and reference. In a pivotal essay first published in 1977, 'Disappearance of the Word, Appearance of the World' (1984), Silliman links lingual transparency with the emergence of capitalist society. When words and meaning are 'surplus,' when they are blindly and blandly consumed, they become transparent. The title of the essay, in fact, says it all; Silliman's contention is that only by dulling the experience of language to a point where one looks through, not at, language, can a capitalist society appear as the 'given' it would like to be. The implication is that an appreciation of the materiality of language could insidiously lead to dissatisfaction with a society that emphasizes a continual abstracting, moving away from the physicality of making, using, doing.

'Surplus-value,' and its resulting consumerism, is passive and inert. The vast majority of people are isolated from the processes of production by it, and, Silliman contends, they are equally isolated from involvement in the production of language. Within a capitalistic system, the material nature of language is transformed, anaesthetized, he suggests, and consequently writing leans more and more towards exposition, description and narration towards ' "realism," the illusion of reality in capitalist thought.' 'These developments,' he continues, 'are tied directly to the function of reference in language, which under capitalism is transformed, narrowed into referentiality' (1987a, 10). As Jerome McGann points out (1987, 640), Silliman makes an important distinction between reference and referentiality. To be fair, given his corpus of essays on this problem, it is referentiality not reference that is the silly corpse Silliman writes of. That words refer is not the problem; the problem is, for Silliman, that capitalism requires words to do nothing *but* refer, to reside inertly on the page with a readily discernible meaning waiting to be culled from them by a reader who demands of her thinking faculties the least possible effort. And capitalism, Silliman suggests, in order to remain preeminent, requires that these words refer to its notion of the world. Lee Bartlett's characterization of the movement's general response to reference is in accord with Silliman's: 'The issue is not, then, reference per se, but a reaction to a prevailing poetics which seems to be unaware of the social implications which hover just above its acceptance as a first given of an unquestioning referentiality' (1986, 748).

Windows are a frequent metaphor for this blandly referential aspect of words. In 'Writing Social Work & Political Practice,' Bruce Andrews puts it this way: 'One mode of writing tips its hat to assumptions of reference, representation, transparency, clarity, description, reproduction, positivism. Words are mere windows, substitutes, proper names, haloed or subjugated by the things to which they seem to point' (1984c, 133). Of course, these windows, one assumes, are well washed – without dirt, grit, or scratches; and no screens, nothing to impede the clarity of view, the transmission of vision. Not all windows, one should be quick to say, can be so easily looked through and dismissed; some, like the stained glass in Hejinian's *My Life,* are beautiful in and of themselves, foreground their own materiality – their colour, texture, subtle imperfections –

while simultaneously offering a transformed view of 'reality' beyond. Hejinian's is a language of colour and artistry, a language that refers to itself as well as to referents; like stained glass, it makes *itself* obvious.

For far too many people, however, language functions in a transparent manner – it informs; it is not continually reformed. To argue in favour of such a use would indicate, at the very least, a naive view of language. But the insistence that this function of language is capitalistic in nature and intent overlooks obvious counterarguments and extends itself into overstatement. For instance, the Socialist Realism of the Stalinist era bred what is arguably the most polemical and uninteresting use of language in this century. Silliman would, I think, lay the blame on the use of 'realism,' capitalism's 'illusion of reality' (1987a, 10); however, even this defence can't deny that the problem is realism more so than capitalism, and that, no matter who developed it, realism is available for the dissemination of *any* sociopolitical viewpoint.[8]

Silliman's idealization of gestural language, something he locates contemporarily in the nonsense syllables of various tribal cultures, seems, at first, to be equally problematical. In the unrevised version of 'Disappearance of the Word,'[9] he praises gesture as the earliest and most independent form of reference: 'In its primary form, reference takes the character of a gesture and an object, such as the picking up of a stone to be used as a tool. Both gesture and object carry their own integrities and are not confused: a sequence of gestures is distinct from the objects which may be involved, as distinct as the labor process is from its resultant commodities' (1984, 125). A gestural language, one assumes, requires activity, production, participation and completely precludes 'consumptive' referentiality.

Silliman's model is *not* a verbal language and does little to suggest what the nature of the reference between object and gesture is, or how that nature can be translated in words; does the picking up of a stone for a tool refer to the stone? To its availability as a tool? Is it perhaps an example of metaphor? Is it a radical example of meaning as use – the picking up of a stone means 'tool' because I use it this way? How does such a model entertain the referential capabilities of nouns? Since all gesture is active, is a gestural language entirely constructed out of active verbs?

His model of how the expressive purity of such gesture is to be carried over into language (through its material nature – rhythm, rhyme, nonsense syllable) creates a tempting solution, however. This is especially true since, as I have already argued, the materiality of language is what, in the usual act of referring, interferes with its abstract referential powers; rhyme, rhythm, alliteration, and other materialist techniques are the scratches and impurities on the referential window. They incorporate process into language, and in doing so they divert attention from pure referentiality. It's a charming paradox – the remnants of a primary form of reference disarm passive referentiality. And it brings quite dramatically to the fore the notion that the importance of the act of referring is not to be dismissed out of hand. Rather an untempered, passive gleaning of reference, the debasing of the word to referentiality (to reference *only*), is.

Ten years after the publication of 'Disappearance of the Word,' Silliman locates in realism, the genre for which a transparent referentiality is central, the sort of conundrum that his earlier views of gestural language implied. 'The utopia of realism,' he writes, 'was not merely one of the transmission of unmediated signifieds but also of a language rendered pure by just this process ... Searching for the signified, the realists discovered the signifier. Seeking to abolish style, they empowered it, in all of its partiality, multiplicity, and omnipresence. Intending to create, at long last, the whole word, the unified sign, they instead blew it apart' (1987b, 37).

The signified, realism, and referentiality rely on the signifier, the very thing they intend the reader to ignore, to look through. Such a reliance has built into it the need for a stylized attention to the signifier, a preservation and polishing of it to ensure its functioning, which results in its appearance, not its disappearance.

Bernstein agrees that it is not the end of reference that 'perceiver-centred' writing seeks; 'Not "death" of the referent,' he writes in 'Semblance,' but 'rather a recharged use of the multivalent referential vectors that any word has, how words in combination tone and modify the associations made for each of them, how "reference" then is not a one-on-one relation to an "object" but a perceptual dimension that closes in to a pinpoint, nail down (*this* word)' (1986, 34).

One way to recharge the use of 'referential vectors' is by '[making] the structures of meaning in language more tangible and in that way allowing for the maximum resonance for the medium' (1986, 35). It is this that 'L=A=N=G=U=A=G=E' poetry and nonsense seek – a reverberating sort of reference, a language that, like Wittgenstein's fly, has not been eschewed, but rather has been shown the way out of the fly-bottle.

'The Condition of Its Wordness':
The Shared Materiality of 'L=A=N=G=U=A=G=E' Writing and Nonsense

One of the premises of this study is that nonsense is analogous to the expression of semiotic materiality erupting into the communicative and rational aspects of language, an eruption that is absolutely simultaneous with the production of language. That is, without the symbolic's transparent repository for language the semiotic *chora* would have no place to erupt; and conversely the symbolic cannot exist without the hypothetical preexistence of the same *chora*. Even more central is an extension of that idea: in all verbal languages dwell the structures of other languages, at some times more obviously than at others. Both types of symbiosis animate the paradoxical relationship often acknowledged between reference and materiality within 'Language-centred' writing.[10] That the principles of nonsense and 'L=A=N=G=U=A=G=E' poetry are so closely aligned is clearest in the extremity of their methods for making language material.

In 'Thought's Measure,' Bernstein speaks of the 'desire: To make language opaque so that writing becomes more and more conscious of itself as world generating, object generating' (1986, 71).[11] Rather than merely list those Nonsense techniques that are shared by 'perceiver-centred' writing, I'll offer a series of parallel examples dramatizing them. My intent is to provide a survey of materialist methods and an indication of the range that the term 'L=A=N=G=U=A=G=E' poetry covers. A brief summation of the function of these techniques follows the examples. Because the outward political intent of Nonsense and 'L=A=N=G=U=A=G=E' writing often differs, the 'content' of the latter may appear to be more sophisticated than that of the former; one might bear in mind that the techniques are as relevant as the content, and that, whether or not these gestures are overtly polemical, they are all linguistically anarchic.

ALLITERATION: One of the many 'musical' techniques employed in both of these styles of writing, as well as in almost every other type of poetry and in many nonpoetic 'texts,' alliteration is found in at least two forms. The traditional form of this technique often appears in Lear's prose, especially as a means of naming: 'Diaphanous Door-scraper,' 'The Co-operative Cauliflower' and 'The Tropical Turnspits' are just a few examples found in 'The Story of the Four Little Children' (1947, 106, 102, 94); however, the best example is the long passage describing the Even-song of the Blue-Bottle Flies quoted in Part One. Carroll's *The Hunting of the Snark* ([1876] 1971) is equally rich with its entirely alliterative cast of Baker, Bellman, Boojum, Barrister, Bandersnatch, Broker, Beaver, and others. Even the Snark turns out to be a Boojum. (Reading the poem from this perspective helps one respond to those critics who claim it is a working through of existential angst: the animating tension of the poem is merely 'to "B" or not to "B".')

This device is also found in such 'L=A=N=G=U=A=G=E' poetry as Susan Howe's *Defenestration of Prague*:

> Right or ruth
> rent
>
> to the winds shall be thrown
> words being wind or web
>
> What (pine-cone wheat-ear
> sea-shell) what
> (quoted in Messerli 1987, 34)

Certainly in Lear's case, sense is directed by the sound; the meaning or applicability of a word is made secondary in importance to an often arbitrarily determined phonic pattern; the door scraper may be labelled 'diaphanous' because the sound of the word fits the patterning of the prose. So the music of a word matters as much as, if not more than, its relatively abstract designatory functions; such an exaggerated material function is typical of nonsense. While the alliteration in Howe's poem does not reach the excesses one often finds in Nonsense verse, one still suspects that word choice has been *limited*, if not entirely governed, by the phonic patterns working within her text.

A more interesting and less common form of alliteration also found in Nonsense and 'L=A=N=G=U=A=G=E' poetry might be called 'alphabetization'; this involves a sequence of 'poems' governed by the alphabet, in which the whole of each 'poem' is built around one letter. Again Lear provides the most obvious Nonsensical example with his many 'alphabets.' Take for instance the letter *V* from *Twenty-Six Nonsense Rhymes and Pictures*:

> The Visibly Vicious Vulture,
> who wrote some Verses to a Veal-cutlet in a
> Volume bound in Vellum
> (1947, 219)

bp Nichol's *Aleph Beth Book* (1970) bases each of its twenty-six concrete poems on a letter of the alphabet (see Figure 15). And Tina Darragh, commenting in 'Procedure' on her interest in the dictionary and alphabetical organization, says, 'But what interests me is the coincidence and juxtaposition of the words on the page in their natural formation (alphabetical order). In reference to each other, they have a story of their own' (1984, 108). In such poems as this one from *On the Corner to Off the Corner*, she meditates on the extra-alphabetical relationships between dictionary entries:

'oilfish' to 'old chap' for 'C'

Performing military service for the king and bearing a child have a common medieval root. The progression to this point is first academic, then technical. Textbooks give way to textiles which lead to T-formations and T-groups. We pause to add 'th' and proceed through Mediterranean anemia, deep seas, Greek muses, pesticides, young shoots and the instinctual desire for death. It is there that we find 'thane' to be followed by all manner of 'thanks', including the 'thank-you-ma'am' – a ridge built across a road so rain will roll off. (Messerli 1987, 156)

Peculiar tensions arise, and unexpected connections are revealed between words, when the alphabet is used as a governing logic for poetry. These tensions indicate simultaneously the arbitrariness of the alphabet, which directs thought and ordering principles, and the chance relationships generated between elements of any order.

HOMONYMS: Both groups of writers explore homonymic constructions, and the disparity between the written form and the sound of words. Lear's most famous example is probably this song found in

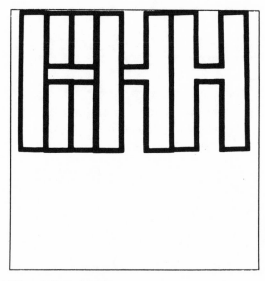

IN   OUR   LIVES.

WE   MUST   BE   TO   FREE

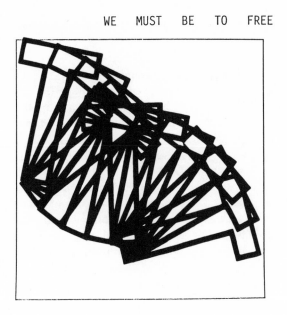

Figure 15 From bp Nichol *The Aleph Beth Book*

his story 'The History of the Seven Families of the Lake Pipple-Popple':

> 'Lettuce! O Lettuce!
> 'Let us, O let us,
> 'O Lettuce leaves,
> 'O let us leave this tree and eat
> 'Lettuce, O let us, Lettuce leaves!'
> (1947, 116)

Silliman uses a homonymic construction to enact one aspect of the very poetic it states: 'Wayward, we weigh words' (quoted in Hartley 1989, 87). These homonyms exploit the sign's arbitrary character, make meaning out of linguistic anomaly. By pitting the sound value of words against the signified, homonyms encapsulate the very spirit of nonsense, and dramatize one aspect of 'L=A=N=G=U=A=G=E' poetry's exploration; both reference *and* materiality are crucial for a homonym to function. Without the signified the examples above would provide merely playful refrains of sound; with the added benefit of reference, they demonstrate the fact that language exists in several different ways simultaneously.

JUXTAPOSITION: Another shared technique, juxtaposition appears most often in nonsense as an anarchic dislocation, or the joining together of phrases or referents that have no clearly articulated, or sensical, connections. It has already been briefly considered in the context of Lilburn's *Pumpkins*. Contemporary Nonsense author/illustrator Edward Gorey, however, uses a juxtaposition more akin to that found in the 'L=A=N=G=U=A=G=E' writers. *The Helpless Doorknob*, a 'Shuffled Story' (1989), is a series of twenty cards that can be read in '2,432,902,736,640,000 different ways' (n.p.) and that is meant to be shuffled into an almost infinite number of non sequiturs and juxtapositions. Its only organizing principle is alliterative; each sentence and every proper name begin with the letter *A*:

Albert left for Peru. Agatha taught Adolphus to dance the one-step. Ambrose took an overdose of sarsaparilla. A mysterious urn appeared in the grounds. Agatha pedalled to the neighbouring village for help. Andrew received a post-card from Amaryllis.

Gorey's story carries Nonsense's use of juxtaposition into the realm of the seemingly random, an area already entered by writers like John Cage, who relies heavily on what he calls 'chance operations,' or bp Nichol, whose anthology of concrete poetry, *The Cosmic Chef* (1970a), and poem *Still Water* (1970b) are boxed books that can be read in a multiplicity of orders.

Other, slightly less radical, examples of juxtaposition abound in the 'L=A=N=G=U=A=G=E' movement. Hejinian's *My Life* shows her use of nonsequitur, and stands as a fine example of her own theory of a realism of 'strangeness' being enacted. A remarkable witty and successful example of juxtaposition and collage is David Bromige's 'My Poetry,' a ten-page prose piece that blends together snatches of reviews (laudatory and damning) of his work with a refreshingly cavalier response to criticism. Here's a short (and metaphorically relevant) excerpt:

> My poetry is 'curiouser & curiouser' as it makes a descent into the rabbit-hole where descent becomes the subject of the poem's concern: a dazzling dimwittedness that makes sense of its mackerel-textured absence. A respectful abstinence from knowing what I'm doing? Therefore, my style seems to have fallen apart, deteriorated in the three-year interim between books; some kind of decadence has set in; it has become problematical, not to say impossible, because if it limits itself to the traditional language & form of a literature it misses the basic truths about itself, while if it attempts to tell those truths it abolishes itself as literature. (1980b, 11)

PALINDROMES, PARAGRAMS, AND PLAY: Reading words backwards or fragmenting them to find other words is another shared technique. Sylvie and Bruno in Carroll's *Sylvie and Bruno Concluded* consider the palindrome EVIL/LIVE ([1893] 1976, 529). Nichol's *The Martyrology* is rife with the disassembling and reassembling of words; one of its basic techniques is the breaking open (and secular personification/ canonization) of words that begin with *st*; 'striking' becomes 'St. Riking,' 'strange,' 'St. Range'; 'stand,' 'St. And,' and so on.[12] Such language play defies traditional orders of reading and regarding words. The word becomes a sequence of elements to be reconfigured, rearranged, reread.

PHONEMIC SHIFTS: Carroll's use of such shifts and their implications has been discussed quite extensively in the context of the 'pig'/'fig' question in *Alice's Adventures in Wonderland*. A similar instance of this shift occurs earlier in the novel when Alice, falling down the rabbit hole, wonders ' "Do cats eat bats? Do cats eat bats?" and sometimes "Do bats eat cats?" for, you see, as she couldn't answer either question, it didn't much matter which way she put it' ([1865] 1971, 20).

Hejinian's *My Life* engages in such phonemic rambunctiousness too: 'Between plow and prow'; 'The grass in my glass' (1987, 65, 68). And Darragh's *'oilfish'* to *'old chap'* for *'C'*, quoted earlier, demonstrates, as Marjorie Perloff points out, 'the vagaries of *words* that can, with the shift of a single phoneme or two, mean such different things as "thane" and "thanks" ' (1985, 216).

REPETITION: Like many of the techniques considered in this section, repetition is commonly found in many other forms of writing. An exaggerated or distorting use of it, however, is typical of Nonsense and 'L=A=N=G=U=A=G=E' poetry. In Nonsense, repetition can take many forms: the repetition of single words, phrases, lines, or refrains. Lear covers the whole range of repetitive styles – from the repeated last words of his self-enclosing limericks, to the more traditionally poetic refrains of *The Pelican Chorus*:

> Ploffskin, Pluffskin, Pelican jee!
> We think no Birds as happy as we!
> Plumpskin, Ploshkin, Pelican jill!
> We think so then, and we thought so still!
> (1947, 232)

In 'L=A=N=G=U=A=G=E' poetry, repetition is rarely a refrain, but words, phrases and lines are frequently repeated or reused in varying contexts. Such repetition is central to *My Life* and is also a major structural factor in Silliman's *Ketjak*. It frees words from a singleness of meaning, allowing them simultaneously to accrue other meanings based on their new contextual uses and to acquire a *structural* and phonic meaning. They begin to mean as textural components, as nodes around which the text composes itself; and perhaps even more important, they begin to mean as sound.

RHYME AND RHYTHM: The importance of these two elements in a Nonsensical writing/reading of poetry has already been argued. In classical Nonsense, rhyme and rhythm are companions as constant as Lear's Owl and Pussy-cat; and 'their' poem is a fine example of this. 'L=A=N=G=U=A=G=E' poetry rarely uses such overt end rhyme, since it resists conventional forms; rather rhyme and rhythm tend to be subtly internalized as in these 'sentences' from *My Life* and *Ketjak* respectively: 'Raisins, cheese, the Japanese' (Hejinian 1987, 64); 'This day's reaches features peaches' (Silliman 1978, 20). The latter example features assonantal as well as true rhyme. Because this use of rhyme is internalized, its subversiveness is more textural, less structural, than the strongly defined and definable rhythmic units found in much classical Nonsense. Yet in both types of rhythmic and rhyming incursion – subtle or overt – sound manipulates, challenges, sense's normal place of privilege. The musical movement of the words vies with their meaning for supremacy.

All of these techniques and many others (such as puns, neologisms, and anagrams) are attempts to centre language and poetry on 'the condition of [their] wordness' (Bernstein 1986, 29–30). When one subscribes to the myth that the referential capacity of language points solely to the exterior object for which each word is a sign, or when one ignores language's innate abilities to point simultaneously to an exterior object and to itself, then language – as the writers of 'perceiver-centred' work argue – is dematerialized. If one's perceptions and understanding of the world are filtered through and expressed by language, then fabricating and privileging a world that is linguistically transparent and transcendental results in the loss of a variety of possible worlds, in the linguistic textures that would make those worlds viable. Through a careful attention to linguistic detail in the process of reading or writing, however, one can dwell in the signifier. A new awareness of language, with a heightened attention to its part in the creation of sense, can allow one to experience the *making* of meaning. Then one can reintegrate her view of the world into a balanced materiality.

Such a material language needs, however, neither to undermine sceptically the material existence of the exterior world nor to nullify the possibility of presence within that world. Bernstein pleads for 'the deeper reality of the interpenetrability and interdependence of all oppositions as appositions' (1986, 287), a simultaneous merger and coexistence that a *Bandar*-logical approach to nonsense maintains is typical of this genre and this type of linguistic deformation. In 'The Objects of Meaning,' Bernstein argues as well for such a bridging, conflating, or blending of the function of the signifier and signified (a very Nonsensical prospect) when he writes, 'One might say, against Derrida, that desiring production is the "primary signified," if that is understood as production of a form of life, where words have truth where they have meaning, in *use*' (1986, 182). Calling attention to the material processes of language as a type of meaning, and splitting or momentarily diverting a reader's attention from (as opposed to destroying) traditional sense in this manner allows for the combination of the functions of signifier and signified and the reconstitution of the sign within a Nonsensical paradigm.[13] The sign becomes a palimpsest that lets both signified *and* signifier show through it; abstract and concrete qualities reside in it simultaneously. When different sign systems are situated upon each other in order to put pressure on the sign – and it should be pointed out that many of the techniques used to heighten a word's nature are as much musical or painterly (for instance, Cubist juxtaposition) as they are lingual – the nature of the sign itself is challenged and changed. To rematerialize language, then, is to redefine the signifying process, to relocate it within the realm of the signified and so fundamentally alter the structure of the sign.

Author a Grammar:
Towards New Grammatical Forms

Such alteration of course causes serious ripples in grammar, but does not call for its overthrow or elimination. While grammatical principles can be used to promote linear and one dimensional language, grammar is not necessarily, as McCaffery claims, 'a huge conciliatory machine [assimilating] elements into a ready structure. This grammatical structure can be likened to profit in capitalism, which is reinvested to absorb more human labour for further profit' (1984a, 160). Grammar is an essential factor in the manufacture of the type of linguistic experiment that interests both Nonsense and 'L=A=N=G=U=A=G=E' writer. Not only does it make possible the expression of those material energies that reestablish language within the body and the physical world, but it also throws into relief the immensity of the avant-garde's subversion of language. If all semblance of structure and reference has been nullified, then the subversiveness of the gesture is overwhelmed by the pure physicality of the moment, the presymbolic wildness of the newborn.

Chomsky's three levels of grammar – grammaticality, semigrammaticality, and ungrammaticality – help illuminate the ripples within signification caused by the creation of the nonsensical, palimpsestic sign in a more practical way. In her insightful study of Gertrude Stein, *A Different Language*, Marianne DeKoven suggests that it is semigrammaticality, not ungrammaticality, that makes possible avant-garde writing.[14] Phrases like Chomsky's example of this second degree of grammaticalness, 'colorless green ideas sleep furiously' are, DeKoven argues, 'meaningful, readable, suggestive, resonant' (1983, 10). Semigrammaticality, she continues, 'not only undermines or fragments coherent meaning, it also subordinates meaning altogether to the linguistic surface, the signified to the signifier: we notice the strangeness or freshness of the verbal combinations themselves – the words "stand out" *as words* – before we register consciously their dedetermined, unresolved articulations of lexical meanings' (1983, 11).

While DeKoven's description of the process of semigrammatical signification differs from my view of the dynamic of nonsense in her insistence on the primacy of the signifier over the signified (a palimpsestic sign requires that uneasy balance that is integral to Nonsense), it should make clear the fact that in semigrammaticality the realigned 'power' structure of signification finds its most cogent expression. Pure grammaticality is a grammar of the old sign, where the referent and referentiality stand as privileged components; ungrammaticality is a grammar of a completely defused sign – defused in terms of potential to function within a signifying system, and defused in terms of its organization, that is, broken apart. If semigrammaticality is to make 'sense,' it requires participatory reading and shared grammar, the authoring of a communal grammar. Before looking at samples of work by Stein and Silliman that engage this semigrammaticality, I'll consider the rules of one communal grammar that has become quite widely accepted within the 'L=A=N=G=U=A=G=E' movement – Silliman's notion of 'the new sentence.'

Silliman's theory takes the sentence as the limit of grammatical or lingual organization. 'The sentence is the horizon,' he contends, 'the border between ... two fundamentally distinct types of integration' (1987a, 87). These types of integration are, on one hand, the arranging of lingual units into sentences, and on the other hand 'higher orders of meaning – such as emotion' (1987a, 87) that integrate collections of related or independent sentences. The paragraph is no longer 'a unit ... of logic or argument' but rather a 'quantity, a stanza' (1987a, 90). That being the case, Silliman suggests, 'the torquing which is normally triggered by linebreaks, the function of which is to enhance ambiguity and polysemy, has moved directly into the grammar of the sentence. At one level, the completed sentence (i.e., not the completed thought, but the maximum level of grammatic/linguistic integration) has become equivalent to a line, a condition not previously imposed on sentences' (1987a, 90).

Silliman's is a unique kind of semigrammaticality. Each sentence, viewed in isolation, appears to be grammatical. But when a group of sentences is read in a sequence, it reveals the nonsequitous nature that generates its energy, and disrupts normal grammar at the level of what linguistic pragmatism calls coreference. These sentences, read as a unit, require a dramatic rereading, reconceiving, and reintegrating. Collectively, new sentences encourage a perpetual parallax, a continually further shift from the traditional semantics in which, individually, they can be read. Silliman wants a syllogistic movement that is 'limited,' and 'controlled'; consequently he tries to create a syllogism that lies between sentences and orchestrates the overall movement of the paragraph in order to '[keep] the reader's attention at or very close to the level of language, that is, most often at the sentence level or below' (1987, 91).

It is precisely this syllogistic movement that makes Silliman's new grammar a forum for the nonsensical sign; the words of this type of sentence stand as referential and as material. This sentence from *Ketjak* – 'But trees are not orderly' (1978, 53) – is a workable, grammatical form, albeit fragmentary; one can cull a referential meaning from this sentence on its own. When, however, such a sentence fragment is juxtaposed with other sentences, its grammatical relations are undermined and the material aspects of the sentences and the words must be consulted to form new patterns of meaning: 'But trees are not orderly. How propose to release the fly from the bottle. Bigger, to serve you better. The moth that destroyed Cleveland. Close cover before striking' (1978, 53). These words don't cease to refer to trees, flies, bottles, moths, Cleveland, covers. However, they do not refer to *just* these things; they also 'refer' to, or enact, slogans or quotations that accumulate without imposed order, to themselves as language with a preexisting and constantly shifting identity. With a reach that stretches in two directions, outward and inward, as a sort of double-headed indicating arrow, each word eclipses the referential and material function within a fluctuating grammar that exists to emphasize that eclipse.

'A continual athleticism':
Tender Buttons *and Nonsense*

Despite Wim Tigges's claim that Gertrude Stein is an Absurdist and not a writer of Nonsense (1988, 41), a nonsensical strategy rewards the reader of Stein, and especially the reader of *Tender Buttons* ([1914] 1962). Considered by many to be Stein's most successful experimental work, this slim volume of prose poems or meditations is divided into three sections – one on objects, one on food, and one on rooms – each of which is further subdivided into individual pieces on, for the most part, examples of objects, food, and rooms, respectively.

This glimpsing of Stein's prose is meant to illustrate a means of reading and not to confront the whole of Stein scholarship with its dramatic split over whether Stein's work has, literally, no coherent meaning (as DeKoven argues throughout her study[15]) and so exists solely to glorify the signifier, or whether it is a cryptic encoding of social and sexual meanings that can be teased out through subtle manipulations or intricate twists of logic and etymology (a position taken in varying degrees by, among others, Rieke, Perloff, and Steiner).

However, I will admit I don't accept the contention that Stein's work in *Tender Buttons* is wholly nonreferential or unrepresentational. In an interview with Robert Hass, Stein discussed her method of writing *Tender Buttons*: 'I used to take objects on a table, like a tumbler or any kind of object and try to get the picture of it clear and separate in my mind and create a word relationship between the word and the things seen' (quoted in Copeland 1975, 88). As opaque as her writing may be in these 'still-lifes' (Perloff 1981, 99) of objects, food, and rooms, Stein *is* attempting to (re)present some external object. But she is trying to do so through the interiorities of language. Her subtitles are not empty gestures; as DeKoven notes, they 'make as well as mock meaning,' for they focus each piece (or poem), and in doing so give the reader a concrete referent as a grounding location (1983, 79). DeKoven argues that these titles are 'arbitrary' (1983, 79), but I would urge that they are so only in terms of Stein's choice of an object to respond to or with; they are not names merely pulled out of the air and appended to writings that are completely separate from them. The pieces in *Tender Buttons* are samples of what Randa Dubnick calls a 'mimesis of the intersection of the present moment of consciousness with an object' (1984, 28); they are samples of the blending of Hejinian's descriptive realism, a realism of 'strangeness' (see note 8), with an associative linguistic presence. The end result of such blending is what Bob Perelman, in an untitled reading of Stein, calls 'a continual athleticism, leaping free of the gravity of the familiar' (1984b, 199). It is a leaping free of gravitational forces (and linguistic ties) that bind one, tightly and permanently, to the earth, the object, and simultaneously a leaping free of the grave seriousness of language. For the most overwhelming qualities of Stein's *Tender Buttons* are its passion for and intimacy with language, and its wit.

Strongly marked by Stein's interest in and understanding of Cubism, *Tender Buttons* 'paints' its subjects in a fractured language that attempts to relate the presentness of the moment in which the subject of the piece is experienced. There is no conventional description in the volume; one doesn't find a piece on potatoes, say, that runs along these lines: 'A potato's shape is usually oval or a rounded oblong. Unripe potatoes are green, new ones have a thin skin, flecked with tan, older ones a thicker brown skin. Inside, potatoes are a whitish-cream colour but they turn quickly to brown when exposed to air. Small protuberances, known as eyes, are really the beginning of roots. The potato grows underground.' Rather, Stein's three potato pieces, printed one after the other, are brief and wholly uninformative, if one is looking for the size, weight, colour, and texture of this tuber. It is the verbal 'reality' of the potato, and how that reality occupies, with sly humour, her ever lively consciousness, that Stein depicts:

POTATOES.
Real potatoes cut in between.

POTATOES.
In the preparation of cheese, in the preparation of crackers, in the preparation of butter, in it.

ROAST POTATOES.
Roast potatoes for.
([1914] 1962, 490)

Stein's decision to include three takes on potatoes, and to put them side by side, may indicate her belief that all things change continually, that nothing, not even a potato, remains the same from one moment to the next. It also indicates that she is not trying for *visual* veracity; these are clearly not attempts to correct each other, but to extend the impressions created, to play the game a bit longer.

None of these pieces are complete sentences, but neither are they ungrammatical. Her language is accessible, simple, and plain as potatoes. *Roast Potatoes*, one of the most often quoted of the pieces, is a fine example of Stein's semigrammaticality.[16] The three words function together as a sentence fragment, and that fragmentary nature makes the role of 'roast' ambiguous: the title suggests that the word is an adjective describing the type of potatoes; a probable alternative, however, is that it is an imperative verb urging someone to roast potatoes for ... whomever. That's left uncertain. As well, considering Stein's extremely rare use of punctuation, especially of commas,[17] it is legitimate to consider 'roast, potatoes' – a sort of list or an unpunctuated, appositional 'menu' – as another possible reading. As Neil Schmitz says in 'Gertrude Stein as Post-Modernist,' 'words as buttons fastening side to side, signifier to signified, become tender, pliable, alive in the quick of consciousness' (1974, 1207).

The fanciest Stein's language gets in these pieces, and that's none too fancy, is in the second piece, which stands like potatoes au gratin (and she includes, one might add, almost all of the ingredients for this dish – cheese, butter, crackers – in the passage) to the plainer boiled and roasted. This second piece involves a rhetorical flourish in the repeated formula of its phrases: 'in the preparation of.' Joining together the three phrases in a single sentence fragment underscores a musical materiality where words, by virtue of their repetition, have their sense underplayed and their sound accentuated. And it encourages a momentum flatly undercut by the very abrupt ending of the pattern 'in it'; the flatness of the ending puts extra weight on 'it' – an ambiguous pronoun with no clearly established antecedent. This may be a tactic for undermining any attempt at a literal decoding of the piece – the reader is left, ultimately, wondering what 'it' is.

Stein also writes a series of four *Chicken* pieces; the final one uses sound very playfully in its two sentences:

Stick stick call then, stick stick sticking, sticking with a chicken. Sticking in a extra succession, sticking in.

([1914] 1962, 493)

Stein's words are pushed quite deep into the realm of sounds. What 'sticking' has to do with 'chicken' is mostly sonal; in fact what each of these phrases has to do with 'chicken' is sonal. To suggest that Stein is flippantly rhyming here, and that the rhyme gets out of control, would be wrong. There are rules operating, but rules that don't necessarily conform to the usual ways of making meaning; Stein doesn't balk at playing havoc with the structures of meaning, or at stretching them to a breaking-point, but she creates such disturbances through a very structured and rigorous sort of play.

'Number' sequences and repetition are vital to the organization of the passage; for instance, twelve is central to the prose poem's configuration. The first sentence is made of three phrases spliced together. The first two phrases each have four syllables, the third has six; the increase in syllables, however, is to accommodate 'chicken,' the 'subject' of the piece, which is mentioned just once at what turns out to be its exact centre. The second sentence has two phrases, one of nine syllables, one of three, making a total of twelve syllables. The phrases are structured so that twelve syllables precede 'chicken' and twelve follow it. The number four is also important since both 'stick' and 'sticking' are repeated four times. This repetition increases the sheer musicality of the passage; if *Chicken* is *about* anything, it may be about the music of the word naming this wholly unmusical bird.

That musicality is carried further by the primary structural feature of the 'poem' – rhyme. Each phrase begins with a word or syllable rhyming with the first syllable of 'chicken' and ends with one rhyming with its final syllable. Consequently each of the phrases has a 'frame' that is little more than a sonal shift from 'chicken,' but that is never used twice: 'stick-then,' 'stick-ing,' 'stick-en,' 'stick-ion,' 'stick-in.' This phrasal framing is quite appropriately rhyme, however, since the 'frame' that contains this piece is entirely made up of rhyme. The passage as a whole is a stretching out of rhymes on 'chicken,' and the phrases are similarly a stretching to the point where other words and rhymes can be inserted into the midst of the elongated rhyme.

The elongation of the rhyme is most noticeable, and most vulnerable, in the first phrase of the second sentence. Previously a pattern had been established – the four syllable phrases followed by the third phrase of six syllables seem regular enough, especially since the extra syllables of 'sticking with a chicken' forcefully reiterate the subject (chicken), rhyme pattern, and movement (the poem as a whole 'sticks' with chicken) of the passage, and as I mentioned above, form its syllabic centre. However, the phrase 'Sticking in a extra succession,' while maintaining the rhyme pattern, completely disrupts any seeming system of four syllable phrases. What Stein does is, quite literally, stick in 'a extra succession' of syllables whose rhythmic flat-footedness is further emphasized by the use of the improper article ('a' not 'an') – this is a phrase that loses the tune. The 'extra succession' is really an overextension; for the twelve syllable rule to be met, 'sticking in,' which is tacked on to the end of the sentence, can have only three syllables. Once again the key is flat.

In a piece like *Chicken*, Stein is not a Nonsense writer; while reference exists at some level, most of the meaning of the poem dwells in the actions of the signifier. There is no delicate tension between the signifier and the signified; the balance is upset. Yet a reader's refusal to abandon reference in the face of *Chicken*'s obvious subversive overload can still serve her reading of it. By retaining a vestige of the title's referent, a reader can counterpoint the music of the poem with the actual music of the bird; in this case the stubborn refusal to admit there is *not* a literal chicken in the poem rewards the reader with what may well be Stein's witty implication – that this poem is about as musical as a chicken gets, and carries a tune for about as long as one can, too.

Balinese *Bandar*-logic:
Silliman's Ketjak

In a parenthetical note to his brief consideration of Ron Silliman's work, Stephen Fredman reveals that ' "Ketjak" is the Balinese monkey chant from the *Ramayana*' (1983, 144). That's an appropriate preface for a nonsensical/*Bandar*-logical reading of Silliman's volume. *Ketjak* is both *Bandar*-logical and musical, perhaps musical because *Bandar*-logical. Fredman observes that 'the experience of reading' *Ketjak*, and Silliman's formally similar work *Tjanting*, 'is akin to the experience of modern music ... or art, in which the exfoliation of formal patterns – of repetition and variation defined by complex operations – gives the aesthetic pleasure' (1983, 144). That there is a formal pattern governing *Ketjak* is easily discernible from a glance at the book's first page; to discern how complex it is takes more careful looking. Silliman established rules for the writing of *Ketjak*, made it a language game that borders on Nonsense. This page has three and a half paragraphs on it – separated from each other by a large white space. Each paragraph is markedly larger than the previous one. A quick counting of sentences proves that the paragraphs' number of sentences is continually doubled: the first paragraph has one sentence, the second two, the third four, the fourth eight, and so on. The twelfth and final paragraph is forty-five pages long and almost one half of the length of the whole book, a far cry from the two-word paragraph that begins the volume.

While Silliman doesn't regulate the length of individual sentences, he does place more demands on his work than just the number of sentences per paragraph. Each sentence, sometimes in its exact form and sometimes slightly modified, is repeated in every paragraph. The first paragraph becomes the first sentence in each succeeding paragraph. As well as being a crucial structural principle, Silliman's use of that placement for this first 'paragraph' ('Revolving door.') provides insight into a reader's experience of the text, since the book often feels like trips through just such a door – each run through longer and faster. Barret Watten compares the work itself, with its fascinating variations on repetition, to 'a fractal curve of an experience that might be reduced to "revolving door"' (1984, 271).

This clearly marked structure of *Ketjak* offers more than 'aesthetic pleasure'; it dramatizes many of the aesthetic principles, and works through many of the problems of reference that have been issues in this chapter. Charles Bernstein, commenting on Silliman's 'poetry of visible borders,' writes, 'Such poetry emphasizes its medium as being constructed, rule governed, everywhere circumscribed by grammar & syntax, chosen vocabulary: designed, manipulated, picked, programmed, organized, & so an artifice, artifact' (1986, 40–1). Silliman's repetitions certainly function this way, revealing a programmatic 'code' behind the self-generating paragraphs; but so too do the other materialist techniques that he uses.

Not surprisingly, there is a good deal of sound play here. Puns like 'the eye is the limit' (26) – which could also be an aesthetic comment – are fairly frequent. And so are clusters of words that seem meditations on sound: 'Wept, swept, slept' (37); 'An harbor, Ann Arbor' (37); 'Ontic antics in the attic' (26); 'Ives jives' (29); 'Cupcake corral' (58); 'Sea-sick sea serpent' (71); 'Never fear, chandelier' (70). Many of these words seem to be grouped together solely because of their sonal affinities, but their humour lies equally in the possibility of their being referentially active as well, in striking a temporary balance between sound and sense. It is not just the sound of 'Cupcake corral' that is funny, but, like Carroll's Looking-Glass entymology, the momentary imagining of such a thing, and, as a friend notes, of the showdown that might occur there.

The same is true of other sentences that are not examples of sound play so much as combinations of words that, because of their improbability or strangeness, emphasize themselves without completely obscuring the often humorous potential of literalness: 'This tapestry concerns the mass capture of rabbits' (15); 'Brushing dry leaves off dead poets' (26); 'Garbage mind pearl diver' (47).

Many of Silliman's sentences are phrases and expressions culled from the world around him; advertising slogans, cartoons, nursery rhymes, popular songs – nothing is free from his borrowing pen. Sylvester the cat, from Warner Brothers' Tweetie Bird cartoon, is represented by his favourite saying 'Suffering succotash' (48); Cecil the sea-sick sea serpent, from the 'Beanie and Cecil' cartoon, also appears (71); a line from a fifties song is altered to 'Who put the bob in the Baba Ram Dass' (50); and almost every matchbook ever made finds a voice in 'Close cover before striking' (53). He not only represents the world as words, he also incorporates the world of public words.

Juxtaposition is probably the most obvious technique Silliman uses, and, when combined with the required repetition of sentences, one of the most humorous, as the following excerpt shows. These are the last few sentences from paragraphs four through eight; while it would be possible to quote the endings in such a way as to incorporate both of the final sentences from paragraph four in each succeeding quotation, for reasons of length, I will restrict myself.

A sequence of object, silhouettes, which to him appears to be a caravan of fellaheen, a circus, dromedaries pulling wagons bearing tiger cages, fringed surreys, tamed ostriches in toy hats, begins a slow migration to the right vanishing point on the horizon line. We ate them. (4)

A sequence of objects, silhouettes, which to him appears to be a caravan of fellaheen, a circus, dromedaries pulling wagons bearing tiger cages, fringed surreys, tamed ostriches in toy hats, begins a slow migration to the right vanishing point on the horizon line. The implications of power within the ability to draw a single, vertical straight line. Look at that room filled with fleshy babies. We ate them. (5)

The implicit power within the ability to draw a single, vertical straight line. That was when my nose began to peel. Look at that room filled with fleshy babies, incubating. A tall glass of tawny port. We ate them. (7)

That was when my nose began to peel. Get aboard. Look at that room filled with fleshy babies, incubating. Points of transfer. A tall glass of tawny port. The shadows between houses leave the earth cool and damp. A slick gaggle of ambassadors. We ate them. (9)

Shadows between houses leave earth cool and damp. Retina burn. A slick gaggle of ambassadors. Astronauts hold hands, adrift in the sky. We ate them. The flag. (14)

Many of Silliman's techniques are evident in a comparison of these passages. The incongruity of juxtaposition and the black humour created by the repeated and abrupt ending – 'We ate them' – is extremely effective. The juxtaposition is especially so, illustrating as it does the working principles of Silliman's theory of the 'new sentence.' A continual barrage of non sequiturs demands that a reader continually shift her stance on the sentences, on how they fit together. Sometimes sentences seem to fit together at first, as in this other example – 'Where is JFK's brain. Yonder' (73).[18] Or in the gruesome 'cannibalism' implicit in one of the examples above: 'Look at that room filled with fleshy babies. We ate them' (5). But the continually expanding context ultimately puts an end to any narrative unity.

Silliman's repetition, or, as the examples above illustrate, his near repetition (sometimes the change is as subtle as the lack of pluralization on one word), requires that each sentence be reintegrated not only within its own paragraph but also within the movement of the paragraphs as a whole. What is demanded, then, is a continually precise attention to the sentences or propositions presented and the structures of meaning that *Ketjak* generates, or requires the reader to generate. It is not enough to have read once about fat, fleshy babies and then to glide over that sentence's other incarnations – to do so would be to lose out on all sorts of meaningful combinations for that sentence.

Silliman intersperses these paragraphs with sentences that may be deemed directly or metaphorically relevant to his aesthetic stance. For instance:

Attention is all. (5)

Every word is either current, or strange, or metaphorical, or ornamental, or newly-coined, or lengthened, or contracted, or altered. (13–14)

Refuse connectedness. (14)

A writing that grows out of itself, a poetry of mould. (16)

Patterns of possibility come together, intersect, disperse. (17)

What if these words don't mean what I believe they do. (57)

Language did not emerge from ratiocination. (57)

But it is wrong to assume that since these seem to be theoretical statements they are more important than any of the other sentences in *Ketjak*. The rapid and eclectic accumulation of sentences and the susceptibility of each to change make clear that no one sentence is to be valued over another, because each is itself a dramatization of problems inherent in the manufacture of meaning.

One of the most frequent ways in which Silliman directly questions reference is by using the demonstrative pronoun 'this.' In 'Language, Realism, Poetry,' he calls 'this' 'a pronoun of presence which foregrounds the referential dimension of language' (1986, xv). 'This' always, or should always, point to something, but in *Ketjak* it generally points to itself.[19] 'This this this this' (1978, 22) is Silliman's most radical example. The repetition isolates the word's sound, but also offers a base for an infinite regress of reference – which this?: this, this this, this this this, this this this this ... Because there is no noun being modified by 'this' the adjective or acting as an antecedent to 'this' the pronoun, one is left with the material presence of a non-referential referral. It is a referral that underscores the tenuousness of lingual reference and the need for language to define itself in terms of other pieces of language, if it is to mean the way one is used to it meaning. Silliman's use of 'this' is an extreme example of the language of the new nonsensical sign.

'This' appears in many other instances where Silliman seeks an immediacy of reference:

This before, this after. (29)

This sentence has five words. (27)

You read this sentence before. (34) [This sentence creates a nice paradox the first time around.]

This sentence is not what I intended. (43)

Here is an empirical fact, this word is used like this. (50)

This list. (50)

In each case, the referential gesture towards an exterior object is turned back upon itself, partially frustrated so that the words of the sentence become the exterior object referred to.

Within the precise structure he sets out for *Ketjak*, Silliman creates a work that is vibrant and strangely lyrical, one whose wit and linguistic particularity is uniquely intertwined with its governing rules. Indeed, the work is almost a paradigm of the fusion of materiality and 'rule,' of semiotic and symbolic. Neither structure nor particular takes precedence over the other; rather they complement each other. By calling this relationship complementary I don't intend to suggest that meaning resides in an easy and static way in *Ketjak*. Sense constantly makes and unmakes itself; meaning is both conservatively coherent (occasionally, temporarily) and constantly constructed. There is a symbiosis that 'resolves' itself naturally even as it revolves; a reader never forgets the presence of the structure, she even reads for it, but that structure is never read to the exclusion of its individual elements. The paragraphs in *Ketjak* are monkey chants, a sort of *Bandar*-logical lingual enactment of the type of discourse the *Bandar-log* brag about in Kipling's 'Road-Song of the *Bandar-log*'; but so, then, is most 'L=A=N=G=U=A=G=E' poetry:

> All the talk we ever have heard
> Uttered by bat or beast or bird –
> Hide or fin or scale or feather –
> Jabber it quickly and all together!
> Excellent! Wonderful! Once again!
> Now we are talking just like men.
> ([1894] 1987, 66)

This talk of sound and word is never precisely referential, but neither can it escape reference; and the people whose verbal universe is jabbered are poets who clearly, whether or not one agrees with their ideas or appreciates their work, are as passionate about language as they are anxious about its socio-political manipulation. While nonsense theory does not necessarily share their political mandate, it most certainly shares their conviction about the importance of the signifier. And can serve the writing of the 'L=A=N=G=U=A=G=E' poets: it exposes and embraces the structures and elements of language with a passion similar to theirs; it alters the sign in such a way that many of their concerns about conventional language can be addressed; it sympathizes with them, plays their games enthusiastically, and enters their community. But it never loses its own unique nature, its individuality.

'What then is a window'

———◆———

Lyn Hejinian's *My Life* meanders lovingly over its own minutiae. Or perhaps leaps is a better word for the vigorous shifts and the continual non sequiturs that mark this 'autobiography,' with its probing and passionate language ebbing and flowing over a lifetime. In both the first and the second editions Hejinian withholds the stable reassurances of genre and form. Rather than titled or numbered chapters, there are long paragraphs – thirty-seven in the first edition, forty-five in the second. Each paragraph begins with an italicized phrase, seemingly unrelated to what follows, and each, Hejinian suggests, is 'a time and place, not a syntactical unit' (1987, 96). Gone are clear divisions between poetry and prose, lyric and narrative. Gone is any clear association of history with memory.

Hejinian belongs to the 'L=A=N=G=U=A=G=E' poetry movement, so it's no surprise that her autobiography challenges the function of verbal expression and the nature of meaning, as well as genre, by overlaying itself with a musical arrangement of language, an emphasizing of the material aspects of words. Meaning is everywhere in this text – and yet nowhere for one unwilling to listen closely. For Hejinian's meaning is neither traditionally conceived nor stable. Her 'life' is a clustering of phrases and fragments, where sequences of more than three clearly and semantically linked sentences are quite rare; it is a dramatic working through of Ron Silliman's theory of the 'new sentence.' The reader must sift and reshape the text. No easy way through or out of the book is offered; nor should it be, because *My Life* is the articulation not just of Hejinian's own life, but of a reader's as well.

'What follows a strict chronology has no memory' (Hejinian 1987, 13).

Charles Olson talks of 'selection' in his essay, 'Human Universe'; writing and even living, he says, are a whittling down of 'that lovely riding thing, chaos' (1966, 59). Each involves the organization of a universe, of poem or person, through selection from an incomprehensibly rich mass of stimulae and sensations, bits and pieces. 'For any of us, at any instant,' he claims, 'are juxtaposed to any experience, even an overwhelming single one, on several more planes than the arbitrary and discursive which we inherit can declare' (1966, 55). Selecting inevitably betrays the flow between these planes, creates a flaw in one's perception of a universe that does not revolve around humanity's limited means of expressing itself.

Since writing and living are a betrayal of one's 'lived' experience, what is memory? Born in. Lived at. Schooled at. Married him. Bore her. Stories of such turning-points or times of shift, even when thick with description, thin one out. Where are: the postcard of Emily Brontë's dog; the red and white package of Hungarian Mammoth Squash seeds (world record – 451 lbs! Absolutely the largest squash you can grow!); the blue plastic E with feet; cobalt therapy, a flying squirrel: postage stamps on a 'S.A.S.E.'; a stamped thin tin bird with fuchsia wings; ants crawling out of peonies my mother cut for my sixth grade teacher; dandelions, from this window, from this angle: blossoms on the maple tree. Where is the language for the plenitude of which such details are only crude indicators?

Lyn Hejinian offers a selection. But what she selects, how she reorganizes her life, produces not a chronology of significant events, but a sonal and visual dramatization of how language constructs one's 'reality' and one's memories. She presents an intuition of the 'pure duration,' the ongoingness, the presentness of time, and simultaneously the wonderful plasticity, the expansive, procreative embrace of both memory and language.

'Thinking about the time in the book, it is really the time of your life' (Hejinian 1987, 55).

Not only is the book the lived time it recounts; it is the time spent writing the book, and reading it. Beyond this, Hejinian's language – her fragments, her repetitions, her memories and echoes – assault the notion of a language whose logic flows with time, that can be read or experienced only in a forward-moving or progressive time frame. By constantly and variously reworking words and phrases so they reappear nonsequentially and seem almost unmotivated, Hejinian tries to break out of narrative and linguistic chronology.

Which is not to suggest that *My Life* has no narrative progression. The subtle movement of language from a distilled child's voice (more recalled than reenacted) to the more 'mature' sensibility of a crafter of words, together with the increase of 'theoretical' asides,[1] produces an understated portrait of the artist. But Hejinian is more immediately concerned with linguistic and temporal 'transgression,' with resisting traditional and staid notions of the time of language, by revealing its spatial nature, rendering it an object to be not remembered so much as *renewed* ('I heard it anew not again' she writes [1987, 82]). Memory is a useful means for renewing language and experience both; it musses up chronology, adjusts or shifts 'reality,' dragging history into (making history into) the present.

'Is that a basis for descriptive sincerity. I am a shard, signifying isolation – here I am thinking aloud of my affinity for the separate fragment taken under scrutiny' (Hejinian 1987, 52).

Hejinian's minutiae: '*A pause, a rose, something on paper*' (7); 'Foxtails, the juice of a peach, have fallen on the flesh of this book' (39); 'What I felt was that figs resemble kidneys' (55); 'Those hard white grains of sand are flea eggs' (62); 'The calves of the cowboy's legs are rubbed shiny, left with no hairs. Pelicans hatch naked from the egg' (86).

Here is an exquisiteness of detail so lyrically precise, so supple, that Hejinian's is not the only life reclaimed. Just saying the title includes the reader. Each time I read this book, I feel the weight and wonder of my own childhood slinking up the skin on my arms, smell the summers of too-many-barbecues and ketchup-cooking-at-the-factory; I find another moment of my life waiting to be rediscovered. Things once extraneous are loved into an intensity that selection had denied them. And more important, words are given an intensity, a thisness, of their own; they begin to exist *as* words, rather than as linguistic referrals to a greater and other 'Outside.'

What helps excavate these 'extraneous' elements and moments in life is the seeming *lack* of selection, the apparent randomness with which fragments seemingly peripheral to the major events of a life are thrown together. For instance, Hejinian doesn't describe giving

birth, but remarks instead, 'When the baby was born I lost considerable importance, surrendered it to him, since now he was the last of
his kind' (1987, 64). The observation is, as usual, a non sequitur: 'Yet
I admit I'm still afraid of something when I refuse to rise for the
playing of the national anthem. The sailor on the flood, ten times the
morning sun, made of wooden goldfish. When the baby was born I
lost considerable importance, surrendered it to him, since now he
was the last of his kind. "Fundamental dispersion," he said, and
then, "no nozzle." The coffee drinkers answered ecstatically, pound-
ing their cups on the table' (1987, 64). This type of dislocation requires that one read not for a definitive meaning, but rather to
engage the process of the making of meaning and to discover the
web of potential relations that resonates between sentences. Their
connection is one of interwoven tissue, the texture of muscle rather
than the firm definition of bone.

'Only fragments are accurate. Break it up into single words, charge
them to combination' (Hejinian 1987, 55).

If this text charts a lifeline, it traces it from one striking detail to
another, from incarnation to new incarnation of individual words,
from point to point. 'A point, in motion, is a line' (1987, 33) for
Hejinian, and the points that constitute her life *are* in constant
motion. 'Strange,' Rilke writes, in the first *Duino Elegy*,

> to see meanings that clung together once, floating away
> in every direction. And being dead is hard work
> and full of retrieval before one can gradually feel
> a trace of eternity. – Though the living are wrong to believe
> in the too-sharp distinctions which they themselves have created
> (1984, 155)

With each recurrence in *My Life* of a phrase, of an image, eventually
of a word, meaning does not merely gather; 'language [becomes]
restless' (Hejinian 1987, 17) and 'meanings ... [float] away / in every
direction' (Rilke 1984, 155) – lodging temporarily with an old friend,
a new companion, until the individuality, the creases and crevices of
each word-image-phrase are momentarily enlivened. 'But a word is
a bottomless pit' (Hejinian 1987, 8). There is always more to retrieve

and imagine. Hejinian's act of retrieval, while it still involves a
degree of selection, undercuts those 'too-sharp' distinctions of the
resolutely or obsessively 'selective,' those living who are so busy
hewing out their own world they neither revel in chaotic source, nor
acknowledge that they have indeed selected, shaped, their world.

'Language which is like a fruitskin around fruit' (Hejinian 1987, 43).

Life as language: 'The dictionary presents a world view ... The bilin-
gual dictionary doubles that, presents two' (Hejinian 1987, 79). Hejinian adds her eloquent 'voice' to the many others insisting that the
world and the self are composed of language. Her version is partly
comprised of theoretical statements. Single sentences (for instance,
'To some extent, each sentence has to be the whole story' [1987, 67])
give outright and as completely as possible her belief that life is built
with and upon language. But these sentences are rarely presented as
something beyond the thoughts of a particular moment. They are
organic with the process of observation from which such asides
grow. And while theoretical statements are signposts, they are not
maps. No one can claim authority on how to interpret the signs
Hejinian leaves. Each reader finds her own paths through this laby-
rinthine text.

In *The dance of the intellect*, Marjorie Perloff talks of Hejinian's
creation of 'a language field that could be anybody's autobiography,
a kind of collective unconscious whose language we all recognize'
(1985, 225). Hejinian mentions 'a portrait bowl' (1987, 25); I think of
a linguistic 'play box,' a first-cousin-once-removed to the one James
Reaney creates in *Colours in the Dark*, and comments upon in his
preface to it: 'The theatrical experience in front of you now is
designed to give you that mosaic-all-things-happening-at-the-same-
time-galaxy-higgledy-piggledy feeling that rummaging through a
play box can give you' (1969, v). But *My Life* doesn't have the 'ances-
tral coffin plates' and 'school relics' (or the eventually cohering world
vision) that are in Reaney's play box (1969, v). Hejinian's toys and
eccentric ephemera are words; her game is language.

'Mischief logic; Miss Chief' (Hejinian 1987, 29).

Hejinian handles words. She picks them up, turns them over, looks at their underbellies. Some she turns over and over – each use a different game, a new possibility; some she discards as broken; some she breaks. This handling allows sound and matter to assert themselves almost continually throughout this text, requiring that its reader at the very least register linguistic disturbance, but more usually revel in such disruption.

Juxtaposition is also part of the game. Her juxtapositions sit a serious meditation next to a commonplace assertion to see what friction comes of such elbow rubbing: 'If I was left unmarried after college, I would be single all my life and lonely in old age. In such a situation it is necessary to make a choice between contempt and an attempt at understanding, and yet it is difficult to know which is the form of retreat. We will only understand what we have already understood. The turkey is a stupid bird. And it is scanty praise to be so-called well-meaning' (1987, 53). The wit here is more subtle than that in Hejinian's conflation of Stein and Williams – 'No ideas but in potatoes' (1987, 70). But the subtlety is invigorating; the reader is called to play along. Rejoice in displacement, illogic; recognize the suppleness, the plasticity, of language and of meaning not firmly bound by conventional expression. 'Collaborate with the occasion' (1987, 29).

Aphorisms abound: 'Pretty is as pretty does ... See lightning, wait for thunder' (1987, 7). As Perloff points out, these aphorisms are 'just slightly out of sync,' a result of 'the language of adults [impinging] on the child's world with all its prescriptions, admonitions, and "wisdoms,"' (1985, 224) and of the often witty juxtaposition of sentences throughout the book. Clichés are questioned too, or at least called to a reader's attention, though not with the unremitting thoroughness of Christopher Dewdney's *The Dialectical Criminal: Hand in Glove with an Old Hat* (1983, 168–9): 'You cannot linger "on the lamb"' (Hejinian 1987, 11); 'We "took" a trip as if that were part of the baggage we carried. In other words, we "took our time"' (1987, 47). Grammatical rules are rephrased: 'Pronouns skirt the subject' (1987, 77). Some are 'contradicted': 'After C, I before, E except' (1987, 68). Hejinian toys with wandering letters, as in 'I've heard that it once was a napron' (1987, 77) or in the frequently repeated phrase 'a name trimmed with colored ribbons' (ibid., 14, passim), which finds its 'source' in 'a pony perhaps, his mane trimmed with colored ribbons' (1987, 15). In all these instances, she calls attention to how language changes, how literalism tampers with meaning and with the world constructed out of language.

She exults in the phonic play of words, the rhyming slip of letters, the compelling nature of rhythm: 'Between plow and prow' (1987, 65); 'Raisins, cheese, the Japanese' (1987, 64). Such phonic play illuminates the limitations of 'sense.' A reader soon finds herself lingering not over meanings, but over the tumble of the words themselves – 'The grass in my glass' (1987, 68); 'I was not afraid in the dark, hearing the low owl, in the light, the bird knocking in the sun. I heard it anew not again' (1987, 82).

'If words matched their things we'd be imprisoned within walls of symmetry' (Hejinian 1987, 70).

Because the narrow language of the symbolic, in its transparency, cannot contain and express the many planes on which any thing exists, such language 'stops' that thing, moves away from its fluctuating reality. Hejinian remarks on this in her essay 'The Rejection of Closure': 'Children objectify language when they render it their plaything, in jokes, puns, and riddles, or in glossolaliac chants and rhymes. They discover that words are not equal to the world, that a shift, analogous to parallax in photography, occurs between thing (events, ideas, objects) and the words for them – a displacement that leaves a gap' (1984b, 138).

This gap shows in *My Life*: 'I insert a description: of agonizing spring morning freshness, when through the open window a smell of cold dust and buds of broken early grass, of schoolbooks and rotting apples, trails the sound of an airplane and a flock of crows' (1987, 48). Self-consciously she names this 'a description' – she is not offering a landscape, a setting. She is giving words instead.

Yet her continual repetition of words in a changing context lets them shimmer with varying resonances and dramatizes how the longing for a union between word and thing can be superseded by the pure power of a word that means itself, fully, intensely. For Hejinian the union between word and object can be had only by making the word itself an object, not by joining it to the object to which it refers. By saying things intensely, she marks the movement away from referential fusion of word and world, and further still, marks the deflection of a potentially stable meaning. The randomness of repetition and reorientation suggests that, despite Hejinian's careful joinings and juxtapositions, meaning travels of its own accord. Words become glorious in their new oldness. They stand intensely as themselves.

'We had been in France where every word really was a bird, a thing singing' (Hejinian 1987, 85).
    'One of my favourite words was birds and will be. If they are but flights to a conclusion, I will wait patiently to look at them' (Hejinian 1987, 89).

Stein claims that language can exist 'as birds as well as words' (1935c, 30), and that words are a part of the strangeness of the world. Certainly, the insistent rise and fall of words is a source of strangeness in *My Life*; the continual repetition (or 'insistence' as Stein suggests – in 'Portraits and Repetitions' [1935b, 166–7] – it might more properly be termed) of the commonplace speech that marks life. Michel Foucault has commented that 'we live in a world completely marked by, all laced with, discourse, that is to say, utterances which have been spoken, of things said, of affirmations, interrogations, of discourses which have already occurred' (Ruas 1986, 177). This is very much Hejinian's world. Her writing of it is an intense listening.

'The obvious analogy is with music, which extends beyond the space the figure occupies' (Hejinian 1987, 57).
    'When you speak you play a language. The obvious analogy is with music' (Hejinian 1987, 82).

It would be a poor listener who did not pick up on Hejinian's 'obvious analogy' with music since it is an important theme (and a theme more musical than literary) throughout *My Life*. Not only because it self-reflexively accounts for the repetitions ('The new cannot be melodic, for melody requires repetition' [1987, 62]), but also because it suggests something important about meaning in this book. Because most statements are decontextualized, and because the reader must 'make' her own sense, meaning is clearly an issue here. Hejinian raises the question of meaning in many of her theoretical musings: '*What is the meaning hung from that depend*' (1987, 16). How much does one need to mean, to be intelligible, and why? What sort of assumptions about language hang on a desire to mean? 'What is one doing to, or with, the statement (the language) or the stated (the object or the idea) when one *means* it' (1987, 42).

Or, *how* does one mean? Ultimately the *how* overrides the what. How Hejinian means is musically – not merely with correspondence between word and thing; not purely referentially. She is not striving for a referential meaning. Sentences, like *A pause, a rose, something on paper* (1987, 7), are themes (in the musical definition of the word); they are repeated in ever changing configurations, and even as they accrue associative and contextual meaning, they develop a potent sound value. Their continual echoes stand as musical ideas, aural images that vary and combine to create an 'intuitive' lyric that speaks intimately, trustingly.

'Sensual,' reverberating sense challenges logical, cerebral sense; dislocating, subverting orders challenge more evident, predictable orders. Despite the rigour, the concentration, the extreme exertion that goes into creating them, music and the musical language of *My Life* move beyond the cerebral. '[But] though I could say the music brought these places "home" to me,' Hejinian writes, 'the composition itself grew increasingly strange as I listened again, less recognizable, in the dark, as when one repeats a word or phrase over and over in order to disintegrate its associations, to defamiliarize it' (1987, 113). A work of this intensity that tries so hard to construct one grammar out of another, to defamiliarize the very substance of one's world and 'self,' is an act of incredible control and precision. What makes Hejinian so successful is her 'lack of clarity,' her leap beyond pure idea to emotion, spirit, rhapsody.

'Through the window of Chartres, with no view, the light transmits the color as a scene. What then is a window' (Hejinian 1987, 65).

A window: transparent. Clear-cut reference. Hejinian offers another take on this metaphor; a 'window-language' that is not transparent, that lets both window and language exist as, and for, themselves, to demonstrate their own beauty. If language must be a window, why not one like the stained glass of Chartres, why not one of colour and texture, a composition that is its own landscape, that adds tincture to the world outside and noticeably alters what little 'reality' one perceives through it?

What then is a window

There's plenty of room' Alice says indignantly to the March Hare, the Mad Hatter, and the Dormouse (Carroll [1865] 1971, 75) when they try to dismiss her from their party. Alice is right about that and, by extension, she is unwittingly right about nonsense too. There *is* plenty of room at the tea-party table: room for Nonsense and nonsensical writers, room for traditional and experimental poets, room for pumpkins and Monkey-Folk. There is room at critical and theoretical tables for nonsense too. In fact, nonsense as a critical and theoretical tool has much to offer literary studies.

It is almost as though there were a game of infinite 'deferral' going on at the March Hare's table. The more room one sees, the more room there is. Let Alice be seated, and suddenly Violet, Guy, Lionel, and Slingsby are there. Soon Kipling, Thibaudeau, Lilburn, Joyce, Hejinian, and Hopkins are pulling up chairs. But nonsense is not *just* a tea-party. It has its own clout, and packs a punch while punch is poured.

Notes

'Loppleton Leery'

1 Thibaudeau's use of an argument makes her text's status as sound poem somewhat ambiguous since it establishes a narrative context for an essentially non-narrative form – that is if one *accepts* her argument as a reliable indicator of events to come rather than as a teasingly false start.

Chapter One

1 Carroll's Looking-Glass insects also demonstrate that, as Sherril Jaffe wittily points out in a lecture/discussion led by David Bromige (1980a, 41), there's a very little gap between *etymology* and *entomology*.

2 Carroll's *Through the Looking-Glass* appeared in December 1871, but was dated 1872; I use the latter date in my citations and the bibliography.

3 It's important to note that neither Nonsense nor nonsense is solely lexical in nature. Syntax often stands as the representative of 'sense,' or maintains its own sort of sense. Its presence is central to the symbiotic nature of both types of nonsense. Nonsense works most effectively when it is either, according to Chomsky's levels of grammaticality, 'grammatical' or 'semigrammatical.' That is, when it preserves at least a moderately accessible/translatable level of syntactic order.

4 For an extended consideration of Nonsense's relationship with visual semiotics, see Wendy Steiner's *The Colors of Rhetoric* (1982).

5 Heath insists, however, that Carroll is not a Nonsense writer but,
  because of his rigid adherence to logical and linguistic rules, an
  Absurdist (1987, 47). While Carroll's delight in following logic to its
  illogical ends may be a technique shared by Absurdist writers, I
  hesitate to label him as such. The reality that he presents is not a
  senseless one, as is that which marks Absurdist literature; rather, as
  Tigges argues, it is a reality made up of senseless language
  (1988, 128). The difference is subtle but important: one uses language
  to create a senseless reality, the other uses senseless language to create
  a reality (1988, 128). As well, his use of the narrator to remind the
  reader continually of the status of Alice's waking world works against
  any desire to read the human situation in the *Alice* books as devoid of
  meaning and order. Alice's world does have order; Carroll uses
  Nonsense to show that, within that order, disorder is necessarily
  found.

6 The tradition of the fool is not one that escaped Edward Lear's notice;
  in his introduction to *The Complete Nonsense of Edward Lear*, Holbrook
  Jackson quotes Lear's letter to his friend Fortescue asking him 'to
  "write to Lord Palmerston to ask him to ask the Queen to ask the
  King of Greece to give" him a "place" specially created, the title to be
  "Lord High Bosh and Nonsense Producer ... with permission to
  wear a fool's cap (or mitre) – three pounds of butter yearly and little
  pig, – and a small donkey to ride on" ' (1947, xvii). Lear connects himself more with the fool than with folly, as may be surmised from
  another letter, this one to his friend Drummond: '(it is not generally
  known,) that I refused the throne of Greece – King Lear the first – on
  account of the conduct of Goneril & Regan my daughters, wh. has
  disturbed me too much to allow of my attention to governing' (Noakes
  [1968] 1985, 181–2). And as Edward Lear playfully prefers domestic
  lunacies (and three pounds of butter) to King Lear's passionate madness, so too do most critics fall back onto George Pitcher's qualification
  that 'nonsense takes on the form of *something like* madness' (1965, 611;
  emphasis added) and ultimately reject madness as a synonym for
  Nonsense.

7 Rieke uses the tradition of folly to connect Nonsense to the
  Shakespearean Fool. Certainly King Lear's madness and his Fool provide obvious connections with the genre. Both characters balance
  sense with incomprehensibility, and would be solid illustrations of the
  common assertion that madness is associated with a hidden truth, that

the cryptic messages of prophecy or the phenomenon of speaking in tongues contains truths that challenge the limitations of verbal expression. They would be illustrations, as well, of the similar tendency on the part of many readers and critics to find 'sense in nonsense' and 'method in madness.' Tigges rightly classes such moments in Shakespeare as 'partial nonsense' (1988, 217), for he points out that the work as a whole is motivated by a desire to do more than contest the hidden mechanizations of sense. Yet it is hard to find anyone who juggles sense and senselessness, order and chaos, clarity of perception and mental upheaval with Shakespeare's grace and precision.

8 Essential to an understanding of nonsense, and of the tenuous blending of these groupings, is the recognition, promoted by Tigges and many other critics, that Nonsense always maintains a delicate tension between (at least) two seemingly incompatible or antithetical concepts. The issue is not one of polarity, but of duality, not of a separable either/or nature but of a multiply inclusive one.

9 Deleuze's very specific use of the word 'sense' lends itself to confusion in certain respects. His definition will not be that used throughout this study, except when he is being discussed. At all other times the less precise definition, that interchangable with 'meaning,' will be intended.

10 For instance, Thibaudeau in *from Throgmoggle & Engestchin* maintains a much more coherent deictical and syntactical than lexical order, although her poetic lines do cause some mild syntactic disruptions.

11 This was certainly a central premise in the sound poetics of Dadaist Hugo Ball, whose work is in several respects comparable to Artaud's radical experiments; for Ball, 'words were still words, units of meaning, even if they were unfamiliar combinations of letters' (Erickson 1984, 74).

12 Given the climate of the Victorian Age and its very staid and didactic approach to children's literature, what Carroll does in the *Alice* books is almost as radical as Artaud's dissolution of language nearly forty years later. Virtually from the time of its publication, *Alice's Adventures in Wonderland* was recognized as pivotal, an exceedingly radical addition to a canon comprised of the distressingly moral books of Sara Trimmer and the like.

13 Lear especially uses violence as part of his work. Take, for instance,

There was an Old Person of Buda,
Whose conduct grew ruder and ruder;
Till at last, with a hammer, they silenced his clamour,
By smashing that Person of Buda.

Figure 16 From Edward Lear *A Book of Nonsense*

'They' is symbolic of society at large (interestingly Lear's illustration shows only one threatening individual much larger than the oppressed Man of Buda), who persecutes innocent and eccentric people. But 'their' actions are qualified by the verse's entropy, its lack of linguistic progression. By encroaching upon the containment of Nonsense verse, by smashing through into the last line which is more often than not a mere repetition of (and so an affirmation of) character, violence is not without its threat. 'They' attack physically, energetically. But the linguistic resilience of 'their' victim undercuts the action; the old Person of Buda is still the last word.

14 Nonsense has often been defined in terms of its relations with itself. Ede defines Nonsense as a 'self-reflexive verbal construction' (1975, 12) throughout her dissertation on Carroll and Lear; Sonstroem, in his article on Lear and Gerard Manley Hopkins, names its strength a 'tidy self-consistency' (1967, 198). And Michael Holquist regards *The Hunting of the Snark* as a poem about itself (1969–70, 147). This is Nonsense as Deleuze construes it: something that means itself.

15 Khlebnikov, a Russian Cubo-Futurist, created *zaum'*, an invented, nonrational language (sometimes translated as 'beyonsense') with Alexei Kruchonykh. Khlebnikov believed it was sense, not nonsense (or beyonsense), that 'destroyed all artistic involvement in language' (1987, I:148). In a section introduction to a short collection of Khlebnikov's works, Charlotte Douglas explains *zaum'*: 'The word must be seen first as a function of its root, the word *um*: intellect, intelligence, reason, the rational faculty of mind. *Um* implies the creation of "pilings," the foundations of the man-made structures that must sooner or later destroy the mind's unity with the natural world. *Um* also implies the separation of thinking man from the natural stuff of language: the shape, sound, and color of words' (Khlebnikov 1985, 113).

16 Rieke insists, throughout her discussion of Joyce's work, on nonsense's excessive meaning. And Stewart, writing of Joyce's language in *Ulysses*, comments: 'Ironically, the "over-loading" of language with significance approaches the limits of language. The point where the discourse bursts with significance is the point of pure ornament and opacity' (1978, 102). Consigning Joyce's language to the limits of language is consigning it to, among other things, the field of Nonsense, a field with which he was quite familiar – if the notable presence of Lewis Carroll, the *Alice* books, and the *Sylvie and Bruno* books in *Finnegans Wake* is any indication.

17 Michael Hancher notes that the drawback to Humpty Dumpty's discussion with Alice (and one assumes with anybody) is not his use of stipulative definition, but his use of it in Looking-Glass Land where all orders are inverted (1981, 50). Humpty Dumpty is subjected to a temporal system that greatly hampers his ability to communicate; seemingly unconcerned about language's intimate relationship with temporal and causal contingencies, he chooses to speak in a manner that directly conflicts with these qualities of language.

18 Susan Stewart makes much of simultaneity in her study of Nonsense. She contends that it is an effective and frequently used method in Nonsensical writing:

It is defined as the quality of existing, happening, occurring at the same time in more than one space; the quality of being coexistent in time while being contiguous in space ... Simultaneity is neither here nor there, but the reconciliation of a paradoxical contradiction between hereness and thereness. It is like the paradox of nothingness, for it cancels itself out – to say that two events are simultaneous is to dis-

solve those events into each other in time while they cannot be dis-
solved in space, and therefore to deny the possibility of simultaneity
by saying 'two events.' (1978, 146)

19 Tigges explicitly locates that balance on the border 'between the
"nightmare of logic" and the "logic of dreams" ' (1987, 26), and Dennis
Lee considers Nonsense to be 'work which unites precise logic and
irrationality so as to make each seamless with the other' (1976, 48).
Such a balance is borne out, as Lisa Ede contends, in the very structure
of *Through the Looking-Glass*, where the dominating precision of the
chess game pattern is subtly undermined from within by the novel's
dream-like movement (1975, 76).

20 Rieke cites Plato in the *Timaeus*, where a lack of reason is associated
with the prophecies of Sibyls, and the Judeo-Christian tradition, in
which prophecies are similarly nonsensical (1984, 9). Both Huxley
(1976, 10) and Hoffstadter (1985, 226) compare Nonsense to the hidden
and seemingly senseless wisdoms of Zen Buddhism. These compari-
sons hold, in part, because of Nonsense's frequent use of 'concealment'
(Byrom 1977, 178) and because of the tendency in most religions to
discuss the ineffable in ways that defy the limitations of sense.

21 He eventually left the group and lived, with Emmy Hennings, a life of
near-seclusion as a devout Catholic.

22 According to George Pitcher in his article 'Wittgenstein, Nonsense, and
Lewis Carroll,' the two 'had radically different attitudes towards nonsense: it tortured Wittgenstein and delighted Carroll' (1965, 611).

23 An example is the game of 'Doublets,' which required its player to
make one word out of another (e.g. 'head' to 'tail') by changing one
letter at a time. The catch: at no time could the player insert a letter
that would not result in an English word. 'Heal' would be an acceptable first move; 'tead' would not.

24 For instance, Pitcher notes the similarities between Wittgenstein's
insistence that knowing what a word means in one context doesn't
ensure knowing what it means in another (one may know how to
measure distance or length, but not how to measure time) (1965, 598).
Similarly both writers attack essentialism, the idea that 'a unique set of
characteristics – constituting an essence – ... is shared by all and only
those individuals to which a certain general term (e.g., "table," "tree,"
"serpent") applies' (Pitcher 1965, 601–2).

25 A metonymic approach to language holds much potential for nonsensical disruption and warrants further investigation. Connections between

écriture féminine and metonymy have opened the way for a highly energized reading of the former, and have been useful in countering criticism of essentialism. A metonymic language based on contiguity and connection is related to nonsense not only because of the similar strategies employed by *écriture féminine* and nonsense, however. The nonsensical overlay that will be discussed in the later chapters of this study could also be construed as metonymic.

26 One needs to consider, too, linguistic versus alphabetic grounds; a transliteration of the words of one language into the alphabet of another can result in seeming nonsense though the words, when pronounced, would have sense for anyone versed in the language that had been transliterated.

'Nobody'

1 For a good part of the cummings section of this interchapter, I'm indebted to James Paul Gee's excellent reading of the poem -- 'anyone's any: A View of Language and Poetry Through an Analysis of *anyone lived in a pretty how town*' (1983).

Chapter Two

1 It almost goes without saying that any use of Kipling is problematical because of his racism and imperialism. While not blind to the offensive aspects of his work, I am unwilling to relinquish it entirely.

2 *Alice's Adventures in Wonderland*, rife as it is with notions of an unstable self, provides another playful illustration of this idea. When Alice, after eating currant cake that she finds in the rabbit hole, '[opens] out like the largest telescope that ever was' ([1865] 1971, 26), she begins talking *to* her far-away feet, and imagines sending them Christmas presents. She dismisses these thoughts, as she does so much else in Wonderland, as 'nonsense' – which is exactly what they are, though nonsense of quite a different sort than she supposes.

3 Lacan's principle of the 'unary signifier' may add to an understanding of how the semiotic functions within language, although his system of thought doesn't include Kristeva's version of the semiotic. Lacan discusses the unary signifier when considering the alienation of the subject inherent in the process of signification. Signification presents the subject with a double-bind, an either/or, which ultimately translates into a neither/nor (1973, 210–1), because it implies a choice between

being and meaning. He argues: 'If we choose being, the subject disappears, it eludes us, it falls into non-meaning. If we choose meaning, the meaning survives only deprived of that part of non-meaning that is, strictly speaking, that which constitutes in the realization of the subject, the unconscious. In other words, it is of the nature of this meaning, as it emerges in the field of the Other, to be in a large part of its field, eclipsed by the disappearance of being, induced by the very function of the signifier' (1973, 211). He depicts the interaction as two circles that overlap slightly. One circle represents being, the other meaning. The area that they share is nonmeaning or the unary signifier. There are several differences between Lacan's unary signifier and Kristeva's semiotic: the relationship of each with preconscious drives (the unary signifier is already a step away from such drives, the semiotic *is* those drives) is one example. Another is that Lacan's model has no room for anything analogous to the semiotic *within* language (Smith 1988, 121). Their similarities are what strike one most, though: each is based on a wholeness in which signifier and signified, self and other are one; and each is outside of meaning but essential to its development.

4 It is important to be aware of a counterdefinition of 'desire' elaborated in *Anti-Oedipus*. In their response to what they consider a Freudian overemphasis on the Oedipal phase, Deleuze and Guattari typify desire as in no way lacking an Other: 'Desire does not lack anything; it does not lack its object. It is, rather, the *subject* that is missing in desire, or desire that lacks a fixed subject; there is no fixed subject unless there is repression. Desire and its object are one and the same thing' (1972, 26).

5 Michel Beaujour (1968, 58) and Michael Riffaterre ([1978] 1984, 14) are among those who comment upon this poetic quality. Susan Vigeurs argues that 'all figurative language [itself an example of linguistic play (1983, 145)] begins in nonsense and depends for its success on retaining an element of that quality' (1983, 143); like figurative language, nonsense 'must be fresh enough to catch the reader off guard' (1983, 144).

6 Noticing that a linguistic device as common as hyphenation is potentially nonsensical indicates that even language that seems purely communicative may show elements of upheaval.

7 This pull to internal sound play is reminiscent of *cynghanedd*, the Welsh metrical form that rigidly requires such rhyming and alliteration.

8 Kaja Silverman explains the theory of connotation, which Barthes

develops in *S/Z* this way: 'A connotative signified or seme perpetuates the play of signification. It represents the antithesis of a transcendental signified ... The connotative signified *always* refers beyond itself, appears ... "pregnant" with additional disclosures. It constitutes a hermeneutic as well as a semic element since it prolongs the search for "truth" ... Reading or viewing ... is thus a process of "skidding" from one signified to another' (1983, 256).

Chapter Three

1 Bakhtin, writing well before Lacan, clearly does not intend his use of 'phallus' to have the meaning that the type of psychoanalytic readings frequently cited in this study would suggest. The term is retained, however, because of its important saturnalian connotations.

2 This statement should be qualified slightly. Certainly Ameslan (American Sign Language) is a physical language, not merely a series of gestures. In 'Deaf Poetics: The Signification of Silence, Poetics of Presence, and Voice of Vision' (1993), Brenda Jo Brueggemann argues cogently and convincingly for connecting a newly emerging deaf poetics with the issues raised by postmodernism, concerns often evinced by and in nonsensical language. Brueggemann outlines a poetic based on a truly physical language, one intimately tied to performance and immanence. She has initiated the theorizing of an important area of poetics, and identified what might will be considered, in the most positive sense of the word, a potentially nonsensical language.

3 For an excellent discussion of Zukofsky's use of mathematics, see Michele Leggott's *Reading 80 Flowers*.

4 Peter Quartermain notices a similar play on the letter *C* in the twelfth poem of Zukofsky's *Anew*. But he reckons Zukofsky to be playing on a wider field of association and connects the letter to, among other things, 'a cathode; an (electric) current; the speed of light; capacitance (i.e., "the ability to store a charge of electricity")' (1992, 46).

5 See Part One for a discussion of the claims by Lecercle and Deleuze.

6 Martin engages here in a rather naive formulation – his valorizing of matriarchy and primitivism becomes too quickly a romanticizing, an idealism of his own. While this does present critical problems, the crux of his argument (if warily used) is nevertheless helpful.

7 It is with some trepidation that I refer to 'this movement,' since feminism is an extremely various field, best referred to as feminisms. However, out of convenience I'll use the singular form of the word, assum-

ing that (as is the case with *all* words) its potential for entertaining difference resonates in the background.

8 It's important to keep in mind, while exploring briefly feminism's contributions to an understanding of how the body relates to nonsense, that there are at least two liberations in progress – the liberation of women (and men) from patriarchal oppression, and that of the body (male as well as female) from a linguistic repression based on limited notions of what sense is, how it functions, and what is appropriate for language to express.

9 A similar attempt to depict the flow of sexuality and desire by using a stream of consciousness technique can be found in Joyce's *Ulysses*, when the rampant physicality of Molly Bloom is evoked in her infamous monologue.

10 It's important to note the limitations of Bakhtin's carnival of genitalia. He makes a concerted effort to justify what has long been considered Rabelais's hostility towards women by tying their debasement to the cycle of birth, by making them symbolically regenerative and walking wombs (1965, 240). Yet he fails, as Wayne Booth points out in 'Freedom of Interpretation' (1982), to prove that women are in any way liberated by this spirit of carnival, by the laughter directed at, and through, them. Irigaray also, it might be argued, offers a carnival of genitalia and, like so many other theorists (Kristeva included – see 1974b 223–5), seeks through laughter an initial form of liberation (1977, 163). Her carnivalesque appeal for a revivification of woman's 'lower stratum,' of her countless erogenous zones has often been accused of being biologically and essentialist-based. But Irigaray's argument provides a scathing critique of the patriarchal thought that initially established the limiting dichotomies it at once adheres to and tries to dismantle.

11 There are problems inherent in this claim, though I stand beside it. Certainly *my* evocation of nonsense – because it grows out of my political and personal convictions – is markedly political. However, this is my own *swaying* of nonsense. Nonsense is a tool for political interpretation, and an amalgam of various political positions, but it is not a form of political interpretation in itself. It becomes such only when used, and according to the *user's* political predisposition. It is effective for precisely this reason: when reading nonsensically one may bring along almost any political agenda (barring perhaps knee-jerk conservatism), but because a nonsensical reading style is so intensely self-probing one may not apply it in the cookie-cutting fashion – roll out the poem, stamp out the ideological shape – which is often so tempting.

12 Actually a diffuse and scattered eroticism is exactly what F. preaches in Cohen's *Beautiful Losers*, though a reader isn't expected to follow his teachings verbatim. Still, a pan-orgasmic body is envisioned – 'Down with genital imperialism! All flesh can come! Don't you see what we have lost? Why have we abdicated so much pleasure to that which lives in our underwear? Orgasms in the shoulder! Knees going off like firecrackers!' (1966, 34).

Chapter Four

1 Lecercle, following Deleuze, explains it this way: 'Nonsense is a meaning-preserving activity: its implicit goal is to save meaning by maintaining the correspondence between signifier and signified which communication requires. Nonsense may fiddle with the upholstery buttons, but only to check that they are sewn on firmly and in their proper places' (1985, 140). His reading of Deleuze condemns Nonsense; not only does he dismiss many important facets of Nonsense, but he also dismisses several Nonsense works from the canon. Many of Lear's limericks, for instance, are implicitly banished – not surprisingly, perhaps, since Lecercle mentions Lear only once, and briefly at that, in his book. Also one can detect a tendency to ignore the many other ways in which nonsense exerts itself linguistically, its points of communion with poetic language.

2 I depart from Deleuze's understanding of Nonsense when I imbue it with a level of materiality that he claims is found only in schizoid language. Nonsense, as Deleuze conceives it, is wholly incorporeal, is in fact a meaning-event. I argue that while nonsense and Nonsense may serve the function that Deleuze attributes to them (stabilizing the continual deferral of sense), they simultaneously reveal the process of sense-making and superimpose upon verbal language other (often more material) systems of meaning. I propose a multiple and material function for nonsense that Deleuze does not accept; he stands here, as does his theory of the event, as an oppositional basis upon which to build.

3 One reason why the term '*Bandar*-logic' fits this theory of nonsense so nicely is that it phonically reflects the way nonsense banders/banters with logocentricism.

4 Foucault attributes this neologism to Deleuze's work because it is very much concerned with orality ('the mouth where the profundity of an oral body separates itself from incorporeal meaning' [1977, 179]), but

Deleuze's continual exploration of the margins of accepted philosophical schools of thought breaks away from the defining and confining traditions of logocentrism.

5 My borrowing of this term from Foucault displaces its sense slightly. Foucault uses it to explain Deleuze's 'event' theory this way: 'This meaning-event is always both the displacement of the present [tense of the verb to which it is fastened and which posits the event] and the eternal repetition of the infinitive' of the same verb that 'introduces meaning into language and allows it to circulate as the neutral element to which we refer in discourse' (1977, 174). I intend its use here to incorporate not only the attribution of some sort of meaning to these noises by their inclusion in the structure of Cage's lectures, but also as a term for the form of the lecture itself. Cage never asserts one crystallized meaning; many of his explorations are aleatory processes that evolve or seek out meaning in their delivery rather than proscribe it. In a way, his method of writing and delivering his lectures reflects the manner in which language grows out of a 'meaning-event' – introducing 'meaning into [his lecture] and [allowing] it to circulate as the neutral element to which we refer in discourse.'

6 To a lesser extent this is also true of the songs that Alice sings and the poems that she recites while in Wonderland. The 'revised' texts of these typically Victorian poems are too pointedly satirical to merit being called pure sound play, but they demonstrate that music has a mind of its own. Or, in more Freudian terms, they demonstrate that music is one outlet for repressed emotion; the songs that Alice sings show the dark side of Victorian morality and capitalism.

7 Velimir Khlebnikov's experiments with language and sound verify such a belief in a musical reconstitution of the sign. As W.G. Weststeijn claims, 'The accentuation of the musical aspect of the word logically resulted in a blurring of the relations between signifier, signified and referent: as regards the musical sign, these relations are basically vague' (1983, 55).

8 One of the ironies of phonocentrism is its tendency to invest sound with a present but separate meaning rather than let sound, in itself, *be* a meaning. Nonsense strives towards such a resonate meaning: sound as sound.

9 Admittedly, deconstruction attempts to break the phoneme down even further to the trace and the arche-trace (Leitch 1983, 28).

10 Winn bases his definition on ideas found in Ezra Pound's *Antheil and the Treatise on Harmony.*

11 Calling this piece Louis Zukofsky's is problematical. Although Zukofsky included it as the final movement of his very long poem *A*, the piece was actually arranged and edited by his wife, Celia, as a surprise gift for Louis. Critics rarely broach the issue of the movement's authorship; while most note with careful asides that Celia prepared the masque, they continue to discuss the piece as exemplary of Louis's work (see, for instance, Charlene Diehl-Jones's otherwise marvellous essay [1989]). In the spirit of orchestration and bricolage, Celia does pillage extant Zukofsky texts, but those very acts of orchestration and bricolage constitute composition in this movement – and often in those movements written by Louis himself.

My inclination is to name Celia as author, and to view Louis's adoption of the text as another example of the collaboration that marked their entire relationship. This view certainly seems more acceptable than Ahearn's suggestion that ' "*A*"-24 wrote itself' more or less (1983, 169). Louis and Celia collaborated frequently: most obviously on their controversial *Catullus*, on *Bottom: On Shakespeare* (the second volume of which was Celia's musical setting for Shakespeare's *Pericles*) and on *Autobiography*. To regard *'A'-24* as another example of such collaboration, but one in which Celia clearly took the lead, is not inconsistent with the Zukofskys' patterns of composition.

12 Contrary to Barry Ahearn's assertion that early in the first scene we find the Son, *Arise, Arise*'s main character, asking 'How do you catch such a bird?' (1983, 169–70), the cousin is the only character who appears – and whose lines appear – in Act One, Scene One. The Son does not appear until the final scene of the masque, Act Two, Scene Four.

13 Celia Zukofsky indicates that at no time are the words to be sung.

14 Henri Meschonnic, in his important study *Critique du rythme: Anthropologie historique du langage*, argues for a different understanding of the term 'rhythm.' For him, it is 'the continuous movement of *signifiance* constructed by the historical activity of a subject' (Bedetti 1988, 93) and 'exposes the subject (*sujet d'énonciation*) through a body language' (1988, 93). Rhythm, as he construes it, is more important than meaning, and 'as the organization of the subject in and by its language, has no further tie, except historically, with structuralism, or with its home, polemics' (1988, 96). Consequently he challenges the binary nature of the sign, its split between '*langage/langue*' and contends that the linking of rhythm and materiality maintains such a split, as does, in his view, Kristeva's definition of rhythm 'in terms of the irrational versus the rational' (1988, 101). While his approach differs from mine,

his intent is, in part, similar – to reconsider the nature of the sign (in my case, the nonsensical sign) through an understanding of how the body can 'dwell' in language.

15 While Sitwell styles her poems as dances, it is perhaps useful to note the disjunction between poem and dance. Dance as gestural, often narrative, expression is also, according to Randy Martin in *Performance as Political Act* (1990), a form of bodily memory, or body reconstruction. Some qualities of dance can't be transposed easily into language. If rhythm, as the common ground between poetry, dance and music, can help infuse one aspect of dance, into language, many of its other elements are achieved only through mimesis and intertextuality.

16 Language, as has been argued throughout this chapter, can never be just sound since even the smallest units of linguistic sound carry the residue of language's sense. Tigges overstates his case in order to emphasis the primacy of sound at times in Carroll's work, as in the Cheshire Cat's 'pig'/'fig' incident, discussed earlier.

17 Rieke indicates that Zukofsky was aware of van Rooten's text; included in his archival papers is a review of *Mots d'Heures* clipped from a newspaper (1992, 214).

18 Thibaudeau's poem poses an interesting problem as a sound poem because it unites linguistic upheaval with narrative frame. The argument triggers interpretative strategies, suggests what a reader might listen for. It provides a possibility for meaning beyond phonemic vigour and so moves the text towards narrative, foregrounding the process of reading. The disjunction between the narrative framework, which is supplied by the argument, and the poem is so obvious, and the connection between them is so tenuous, a reader cannot avoid facing the arbitrariness inherent in interpretation. This is even more evident in two of Thibaudeau's other *Throgmoggle* poems; their 'arguments' read: 'Inwhich Throgmoggle and Engestchin spend an Evening with the Bird People and hear of varieties they never knew existed,' and 'Inwhich Throgmoggle and Engestchin are Expecting a Light, Refreshing Comedy.'

19 McCaffery might also have called for a new critical form, as well as vocabulary, to treat sound poetry appropriately, though it is perhaps just that a written paper cannot possibly do justice to any actual sound poem since it can't 'reproduce it.' These poems participate entirely in Ong's presence of evanescence; even their textual notation (which often borders on concrete poetry or abstract art) can give no precision. In sound poetry, the moment of performance is everything.

20 McCaffery's article suggests that both Paula Claire and Bob Cobbing work together on this sounding of objects; Claire, however, claims this is an inaccuracy that has lead to some confusion in the past. While the two have collaborated, they have not done so on the projects mentioned in the context of McCaffery's statement. Those works were Claire's *Cabbage Brain, 1978* and *Stonetones, Writers Forum, 1974*. Claire observes this in a letter of 9 April 1993, and adds 'When I improvise with natural objects, I yearn to become one with them, express their being in sound. Sound is spirit in substance, animates substance.'

'O jongleurs, O belly laughs'

1 I don't intend to suggest that all versions of the nonsensical body are theological or pose proofs for the doctrines of transubstantiation, consubstantiation, or Incarnation. However, given Lilburn's theological background (he was a Jesuit priest for years) and the influence that that background appears to have upon his poetic statements, it seems appropriate to note the affinities that the nonsensical body has with the doctrines mentioned above. All of these require one to reconsider the orientation of specific bodies within the world as a result of the (metaphorical, in some cases) merger or union of seeming oppositions, be it spirit and flesh or symbolic and semiotic modes.

Chapter Five

1 Here the 'L=A=N=G=U=A=G=E' writers follow the lead of Khlebnikov, who Charlotte Douglas says 'managed to create an entire poetics in that area of language the Anglo-Saxon tradition tends to belittle as "play" – neologisms, palindromes, riddles, puns' (Khlebnikov 1985, 6).
2 The poem, with its scattered appearance, presents the illusion of randomness, but is not an actual random or chance text. There is some element of conscious choice that determines at least one axis of the poem – for instance, Andrews chose the words of the poem, and chose ones that could be configured into a more or less meaningful text. Such a contention implicitly challenges the possibility of the random text; even the chance works Cage produced using the I Ching have behind them the conscious choice to *use* the I Ching as a method for producing a text.
3 George Hartley has recently suggested to me that McCaffery's fly be

read not as meaning per se, but as a metaphor for the self. Such a reading suggests that rather than seeking a nonreferential language, McCaffery may be challenging the illusion of the stable and fully formed 'self,' and would certainly be consistent with many of McCaffery's other writings. Hartley's take on this metaphor is both intriguing and useful, and deserves far more consideration than time constraints allow me to give it here.

4 This essay appeared in an earlier version titled 'The Death of the Subject: The Implications of Counter-communication in Recent Language-Centered Writing.'

5 It is important to note that while Hartley offers a sound analysis of some of McCaffery's work, he ultimately presents a somewhat lopsided view, wholly ignoring all of McCaffery's more 'conventional' writing – conventional in the sense that he uses whole words, phrases, sometimes even syntactically correct sentences. Every piece by McCaffery, that Hartley refers to is a graphemic 'collage' or sound poem. Thus, while Hartley gives a good reading of McCaffery's theoretical stances (better of his earlier ones than his later ones), he fails to consider many of McCaffery's writings that are more muted, less radical. McCaffery is willing and able to use referential language in exciting and innovative ways; he doesn't limit himself solely to a pure materiality.

6 Jackson Mac Low offers a telling response to McCaffery's original claim of fetishism in 'Language-centred' when he asks: 'What could be more of a fetish or more alienated than slices of language stripped of reference?' – if it *could* be, that is. Mac Low contends that it's impossible to subtract all reference from language (1986, 492).

7 One of the most problematical aspects of relating reference with capitalism is the fact that reference existed as a central function of language long before capitalism existed. While some 'L=A=N=G=U=A=G=E' poets might defend their position by suggesting that the advent of written language initiated a division in society between the literate and the nonliterate, and by extension the upper and the lower classes, such a defence seems naive, and uses an extremely loose definition of capitalism. The capitalist system may not urge an engagement with language's materiality, but neither do many noncapitalist societies. At best, then, the terminology criticizing and explaining capitalism can be used *metaphorically* to provide one way of interpreting how language may function.

8 In a fascinating essay, 'Strangeness,' Lyn Hejinian meditates on the

possibilities of another form of realism. She says, 'I don't mean after-the-fact realism, with its emphasis on the world described (the objects of description), nor do I want to focus on an organizing subjectivity (that of the perceiver-describer); nor, finally, am I securing the term to a theory of language. I propose description as a method of invention and of composition' (1989, 32). Hejinian uses the analogy of scientists or early explorers who, not knowing what would be valuable about their new discoveries, made note of all things equally. Such realism revels not in ordering the world, but in pointing to it. She suggests, 'it is exactly the strangeness that results from a description of the world given in the terms "there it is," "there it is," "there it is" that restores realness to things in the world and separates things from ideology' (1989, 44). What she calls for is a realism that escapes the constraints of genre and that, recognizing the fullness of language, presents a reality 'ordered' sensually and linguistically. This, as will be seen, is the order of *My Life*.

9 Silliman's text, originally printed in *A Hundred Posters* 14 appears in its unrevised version in *The L=A=N=G=U=A=G=E Book* (1984a, 121–32). A slightly modified version is in Silliman's volume of collected essays, *The New Sentence*. All references to the essay, except the one to which this note is appended, are from the modified version. Part of the quotation that follows has been removed in the newest version of the essay; this removal does not alter Silliman's stance about gestural language. Because the unrevised version fits more smoothly and clearly into the process of my argument, I have chosen to use it here.

10 I should reiterate that this 'movement,' like any other group of people, is not in complete agreement over any of the issues raised. This generalization indicates a point of relative consensus that is attended by a great many subtleties and points of contention.

11 Clearly Bernstein makes a distinction between critical and creative writing here. While many 'L=A=N=G=U=A=G=E' poets, including Bernstein, produce theoretical and critical writings that defy the traditional and communicative norms of such genres, the attempt to write about abstractions in a rematerialized language emphasizes the limitations of a fully material means of communication. The quotation from Bernstein to which this note is appended, for instance, would be vastly different (and possibly less effective) if he used language that approached the level of materiality that McCaffery originally sought.

12 Nichol's playful reconfiguration of language here uses another technique, abbreviation, which is also potentially nonsensical since it alters

and draws attention to a word's material nature (visual, phonic) while maintaining its referential nature.

13 Khlebnikov also suggested that the focusing on the material nature (or musical aspect) of language resulted in an altering of relations between the signifier and the signified. (See Weststeijn 1983, 46–7; 84–5.)

14 It should be noted that the text of sound poetry constitutes a special case that is, if anything, agrammatical – especially if McCaffery's characterization of the texts for sound poetry as a thetic interface is accepted. Since the thetic is *not* a part of the symbolic, merely the point of transition into, or the point of creation of, the symbolic, the thetic can claim no real degree of grammaticality. Rather it has a peripheral relationship that does not actively participate in grammatical production or destruction. Such is the *text* of the sound poem; the actual performance, however, is, according to McCaffery, the oral release of libidinal drives and so is usually an ungrammatical assault on meaning and order.

15 Although I don't agree with all of DeKoven's conclusions, her study is a fine application of Kristeva's theory of poetic language to Stein's work and well worth the careful consideration of anyone interested in reading Stein's work from either a Kristevan or a nonsensical point of view.

16 Peter Quartermain (1992, 23) offers a brief but lively reading of *Roast Potatoes* that both complements and extends my small efforts here.

17 In 'Poetry and Grammar,' Stein outlines her contempt for the comma:

As I say commas are servile and they have no life of their own, and their use is not a use, it is a way of replacing one's own interest and I do decidedly like to like my own interest my own interest in what I am doing. A comma by helping you along holding your coat for you and putting on your shoes keeps you from living your life as actively as you should lead it and to me for many years and I still do feel that way about it only now I do not pay as much attention to them, the use of them was positively degrading. (1935a, 219–20)

Stein's ironic use of commas in the midst of such scathing condemnation is a delightful poke at herself.

18 Silliman's choice not to use question marks in *Ketjak* qualifies the referentiality of some of its sentences; interrogative words don't function in their traditional sense.

19 Since *Ketjak* is published by This, a small press in San Francisco, Silliman's many references to 'this' may be playfully self-referential too.

They may also 'refer' to the magazine by the same name. It is actually *This* magazine which Silliman is discussing in 'Language, Realism, Poetry' when he comments on the nature of the word 'this.'

'What then is a window'

1 These theoretical statements, like those in Silliman's *Ketjak* (1978), are of no more or less importance than any other sentence in this text. To privilege any one of them would be to undermine one of the book's (and the movement's) premises – that language is valuable as much for what it *is* as for what it points to or means.

Bibliography

—◆—

Ahearn, Barry. 1983. *Zukofsky's 'A': An Introduction*. Berkeley: University of California Press

Albert, Jonathan. 1982. 'A Language of Spoken Movement.' *Open Letter* 5.3: 11–16

Altman, Charles F. 1981. 'Intratextual Rewriting: Textuality as Language Formation.' In *The Sign in Music and Literature*, edited by Wendy Steiner, 39–51. Austin, Texas: University of Texas Press

Andrews, Bruce, and Charles Bernstein. 1984a. 'Repossessing the Word.' In *The L=A=N=G=U=A=G=E Book*, edited by Bruce Andrews and Charles Bernstein, ix–xi. Carbondale, Illinois: Southern Illinois University Press

Andrews, Bruce. 1984b. 'Text and Context.' In *The L=A=N=G=U=A=G=E Book*, 31–8

– 1984c. 'Writing Social Work & Political Practice.' In *The L=A=N=G=U=A=G=E Book*, 133–6. See Andrews and Bernstein 1984a

Arthos, John. 1974. *Masque*. In *Princeton Encyclopedia of Poetry & Poetics*. Enl. ed., edited by Alex Preminger et al. Princeton: Princeton University Press, 474–5

Auden, W.H. 1979. *In Memory of W.B. Yeats*. In *Selected Poems*, edited by Edward Mendelson, 80–3. New York: Vintage-Random House

Baier, A.C. 1967. 'Nonsense.' In *Encyclopedia of Philosophy*, edited by Paul Edwards, Vol 5:520–2. New York: Macmillan Company & The Free Press

Bakhtin, Mikhail. 1965. *Tvorcestvo Fransua Rable i narodnaja kul'tura srednevekov'ja*. Moscow: Khudozhestvennia literature. Translated by Hélène Iswolsky under the title *Rabelais and His World*. 1968; Bloomington, Indiana: Midland Book – University of Indiana Press, 1984

Ball, Hugo. 1927. *Die Flucht aus der Zeit*. Munich: Duncker und Humblot. Translated by Ann Raimes under the title *Flight Out of Time*, edited by John Elderfield. New York: Viking Press, 1974

Baring-Gould, Ceil, and William S. [1962] 1967. *The Annotated Mother Goose*. New York: Meridian–World Publishing

Barthes, Roland. 1964. *Elements de Sémiologie*. Paris: Éditions du Seuil. Translated by Annette Lavers and Colin Smith under the title *Elements of Semiology*. In *Writing Degree Zero and Elements of Semiology*, 1967. Boston: Beacon Press, 1970

– 1970. *S/Z*. Paris: Éditions du Seuil. Translated by Richard Miller. New York: Hill and Wang, 1974

– 1973. *Le Plaisir du texte*. Paris: Éditions du Seuil. Translated by Richard Miller under the title *The Pleasure of the Text*. New York: Hill and Wang, 1975

– 1977. 'The Grain of the Voice.' In *Image-Music-Text*, translated by Stephen Heath, 179–89. Glasgow: Fontana–Wm. Collins and Sons, Ltd

Bartlett, Lee. 1986. 'What is "Language Poetry"?' *Critical Inquiry* 12:741–52

Baum, Alwin L. 1987. 'Carroll's *Alices*: The Semiotics of Paradox.' In *Lewis Carroll: Modern Critical Views*, edited by Harold Bloom, 65–81. New York: Chelsea House

Beaujour, Michel. 1968. 'The Game of Poetics.' *Yale French Studies* 41:58–67

Bedetti, Gabriella. 1988. 'Interview: Henri Meschonnic.' *Diacritics* 18.3:93–111

Bernstein, Charles. 1986. *Content's Dream: Essays, 1975–1984*. Los Angeles: Sun & Moon Press

Binhammer, Katherine. 1991. 'Metaphor or Metonymy? The Question of Essentialism in Cixous.' *Tessera* 10:65–79

Blacking, John. 1981. 'The Problem of "Ethnic" Perceptions in the Semiotics of Music.' In *The Sign in Music and Literature*, 184–94. See Altman 1981

Bloom, Harold. 1987. Introduction. In *Lewis Carroll: Modern Critical Views*, 1–11. See Baum 1987

Bogue, Ronald. 1989. *Deleuze and Guttari*. London: Routledge

Booth, Wayne C. 1982. 'Freedom of Interpretation: Bakhtin and the Challenge of Feminist Criticism.' *Critical Inquiry* 9:45–76

Boulez, Pierre. 1966. *Relevés d'apprenti*. Paris: Éditions du Seuil. Translated by Herbert Weinstock under the title *Notes of an Apprenticeship*, edited by Paul Thevenin. New York: Alfred A. Knopf, 1968

Bowering, George. 1979. 'Given This Body: An interview with Daphne Marlatt.' *Open Letter* 4.3:32–88

Bringhurst, Robert. 1986. *Pieces of Map, Pieces of Music*. Toronto: McClelland and Stewart

Bromige, David. 1980a. 'Intention & Poetry.' *TALKS: Hills* 6/7:25–49

– 1980b. 'My Poetry.' In *My Poetry*, 11–20. Berkeley, California: The Figures

Brossard, Nicole. 1985. *La Lettre aérienne*. Montreal: Les éditions du remue ménage. Translated by Marlene Wildeman under the title *The Aerial Letter*. Toronto: The Women's Press, 1988

Brueggemann, Brenda Jo. 1993. 'Deaf Poetics: The Significance of Silence, Poetics of Presence, and Voice of Vision.' A paper presented at the 21st Annual Twentieth-Century Literature Conference, University of Louisville, Louisville, Kentucky, 25–27 February

Bruns, Gerald L. 1974. *Modern Poetry and the Idea of Language: A Critical and Historical Study*. New Haven: Yale University Press

Bush, Jamie. 1987. 'Ted Hughes's Concept of Language: Beyond Inscription.' Unpublished essay

Byrd, Don. 1983. 'The Poetry of Production.' *Sagetrieb* 2.2:7–43

Byrom, Thomas. 1977. *Nonsense and Wonder: The Poems and Cartoons of Edward Lear*. New York: Brandywine Press–E.P. Dutton

Cage, John. 1961. *Silence*. Middletown, Connecticut: Wesleyan University Press

– 1979. *Empty Words: Writings '73–'78*. Middletown, Connecticut: Wesleyan University Press

Cammaerts, Emile. 1925. *The Poetry of Nonsense*. London: George Routledge & Sons Ltd

Carroll, Lewis. [1865] 1971. *Alice's Adventures in Wonderland*. In *Alice in Wonderland*, edited by Donald J. Gray, 1–99. New York: W.W. Norton & Co

– [1872] 1971. *Through the Looking-Glass*. In *Alice in Wonderland*, 101–209. *See* Carroll [1865] 1971

– [1876] 1971. *The Hunting of the Snark*. In *Alice in Wonderland*, 211–30. *See* Carroll [1865] 1971

– [1889] 1976. *Sylvie and Bruno*. In *The Complete Works of Lewis Carroll*, 277–503. 1936; New York: Vintage–Random House

– [1893] 1976. *Sylvie and Bruno Concluded*. In *The Complete Works of Lewis Carroll*, 509–749. *See* Carroll [1989] 1976

Chesterton, G.K. 1913. 'A Defence of Nonsense.' In *A Century of English Essays: An Anthology Ranging from Caxton to R.L. Stevenson & the Writers of Our Own Time*, edited by Ernest Rhys and Lloyd Vaughan, 446–50. London: J.M. Dent & Sons Ltd

– 1953a. 'How Pleasant to Know Mr. Lear.' In *A Handful of Authors: Essays on Books and Writers*, edited by Dorothy Collins, 120–4. London: Sheed and Ward

– 1953b. 'Lewis Carroll.' In *A Handful of Authors*, 112–19. *See* Chesterton 1953a

Chilton, Harrison Randolph. 1981. 'The Object beyond the Image: A Study of Four Objectivist Poets.' Ph.D. diss., University of Wisconsin, Madison

Chukovsky, K. 1968. *From Two to Five*. Berkeley: University of California Press

Cixous, Hélène. 1975. *La Jeune Née* by Hélène Cixous and Catherine Clément. Paris: Union Generale d'éditions. Translated by Betsy Wing under the title *The Newly Born Woman*. Minneapolis: University of Minnesota Press, 1986

Claire, Paula. 1984. 'The Notation of My Sound Poetry.' *Open Letter* 5.7:56–74

– 1993. Letter to Marnie Parsons, 9 April

Clark, Katerina and Michael Holquist. 1984. *Mikhail Bakhtin*. Cambridge, Massachusetts: Belknap Press–Harvard University Press

Clement, Catherine. 1975. *La Jeune Née* by Hélène Cixous and Catherine Clément. *See* Cixous 1975

Cobbing, Bob. 1978. 'Some Statements on Sound Poetry.' In *Sound Poetry: A Catalogue for the Eleventh International Sound Poetry Festival*, edited by Steve McCaffery and bp Nichol, 39–40. Toronto: Underwhich Editions

Cohen, Leonard. 1966. *Beautiful Losers*. Toronto: NCL–McClelland and Stewart

Cohen, Morton N., ed. 1979. *The Letters of Lewis Carroll*, Vol. 1. New York: Oxford University Press

Cooke, Raymond. 1987. *Velimir Khlebikov: A Critical Study*. Cambridge: Cambridge University Press

Copeland, Carolyn Faunce. 1975. *Language & Time & Gertrude Stein*. Iowa City: University of Iowa Press

Corman, Cid. 1979. 'In the Event of Words.' In *Louis Zukofsky: Man and Poet*, edited by Carroll F. Terrell, 305–36. Orono, Maine: National Poetry Foundation/University of Maine at Orono

Coward, Rosalind, and John Ellis. 1977. *Language and Materialism*. London: Routledge and Kegan Paul

Crewes, Judith. 1987. 'Plain Superficiality.' In *Lewis Carroll: Modern Critical Views*, 83–102. *See* Baum 1987

Culler, Jonathan. 1982. *On Deconstruction: Theory and Criticism after Structuralism*. Ithaca, New York: Cornell University Press cummings, e.e. 1959. 'anyone lived in a pretty how town.' In *100 Selected Poems*, 73–4. New York: Grove Press Inc

Darragh, Tina. 1984. 'Procedure.' *The L=A=N=G=U=A=G=E Book*, 107–8. See Andrews and Bernstein 1984a

– 1987. 'oilfish' to 'old chap' for 'C'. In *'Language' Poetries: An Anthology*, edited by Douglas Messerli, 156. New York: New Directions Press

Davenport, Guy. 1974. 'Zukofsky's "A"-24.' *Parnassus* 2 (Spring/Summer): 15–24

– 1979. 'Zukofsky's English Catullus.' In *Louis Zukofsky: Man and Poet*, 365–70. See Corman 1979

DeKoven, Marianne. 1983. *A Different Language: Gertrude Stein's Experimental Writing*. Madison, Wisconsin: University of Wisconsin Press

Deleuze, Gilles. 1969. *Logique du Sens*. Paris: Les éditions de Minuit. Translated by Mark Lester and Charles Stivale under the title *The Logic of Sense*, edited by Constantin V. Boundas. New York: Columbia University Press, 1990

Deleuze, Gilles, and Félix Guattari. 1972. *L'anti-Oedipe*. Paris: Les éditions de Minuit. Translated by Robert Hurley, Mark Seem, and Helen R. Lane under the title *Anti-Oedipus*, 1977. Minneapolis: University of Minnesota Press, 1983

Dembo, L.S. 1979. 'Louis Zukofsky: Objectivist Poetics and the Quest for Form.' In *Louis Zukofsky: Man and Poet*, 283–303. See Corman 1979

Derrida, Jacques. 1967a. *De la grammatologie*. Paris: Les éditions de Minuit. Translated by Gayatri Chakravorty Spivak under the title *Of Grammatology*. Baltimore and London: The Johns Hopkins University Press, 1974

– 1967b. *La Voix et le Phénomène*. Paris: Presses Universitaires de France. Translated by David B. Allison under the title *Speech and Phenomena*. Evanston, Illinois: Northwestern University Press, 1973

– 1967c. *L'écriture et la différance*. Paris: Éditions du Seuil. Translated by Alan Bass under the title *Writing and Difference*. Chicago: University of Chicago Press, 1978

Dewdney, Christopher. 1983. *Predators of the Adoration: Selected Poems, 1972–82*. Toronto: Modern Canadian Poets Series, McClelland and Stewart

Diehl-Jones, Charlene. 1989. 'Sounding "A".' *Line* 14 (Fall): 52–71

Dubnick, Randa. 1984. *The Structure of Obscurity: Gertrude Stein, Language and Cubism*. Urbana and Chicago: University of Illinois Press

Dutton, Paul. 1989. 'bp Nichol and the Past-Present of a Future Music.' *Musicworks* 44:4–16

Ede, Lisa S. 1975. 'The Nonsense Literature of Edward Lear and Lewis Carroll.' Ph. D. diss., Ohio State University, Columbus, Ohio

Eliot, T.S. 1942. *The Music of Poetry*. Folcroft, Pennsylvania: The Folcroft Press, Inc

– 1951. 'Dante.' In *Selected Essays*, 237–77. London: Faber and Faber

Erickson, John D. 1984. *Dada Performance, Poetry, and Art*. Boston: Twayne Publishers

Farwell, Marilyn R. 1977. 'Adrienne Rich and an Organic Feminist Criticism.' *College English* 39.2:191–203

Forrest-Thomson, Veronica. 1978. *Poetic Artifice: A Theory of Twentieth-Century Poetry*. Manchester: Manchester University Press

Foucault, Michel. 1961. *Histoire de la Folie*. Paris: Librairie Plon. Translated by Richard Howard under the title *Madness and Civilization: A History of Insanity in the Age of Reason*, 1965. New York: Vintage–Random House, 1973

– 1977. 'Theatrum Philosophicum.' In *Language, Counter-Memory, Practice: Selected Essays and Interviews*, translated by Donald F. Bouchard and Sherry Simon, 165–96, edited by Donald F. Bouchard. Ithaca, New York: Cornell University Press

Fredman, Stephen. 1983. *Poet's Prose: The Crisis in American Verse*. Cambridge, England: Cambridge University Press

Freud, Sigmund. 1900. *Die Traumdeutung*. Leipzig und Wien: Franz Deuticke. Translated by A.A. Brill under the title *The Interpretation of Dreams*, 1913. New York: The Modern Library, 1950

– 1905. *Der Witz und seine Beziehung zum Unbewussten*. Leipzig und Wien: Franz Deuticke. Translated by James Strachey under the title *Jokes and Their Relation to the Unconscious*, edited by Angela Richards, 1960. London: Penguin–Viking Books, 1976

Frye, Northrop. 1957. *Anatomy of Criticism: Four Essays*. Princeton: Princeton University Press

Fuss, Diana. 1989. *Essentially Speaking: Feminism, Nature and Difference*. New York: Routledge

Gardner, Martin, 1970. *The Annotated Alice*. Harmondsworth, England: Penguin Books

Gee, James Paul. 1983. 'anyone's any: A View of Language and Poetry Through an Analysis of "anyone lived in a pretty how town." ' *Language and Style* 16.2:123–37

Gorey, Edward. 1989. *The Helpless Doorknob: A Shuffled Story*. n.p

Gott, Richard. 1988. Review of Hugh Haughton's *The Chatto Book of Nonsense*. *The Manchester Guardian* (4 December): 37

Grenier, Robert. 1986. 'Notes on Coolidge, Objectives, Zukofsky, Romanticism, And &.' In *In The American Tree*, edited by Ron Silliman, 530–43. Orono, Maine: National Poetry Foundation-University of Maine at Orono

Haas, Robert. 1978. *Twentieth Century Pleasures*. New York: Random House

Haight, M.R. 1971. 'Nonsense.' *British Journal of Aesthetics* 11.3:247–56

Hancher, Michael. 1981. 'Humpty Dumpty and Verbal Meaning.' *Journal of Aesthetics and Art Criticism*. 40.1:49–58

Hanslick, Eduard. 1922. *Vom Musikalisch-Schonen*. (13th–15th edition). Leipzig: Breitkopf und Hartel. Translated by Gustav Cohen under the title *The Beautiful in Music*, edited by Morris Weitz. New York: Bobbs-Merrill Co., Inc., 1957

Hartley, George. 1989. *Textual Politics and the Language Poets*. Bloomington and Indianapolis: Indiana University Press

Hatlen, Burton. 1979. 'Zukofsky as Translator.' In *Louis Zukofsky: Man and Poet*, 345–64. *See* Corman 1979

Haughton, Hugh, 1988. *The Chatto Book of Nonsense Poetry*. London: Chatto & Windus

Hayman, Ronald. 1977. *Artaud and After*. Oxford: Oxford University Press

Heath, Peter. 1987. 'The Philosopher's Alice.' In *Lewis Carroll: Modern Critical Views*, 45–52. *See* Baum 1987

Hejinian, Lyn. 1984a. 'If Written is Writing.' In *The L=A=N=G=U=A=G=E Book*, 29–30. *See* Andrews and Bernstein 1984a

– 1984b. 'The Rejection of Closure.' *Poetics Journal* 4:134–43

– 1987. *My Life*. Los Angeles: Sun & Moon Press

– 1989. 'Strangeness.' *Poetics Journal* 8:32–45

Henkle, Roger B. 1973. 'The Mad Hatter's World.' *The Virginia Quarterly Review* 49.1:99–117

Hoffstadter, Douglas. 1985. *Metamagical Themas: Questing for the Essence of Mind and Pattern*. New York: Basic Books, Inc

Holquist, Michael. 1969–70. 'What is a Boojum?: Nonsense and Modernism.' *Yale French Studies* XLIII:145–64

Hopkins, Gerard Manley. 1970. *The Poems of Gerard Manley Hopkins*. (Fourth Edition), edited by W.H. Gardner and N.H. MacKenzie. Oxford: Oxford University Press

Howe, Susan. 1987. '*from* Speeches at the Barriers.' In *'Language' Poetries: An Anthology*, 34–6. *See* Darragh 1987

Huizinga, Johan. [1950] 1955. *Homo Ludens: A Study of the Play-Element in Culture*. Boston: Beacon Press

Huxley, Francis. 1976. *The Raven and the Writing Desk*. London: Thames and Hudson

Irigaray, Luce. 1974. *Speculum de l'autre femme*. Paris: Les éditions de Minuit. Translated by Gillian C. Gill under the title *Speculum of the Other Woman*. Ithaca, New York: Cornell University Press, 1985

– 1977. *Ce Sexe qui n'en est pas un*. Paris: Les éditions de Minuit. Translated by Catherine Porter and Carolyn Burke under the title *This Sex Which Is Not One*. Ithaca, New York: Cornell University Press, 1985

Joyce, James. [1939] 1976. *Finnegans Wake*. New York: Penguin–Viking Books

Khlebnikov, Velimir. 1976. *Snake Train: Poetry and Prose*, edited by Gary Kern. Introduction by Edward J. Brown. Translated by Gary Kern, Richard Sheldon, Edward J. Brown, Neil Cornwell, Lily Feiler. Ann Arbor, Michigan: Ardis Press

– 1985. *The King of Time: Selected Writings of the Russian Futurian*. Translated by Paul Schmidt, edited by Charlotte Douglas. Cambridge, Massachusetts: Harvard University Press

– 1987. *Collected Works* Vol. I. Translated by Paul Schmidt, edited by Charlotte Douglas. Cambridge, Massachusetts: Harvard University Press

Kipling, Rudyard. [1894] 1987. *The Jungle Book*. London: Puffin–Penguin Books

Korg, Jacob. 1979. *Language in Modern Literature: Innovation and Experiment*. New York: Barnes and Noble

Kristeva, Julia. 1974a. *Des Chinoises*. Paris: édition des Femmes. Translated by Anita Barrows under the title *About Chinese Women*. London: Marion Boyars, 1974

– 1974b. *La révolution du poétique langue*. Paris: Éditions du Seuil. Translated by Margaret Waller under the title *Revolution in Poetic Language*. New York: Columbia University Press, 1984

– 1980. *Desire in Language: A Semiotic Approach to Literature and Art*, edited by Leon S. Roudiez. Translated by Thomas Gora, Alice Jardin, Leon S. Roudiez. New York: Columbia University Press

– 1981. *La langue, cet inconnu*. Paris: Éditions du Seuil. Translated by Anne M. Menke under the title *Language: The Unknown*. New York: Columbia University Press, 1989

– 1983. *Histoires d'amour*. Paris: Éditions Denoel. Translated by Leon S. Roudiez under the title *Tales of Love*. New York: Columbia University Press, 1987

– 1985. 'The Speaking Subject.' In *On Signs*, edited by Marshall Blonsky, 210–20. Baltimore: Johns Hopkins University Press

Lacan, Jacques. 1973. *Les Quatre Concepts Fundamentaux de la Psychanalyse*. Paris: Éditions du Seuil. Translated by Alan Sheridan under the title *The Four Fundamental Concepts of Psycho-Analysis*, edited by Jacques-Alain Miller. New York: W.W. Norton & Co., 1977

Lear, Edward. 1947. *The Complete Nonsense of Edward Lear*, edited by Holbrook Jackson. London: Faber and Faber Ltd

Lecercle, Jean-Jacques. 1985. *Philosophy through the Looking-Glass: Language, Nonsense, Desire*. La Salle, Illinois: Open Court

Lechte, John. 1990. *Julia Kristeva*. London: Routledge

Lee, Dennis. 1976. 'Roots and Play: Writing as a 35-Year-Old Children.' *Canadian Children's Literature* 4:28–58

– 1977. *Garbage Delight*. Toronto: Macmillan of Canada

Leggott, Michele. 1989. *Reading Zukofsky's '80 Flowers.'* Baltimore and London: Johns Hopkins University Press

Leitch, Vincent B. 1983. *Deconstructive Criticism: An Advanced Introduction*. New York: Columbia University Press

Lennon, John. 1964. *In His Own Write*. London: Jonathan Cape

– 1965. *A Spaniard in the Works*. London: Jonathan Cape

Lilburn, Tim. 1986. *Names of God*. Lantzville, British Columbia: Oolichan Books

– 1987. 'Thoughts toward a Christian Poetics.' *Brick: A Journal of Reviews* 29:34–6

Livingston, Myra Cohn. 1981. 'Nonsense Verse: The Complete Escape.' *Celebrating Children's Books*, edited by B. Hearne, M. Kaye, 122–39. New York: Lothrop, Lee and Shepherd Books

Mac Low, Jackson. 1986. 'Language-centered.' *In The American Tree*, 491–5. See Grenier 1986

Marlatt, Daphne. 1984. *Touch to My Tongue*. Edmonton, Alberta: Longspoon Press

Martin, Randy. 1990. *Performance as Political Act: The Embodied Self*. New York: Critical Perspectives in Social Theory, Bergin and Garvey Publishers

Martin, Stephen-Paul. 1988. *Open Form and the Feminine Imagination. (The Politics of Reading in Twentieth-Century Innovative Writing)*. Washington, DC: Maisonneuve Press

McCaffery, Steve. 1978a. 'Sound Poetry: A Survey.' In *Sound Poetry: A Catalogue*, 6–18. See Cobbing 1978

– 1978b. 'Text-sound, Energy and Performance.' *Sound Poetry: A Catalogue*, 72–3. See Cobbing 1978

– 1984a. 'From the Notebooks.' In *The L=A=N=G=U=A=G=E Book*, 159–62. See Andrews and Bernstein 1984a

- 1984b. 'Intraview.' In *The L=A=N=G=U=A=G=E Book*, 189. *See* Andrews and Bernstein 1984a
- 1986. *North of Intention: Critical Writings, 1973–1986*. New York and Toronto: Roof Books/Nightwood Editions
- 1987. *Evoba: The Investigations Meditations, 1976–78*. Toronto: Coach House Press

McGann, Jerome J. 1987. 'Contemporary Poetry, Alternate Routes.' Critical Inquiry 13:624–47

McHale, Brian. 1992. 'Making (Non)sense of Postmodernist Poetry.' In *Language, Text and Context: Essays in Stylistics*, edited by Michael Toolan, 6–35. London and New York: Routledge

McKay, Don. 1989. 'Notes on Poetic Attention.' In *The Second MacMillan Anthology*, edited by John Metcalf and Leon Rooke, 207–08. Toronto: MacMillan.

Messerli, Douglas. 1987. 'Introduction.' In *'Language' Poetries: An Anthology*, 1–11. *See* Darragh 1987

Miller, Edmund. 1987. 'The *Sylvie and Bruno* Books as Victorian Novel.' In *Lewis Carroll: Modern Critical Views*, 53–63. *See* Baum 1987

Minh-ha, Trinh T. 1989. *Woman, Native, Other: Writing Postcoloniality and Feminism*. Bloomington, Indiana: Indiana University Press

Moi, Toril. 1985. *Sexual/Textual Politics: Feminist Literary Theory*. London: New Accents Series Methuen

Nichol, bp. 1969. *The Aleph Beth Book*. Ottawa: Oberon Press
- 1970a. *The Cosmic Chef: An Evening of Concrete*. Ottawa: Oberon Press
- 1970b. *Still Water*. Vancouver, British Columbia: Talonbooks
- 1982. *The Martyrology Book 5*. Toronto: Coach House Press
- 1987. 'Primary Days: Housed with the Coach at the Press, 1965 to 1987.' *Provincial Essays* 4:19–25

Noakes, Vivien. [1968] 1985. *Edward Lear: The Life of a Wanderer*. London: Ariel Books-BBC

Norris, Christopher. 1982. *Deconstruction: Theory and Practice*. London: Methuen

Olson, Charles. 1965. *Proprioception*. San Francisco: Writing–Four Seasons Foundation
- 1966. *Selected Writings*, edited by Robert Creeley. New York: New Directions Press

Ong, Walter. 1967. *The Presence of the Word*. New Haven: Yale University Press

Orlov, Henry. 1981. 'Towards a Semiotics of Music.' In *The Sign in Music and Literature*, 131–7. *See* Altman 1981

Paget, Richard Arthur. [1930] 1963. *Human Speech*. London: Routledge and Kegan Paul

Palmer, Michael. 1987. 'The man by contrast is fixed symmetrically.' In *Talking Poetry: Conversations in the Workshop with Contemporary Poets*, edited by Lee Bartlett, 125–48. Albuquerque, New Mexico: University of New Mexico Press

Partridge, Eric. 1950. 'The Nonsense Words of Edward Lear and Lewis Carroll.' In *Here, There and Everywhere: Essays Upon Language*, 162–88. London: Hamish Hamilton

Peake, Mervyn. [1972] 1983. *A Book of Nonsense*. Harmondsworth: Penguin Books

Perelman, Bob. 1984a. ' "*A*"-24.' In *The L=A=N=G=U=A=G=E Book*, 292–3. See Andrews and Bernstein 1984a

– 1984b. Untitled. In *The L=A=N=G=U=A=G=E Book*, 199–200. See Andrews and Bernstein 1984a

Perloff, Marjorie. 1981. *The Poetics of Indeterminacy: Rimbaud to Cage*. Princeton: Princeton University Press

– 1985. *The dance of the intellect: Studies in the poetry of the Pound Tradition*. Cambridge: Cambridge University Press

– 1990. *Poetic License: Essays on Modernist and Postmodernist Lyric*. Evanston, Illinois: Northwestern University Press

Pitcher, George. 1965. 'Wittgenstein, Nonsense, and Lewis Carroll.' *The Massachusetts Review* VI:591–611

Pound, Ezra. 1937. *Polite Essays*. London: Faber and Faber

Quartermain, Peter. 1992. *Disjunctive Poetics: From Gertrude Stein and Louis Zukofsky to Susan Howe*. Cambridge, England: Cambridge University Press

Reaney, James. 1969. *Colours in the Dark*. Vancouver, British Columbia: Talonbooks

Rich, Adrienne. 1984. 'Our Whole Life.' In *Facts of a Doorframe: Poems Selected and New 1950–1984*, 133. New York: W.W. Norton & Co

Rieke, Alison Rae. 1984. 'Sense, Nonsense, and the Invention of Languages: James Joyce, Louis Zukofsky, Gertrude Stein.' Ph. D. diss., University of Kentucky, Lexington, Kentucky

– 1992. *The Senses of Nonsense*. Iowa City: University of Iowa Press

Riffaterre, Michael. [1978] 1984. *Semiotics of Poetry*. Bloomington, Indiana: Midland Books–Indiana University Press

Rilke, Rainer Maria. 1984. *Duino Elegies*. In *The Selected Poetry of Rainer Maria Rilke*. Translated by Stephen Mitchell, 151–211. New York: Vintage-Random House

Ross, Angus. 1982. *Selections from 'The Tatler' and 'The Spectator' of Steele and Addison*. New York: Penguin-Viking

Ruas, Charles. 1986. 'Postscript: An Interview with Michel Foucault.' In *Death and the Labyrinth: The World of Raymond Roussel*. Translated by Charles Ruas, 169–86. Berkeley: University of California Press

Schafer, R. Murray. 1988. *The Thinking Ear*. Toronto: Arcana Editions

Schmitz, Neil. 1974. 'Gertrude Stein as Post-Modernist: The Rhetoric of *Tender Buttons*.' *Journal of Modern Literature* 3.5:1203–18

Sewell, Elizabeth. 1952. *The Field of Nonsense*. London: Chatto and Windus.

Sheringham, Michael. 1977. 'From the Labyrinth of Language to the Language of the Senses: the Poetry of André Breton.' In *Sensibility and Creation*, edited by Roger Cardinal, 72–102. New York: Barnes and Noble–Harper & Row.

Silliman, Ron. 1978. *Ketjak*. San Francisco: This

– 1984. 'Disappearance of the Word, Appearance of the World.' In *The L=A=N=G=U=A=G=E Book*, 121–32. See Andrews and Bernstein 1984a

– 1986. 'Language, Realism, Poetry.' In *In the American Tree*: xv–xxiii. See Grenier 1986

– 1987a. *The New Sentence*. New York: Roof Books

– 1987b. ' "Postmodernism": Sign for a Struggle, Struggle for the Sign.' *Poetics Journal* 7:18–39

Silverman, Kaja. 1983. *The Subject of Semiotics*. New York: Oxford University Press

Sitwell, Edith. [1957] 1982. *Collected Poems*. London: Papermac–Macmillan and Co

Smith, A.C.H. 1972. *Orghast at Persepolis*. London: Eyre Methuen

Smith, Paul. 1988. *Discerning the Subject*. Minneapolis, Minnesota: University of Minnesota Press

Sonstroem, David. 1967. 'Making Earnest of the Game.' *Modern Language Quarterly* 28:192–206

Springer, George P. 1956. 'Language and Music: Parallels and Divergences.' In *For Roman Jakobson: Essays on the Occasion of His Sixtieth Birthday*, edited by Morris Halle et al, 504–13. The Hague: Mouton & Co

Stein, Gertrude. [1914] 1962. *Tender Buttons*. In *Selected Writings of Gertrude Stein*, edited by Carl Van Vechton. New York: Vintage–Random House

– 1935a. 'Poetry and Grammar.' In *Lectures in America*, 209–46. Boston: Beacon Press

– 1935b. 'Portraits and Repetition.' *Lectures in America*, 165–206. See Stein 1935a

– 1935c. 'What Is English Literature.' *Lectures in America*, 11–55. See Stein 1935a

Steiner, Wendy. 1982. *The Colors of Rhetoric: Problems in the Relation between Modern Literature and Painting*. Chicago: University of Chicago Press

Stevens, Wallace. 1951. *The Necessary Angel: Essays on Reality and the Imagination*. London: Faber and Faber

– 1972. 'Notes Toward a Supreme Fiction.' In *The Palm at the End of the Mind: Selected Poems and a Play*; edited by Holly Stevens, 207–34. New York: Vintage Books-Random House

Stewart, Susan. 1978. *Nonsense: Aspects of Intertextuality in Folklore and Fiction*. Baltimore: The Johns Hopkins University Press.

Sutherland, Robert D. 1970. *Language and Lewis Carroll*. The Hague: Mouton

Thibaudeau, Colleen. 1991. *The Artemesia Book: Poems Selected and New*. London, Ontario: Brick Books

Thomas, Dylan. 1965. 'Notes on the Art of Poetry.' *Modern Poetics*, edited by James Scully, 185–94. New York: McGraw-Hill Book Co

– 1971. *The Poems*, edited by Daniel Jones. London: Everyman's Library, Dent

Tigges, Wim. 1987. 'An Anatomy of Nonsense.' In *Explorations in the Field of Nonsense*, edited by Wim Tigges, 23–46. Amsterdam: Rodopi Editions

– 1988. *An Anatomy of Literary Nonsense*. Amsterdam: Rodopi Editions

Treece, Henry. 1956. *Dylan Thomas: 'Dog Among the Fairies'* (Second Edition). London: Ernest Benn Ltd

Valéry, Paul. 1958. *The Art of Poetry*. Translated by Denise Folliot. *The Collected Works of Paul Valéry*, Vol. VII. New York: Pantheon

van Rooten, Luis d'Antin. [1967] 1980. *Mots d'Heures: Gousses, Rames The d'Antin Manuscript*. New York: Penguin Books

Vigeurs, Susan T. 1983. 'Nonsense and the Language of Poetry.' *Signal* 42:137–49

Watkins, Vernon, [1957] 1982. *Letters to Vernon Watkins*. Westport, Connecticut: Greenwood

Watten, Barrett. 1984. 'Ron Silliman, *Mohawk* and *Ketjak*.' *The L=A=N=G=U=A=G=E Book*, 270–1. See Andrews and Bernstein 1984a

Welsh, Andrew. 1978. *Roots of Lyric: Primitive Poetry and Modern Poetics*. Princeton: Princeton University Press

Wendt, Larry. 1978. 'Metropolitan Fractalizations: Six Text-Sound Compositions.' In *Sound Poetry: A Catalogue*, 69–70. See Cobbing 1978

Weststeijn, W.G. 1983. *Velimir Chlebnikov and the Development of Poetical*

Language in Russian Symbolism and Futurism. Amsterdam: Rodopi Editions

Winn, James Anderson.1981. *Unsuspected Eloquence: A History of the Relations between Poetry and Music*. New Haven: Yale University Press

Wittgenstein, Ludwig. [1953] 1958. *Philosophical Investigations*. Translated by G.E.M. Anscombe. London: Basil Blackwell

Woolf, Virginia. [1929] 1977. *A Room of One's Own*. London: A Triad Grafton Book, Collins Publishing Co

Young, Alan. 1981. *Dada and After: Extremist Modernism and English Literature*. Manchester: Manchester University Press

Zukofsky, Celia, and Louis Zukosfsky. 1969. *Catullus*. London: Cape Goliard Press

Zukofsky, Louis. 1963. *Bottom on Shakespeare*, Vol. 1. Austin, Texas: The Ark Press

– 1971. *ALL: The Collected Short Poems, 1923–1964*. New York: W.W. Norton & Co

– 1978a. *'A'*. Berkeley: University of California Press

– 1978b. *80 Flowers*. Lunenberg, Vermont: The Stinehour Press

– 1979. '[Sincerity & Objectification].' *Louis Zukofsky: Man and Poet*, 265–81. *See* Corman 1979

– 1981. *Prepositions: The Collected Essays of Louis Zukofsky*, Expanded Edition. Berkeley: University of California Press

– 1991. *Complete Short Poetry*. Foreword by Robert Creeley. Baltimore: Johns Hopkins University Press

Index

—◆—